Studying Western Civilization

Reading Maps • Interpreting Documents • Preparing for Exams

A STUDENT'S GUIDE
VOLUME II: SINCE 1320

for

The Challenge of the West

Hunt • Martin • Rosenwein • Hsia • Smith

Richard M. Long

Hillsborough Community College

D. C. Heath and Company
Lexington, Massachusetts   Toronto

Address editorial correspondence to:

D. C. Heath and Company
125 Spring Street
Lexington, MA 02173

International Standard Book Number: 0-669-35366-3

10 9 8 7 6 5 4 3 2 1

To the Student

About *The Challenge of the West*

Imagine trying to write a narrative for a friend from abroad about the most recent American presidential campaign. Should you adopt a partisan point of view or try to be objective (though that might be difficult)? How much did the voters' memories of the nation's past—remote and recent—affect their attitudes and behavior? Should you start by giving a demographic and social overview of the country as a whole? or perhaps with the economic condition of the country, because you believe that such matters dictate political outcomes? Or should you narrate the political rhetoric and its effect on the voters, implying that economic and social results are determined mainly by political processes and decisions? Which parts of the country had the greatest impact on the election and therefore deserve special attention? Should you integrate the issues of women and minority groups throughout your discussion or deal with them in a special addendum afterwards? What newspapers, magazines, and other sources give trustworthy accounts of the events that you did not witness personally? And, given limitations of time and space, what information can you omit without damaging the coherence of your narrative?

The authors of *The Challenge of the West* faced all these questions, but the narrative they have written is far more ambitious: a history of Western civilization from prehistoric times to the present. This text does not define "the West" narrowly; it acknowledges that the peoples of the Mediterranean and of western Europe were in constant contact with the peoples of eastern Europe, western Asia, and north Africa, and later with the native peoples and immigrants' offspring in the Americas. The authors have covered all of the traditional material of a Western Civilization course, but *The Challenge of the West* differs from traditional textbooks in several important respects. The historical perspectives of the authors are best expressed in their own introduction, but several features of the book should be mentioned here.

Historical Perspectives

In the past, most history textbooks concentrated on political and diplomatic history to the point that the past seemed little more than a succession of monarchs and wars, with a nod from the occasional philosopher. Historians also concentrated on the elites—the literate ruling classes who left behind written evidence of their lives—because history was traditionally based on written records. Many modern historians, aware that such an approach ignored the vast majority of the human race, have been creative in unearthing evidence about the "inarticulate masses" and have taken advantage of new methodologies, from archaeology to computers, to try to study the whole of past society. In *The Challenge of the West*, the wealth of new information uncovered in the last few decades—about everyday life, the views of ordinary people, and the experiences of women and the poor—has replaced the "wars and kings" approach as the basis of the historical narrative. Rather than being separated from the traditional political narrative, the new social history has been woven into the fabric of each chapter from the beginning.

Chronological Divisions

For convenience, historians have always carved up the past into "periods" such as the Middle Ages, the Renaissance, and the Scientific Revolution. Of course, a person living in the Middle Ages was not aware that some historian would eventually label the age in such a way, nor was the end of the Middle Ages and the beginning of the Renaissance an event noted by contemporaries. The units of Western history have traditionally been defined by developments in political or intellectual history, even though ordinary people were often unaffected by these events.

Because *The Challenge of the West* is an original narrative of Western history, the authors have selected new criteria for defining historical periods. You will immediately perceive advantages in dividing the past into smaller units defined primarily by a specific time span. Some textbooks, for example, discuss all of ancient Egypt as a single unit or chapter, from the Neolithic period through the decline of the New Kingdom. In this way, the 3,000-year flow of Egyptian history is readily grasped: Old Kingdom, Intermediate Period, Middle Kingdom, Intermediate Period, New Kingdom. On the other hand, students may then be confused about which peoples in Mesopotamia, discussed in the previous chapter, were contemporaneous with the Old Kingdom, or which people in Anatolia (discussed in the following chapter) were in contact with the New Kingdom, or which period in Egyptian history paralleled Minoan civilization, discussed in still another chapter. *The Challenge of the West* should make chronological connections such as these much easier to learn.

How to Use Your Text

Reading the Textbook for General Comprehension

There is a difference between carefully *reading* a chapter and *studying* a chapter. After a careful reading, you can expect to retain a general overview but not necessarily minute details, such as dates. Reading should be done in good light, in a comfortable, straight-backed chair (not so comfortable that you fall asleep!), and without distractions, such as radio or television in the background. It should not be hurried (for example, don't begin your reading the night before the test), and you shouldn't try to do all your reading in large blocks of time. If you find yourself having difficulty concentrating or becoming fatigued quickly, you may need to change your habits—get more sleep, don't try to study immediately after eating a big meal—or you may even need to have your eyes examined! Passing the eye exam for a driver's license is no guarantee that you don't need reading glasses.

Like any other skill, reading for comprehension improves with practice. When you have finished a careful reading of the Prologue, for example, you should be able to answer the following questions without referring back to the text: What does *paleolithic* mean? Who were these hunter-gatherers? How did they live? Why is this significant? What does *neolithic* mean? How does it differ from paleolithic? What does the neolithic lifestyle have in common with a modern way of life? Why is this significant? What and where was Çatal Hüyük? Approximately when was it inhabited and by whom? Why is it significant? Notice that all of these questions were implicit in the various subheadings. In a well-written book, chapter divisions reveal the logic behind the organization of the material. They indicate the general topics that the authors consider most important and how these topics are interrelated. One good approach to reading a text is to use these subtitles to pose questions for yourself—Who were these hunter-gatherers? How did they live?—and then read for the answers. An outline for each chapter is provided in this *Student's Guide* for your convenience.

Taking Notes in Class

Whenever possible, read the appropriate information in your text before attending lectures on a given topic. You will notice an enormous difference in how well you comprehend lectures on totally unfamiliar material as opposed to lectures on material with which you are already somewhat familiar. You will also find it easier to participate in class and ask good questions. Your note taking will improve, too, because you will know which material requires detailed notes and which is covered adequately in the text. Soon after taking notes in class, you should rewrite them so that they will be legible and coherent when you study them later; the rewriting is also a useful reinforcement for learning and understanding the material.

Studying the Textbook

Every instructor has his or her own emphases; ask your instructor about his or her special interests, which material will be covered in tests, and the sorts of questions that will be asked. A single reading of the text will probably not be sufficient to absorb all of the details an instructor will expect you to learn. When you study the textbook, the same guidelines apply as for your first reading of it: adequate rest, reasonable blocks of time, no distractions, good lighting, and a comfortable, straight-backed chair. It can be useful to keep a journal or take notes on the material you want to learn. Whether you are studying for an essay examination or an objective test (multiple-choice, matching, fill-in-the-blank, and short-answer questions) you will need a command of facts and details—people, events, dates. Compile a list of the terms likely to be on the test and make certain you know enough about each to answer questions. Quizzing yourself with flashcards or studying with a classmate will work better than rereading lists of terms again and again. Underlining or highlighting in the text is not recommended because studies have shown that it simply doesn't work for most people. If you find that your study skills are deficient (your first tests should provide this information), most instructors will be happy to give advice, and most colleges and schools offer counseling services and tutorial assistance. Find out what resources are available, and make use of them.

How to Use This *Guide*

This *Student's Guide* is designed to help you by providing reinforcement and self-testing based on the textbook as well as some complementary exercises. Every chapter of the text has a corresponding chapter in the *Student's Guide,* each with the following features:

Chapter Outline: a list of the topics in the chapter, in the order in which they are covered. If you read the outline first, you will know what to expect when you read the chapter. If you then carefully read the chapter, when you reread the outline you should be reminded of certain basic information about each topic and its significance. If you cannot recall basic information about each topic, reread the section in question.

Chapter Summary: a brief overview of the period discussed in the chapter. The summaries are intended to assist you by placing the chapters in broad historical and chronological perspective. They are not simply abridgements of the chapter, nor are they substitutes for reading the chapter. They may be helpful when preparing for an exam.

Vocabulary: a checklist of words with which you might not be familiar. You should always look up unfamiliar words you encounter, not only to make certain you understand what you are reading, but also to improve your ability to communicate with clarity and precision.

Self-Testing and Review Questions: quizzes in several formats, designed to provide a comprehensive review of the material in the chapter and to help you prepare for tests.

Identifications To write a complete identification of a term, always include *who* or *what, when, where,* and *why significant.* For example, if asked to identify Aristotle, you should indicate that he was a Greek philosopher who lived in the fourth century B.C. and something about what he did, said, wrote, or thought that made him historically significant. *Hint:* On a test, students frequently forget to write the obvious—for example, that Julius Caesar was a Roman—and many instructors will deduct points for such omissions.

Chronology Dates are the mileposts along the road of the past; historians use them to record and measure change in the same way that scientists use rulers and scales. Just as a marine biologist knows what kind of ocean life to expect at a depth of three miles, a historian knows what kind of technology, architecture, and literature to expect in central France in the year 1022. Even if your instructor does not test you on dates, your understanding of the past will be greatly enhanced by learning some of them, especially those important "watershed" dates that are turning points in several different fields or regions—dates like 1492 or 1688–1689.

Matching Exercises These questions test your recall and recognition of facts and details. Read all the choices in both columns before answering. If you cannot recognize all of the items in a group, you can improve your odds of guessing correctly by matching the ones you *do* know. You should be able to answer at least half of these correctly after a single, careful reading of the chapter, and you should be able to answer all of them after studying it.

Multiple-Choice Questions In some multiple-choice tests, the student is asked to choose the "best" of several more-or-less-correct answers, but in *Studying Western Civilization* the multiple-choice questions are formulated so that one answer is clearly correct and the others are clearly false. Read the question and try to *think* of the correct answer before carefully *reading* the answers. If you cannot immediately recognize the correct answer among those provided, you can improve your odds of guessing correctly by eliminating the choices you know to be false. As with the matching exercises, you should be able to answer at least half of these correctly after a single, careful reading of the chapter, and you should be able to answer all of them after studying it.

Practice Essay Questions In addition to essay questions within each chapter, *Studying Western Civilization* gives you essay questions covering larger units of the text, rather like midterm exams. In this age of standardized tests and answer forms, students sometimes feel intimidated by essay tests simply because they are afraid their blind spots will be revealed to the instructor. In fact, it is the matching and multiple-choice questions that show what facts you have *not* learned. Essay tests instead give you the opportunity to demonstrate, and to get credit for, what you *have* learned. They place a premium on your ability to organize and communicate your thoughts, and these are skills that, like any others, improve with practice.

Before answering any essay question on a test, consider the question very carefully and try to understand precisely what the instructor is asking. Take a little time to plan and outline your answer before you begin to write. Give specific examples to illustrate the points that you make; remember that this is your opportunity to show off what you have learned, so don't skimp on facts and details—but include only those appropriate to your topic. Answer all of the question; plan your time so that you are not still answering the first half of a question when time runs out. Above all, focus on the question that you were asked. Always remember that the instructor will evaluate your answer to see what you have learned; write the kind of answer you would want to read if you were the instructor.

There are many different kinds of essay questions, and each requires a different type of answer. Some ask you to summarize what you have learned; these require the least original thought but emphasize comprehensive and detailed knowledge. Others require you to summarize the material differently from the way it was originally presented; for example, after reading three chapters on the Middle Ages throughout Europe, the student might be asked to write an essay on the course of French history during the period. Questions like these can be daunting, but taking a little time to plan and outline your answer will help you to write a good essay. Still others ask provocative questions that reward originality rather than rote memorization or organizing skills. In this *Student's Guide* you will find all of these kinds of questions and more.

If you need further practice writing essays, try this: immediately after you have read a new chapter in the text, make up several essay questions that you think are challenging but reasonable summations of the material. Later, when you are preparing for a test, return to these questions and see if you can answer them.

Skill Building: Maps
The events of history are closely tied to geographical factors. Rivers were the focus of the earliest civilizations, and they long continued to be conduits for trade, language, and culture. The Mediterranean Sea served this function for classical European civilization, and by the eighteenth century the Atlantic Ocean performed the same function for western Europe and the Americas. The fertility and topography of the land often determined whether people would be hunters, nomads, herdsmen, or farmers, and also whether they would be warriors. Your text provides dozens of geographical references and maps. This *Student's Guide* gives you the opportunity to test your map skills. Notice that wars and migrations will change the boundaries of certain states—such as Burgundy, Poland, or Lithuania—hundreds of miles from one chapter to the next. Cities and rivers remain constant, so the fact that you are repeatedly asked to locate Rome, Paris, the Rhine, or the Danube on the map not only reflects their perennial significance but also provides fixed reference points from which to measure political and other kinds of changes.

Enrichment Exercises
These exercises suggest books, plays, films, and other resources that will enable you to go beyond the material presented in the text. We can often gain a more accurate picture of, say, human relations in a given century—father and son, husband and wife, mistress and slave—by reading the literature of the age than by studying the laws. And although a modern novel or film about the past may not always be historically accurate, it does demonstrate how we use our memories and perceptions of the past to provide insight, meaning, and perspective in our own lives and for our own era. The reason the past remains important is that it improves our understanding of the present or affects us still. You might ask yourself whether an incorrect perception of the past that is widely held and influential is less important than a true perception of the past that is little known.

Document Analysis
Written records are the traditional basis of history, but often the historical records are incomplete, mistaken, self-serving, or even intentionally falsified. Even the most straightforward piece of evidence can be subject to sharp differences of interpretation. In this section, you have the opportunity to be the historian, to draw conclusions based on documentary information. Nearly all of the documents were suggested and introduced by the textbook authors, but the questions were added by the author of this *Student's Guide*. Observant students might notice some friendly differences of opinion among the various writers on how these documents should be interpreted.

Many books in your college library and bookstore can help you to improve your study skills. The following books are especially recommended for students who want advice on how to study Western civilization:

Jules R. Benjamin, *A Student's Guide to History,* 5th edition (New York: St. Martin's Press, 1991).

Norman F. Cantor and Richard I. Schneider, *How to Study History* (New York: Thomas Y. Crowell, 1967).

Robert V. Daniels, *Studying History: How and Why* (Englewood Cliffs, N. J.: Prentice-Hall, Inc., 1966).

Your course in Western civilization can lay the foundation for a lifetime of studying and enjoying history. Remember, history is not the past. History is stories about the past told by storytellers with their own points of view. Always ask who is telling the story and why. Ask what they might have left out and why. Keep an open mind but think critically, and you should do well in your study of history. Learn from—and enjoy—the journey!

R. M. L.

Contents

CHAPTER

13

The Collapse of Medieval Order, 1320–1430

Chapter Outline

TOWARD THE RENAISSANCE: THE SOCIAL ORDER AND CULTURAL CHANGE
The Household
The Underclasses
Middle-Class Writers and the Birth of Humanism

Chapter Summary

In the fourteenth century, social and economic trends were driven by three complex and intimately related events—the Hundred Years' War, the Black Death, and the schism. The century began with famine, financial contraction, an ill-fated French invasion of Flanders, and the surprising establishment of the Papal Curia at Avignon (see Chapter 12). The conflict between France and England over Flanders festered. Eventually Edward III of England, a grandson of Philip IV, claimed the throne of France and invaded that country, thus starting more than a century of intermittent warfare. After the French feudal nobility suffered military humiliation at Crécy in 1346, the English established themselves on French soil. Even before the arrival of the Black Death, the western Christian world was divided by the Avignon papacy. As early as 1327, Marsilius of Padua denounced the papacy for its absence from Rome, and in the 1340s Cola di Rienzo led a rebellion in the depressed Eternal City. The enemies of France assumed that the popes were under the French thumb and acted accordingly. Nevertheless, the papal court at Avignon exposed Italians such as Petrarch and Boccaccio to the brilliant culture of Provence.

The arrival of the Black Death in the late 1340s was an overwhelming event that quickly became the most important historical force of the age. Spread by fleas and rats, its effects varied from place to place, but it tended to be most destructive in crowded urban settings. In all, it probably killed over a third of Europe's population and further outbreaks continued for centuries. Besides widespread death, the plague brought social hysteria, anti-Jewish violence, religious fanaticism, and economic dislocation. Ironically, the scarcity of labor that it caused often drove up wages in the cities and increased individual wealth, but elsewhere it caused economic depression, depopulation, and decreased revenues from agriculture.

The English continued their oppression of the French in the 1350s, and the desperate French peasants were driven to revolt by war and mistreatment. During the second half of the century, however, the French began to rally. Social and economic problems after the plague led to more rebellions, urban and rural, from London to Florence. In 1356 the Golden Bull redefined the election of emperors in Germany, insulating them from papal meddling.

In 1378 the efforts of Gregory XI to move the papacy back to Rome resulted in a disastrous schism—two rival popes, whose bickering undermined lay respect for the clergy throughout Europe. Such disunity also ruled out the remote possibility of organized resistance to the Turkish invasion of the Balkans. Anticlerical movements, such as those of the Lollards in England and the Hussites in Bohemia, questioned the role of the clergy in salvation and favored Scripture over church tradition. Others looked to church councils to solve the church's problems. The Council of Constance finally reunited the western church under a single Roman pope; it also burned Hus as a heretic.

The English victory at Agincourt in 1415 and an Anglo-Burgundian alliances brought most of northern France under English control. The war seemed to be over. But the remarkable career and martyrdom of Joan of Arc brought Armagnac victories, unsettled the alliance with Burgundy, and eventually inspired the French armies to victory.

The contradictions of the rage were reflected in its literary trends. The tradition of classical scholarship and a revival of Latin and Greek in some ways contrasted with but also enriched a new golden age of secular, vernacular literature.

Vocabulary

flagellant Member of a group (organized or otherwise) that practiced "mortification of the flesh," often mutual scourging, as a religious ritual.

anticlerical Opposed to the clergy. In this chapter, anticlericalism included criticizing the wealth and privilege of the clergy, especially questioning whether the clergy and sacraments were necessary for salvation.

dauphin Heir to the French throne. The assumption of this title was a precondition to claiming the Dauphiné region in southeastern France, and so the title became synonymous with the eldest son of the French monarch.

excommunication A form of church censure by which one is forbidden the sacraments, and as a consequence, denied salvation.

viticulture The cultivation of grapes; also wine making.

misogyny Hatred of women. Hatred of men is called misandry.

sonnet A short poem usually consisting of fourteen lines with a fixed rhyme pattern and meter. The origin of the form is either Italian or Provençal, and Petrarch is considered one of its inventors.

novella A prose tale midway in length between a short story and a novel.

Conclave The College of Cardinals, meeting for the purpose of selecting a new pope.

poet laureate The most eminent poet of the land, nation, or age, so named because a laurel wreath was a reward for uncommon achievement in ancient Greece. Both Dante and Petrarch were often depicted wearing such a wreath.

Self-Testing and Review Questions

Identification

After reading Chapter 13, identify and explain the historical significance of each of the following:

1. Petrarch

2. Janissaries

3. Council of Constance

4. John of Gaunt

5. Book of Hours

6. Lollardy

7. Taborites

8. Jacquerie

9. Ciompi revolt

10. Golden Bull

11. Hanseatic League

12. Casimir III

13. Pius II

14. La Pucelle

15. humanism

16. Fraticelli

17. Bertrand du Guesclin

18. Armagnacs

19. Swiss Confederation

20. Fernando Martínez

21. Ockham's razor

22. Procop the Shaven

23. Jogailo

24. Battle of Kossovo

25. Osman I

26. *Decameron*

27. John Hus

Chronology

Identify the events or issues associated with the following dates. Some dates may be significant for more than one reason. After you finish, answer the questions that follow.

1315–1317

1327

1346

1348–1350

1356

1358

1378

1381

1389

1415

1431

1. Why did so many popular rebellions, both urban and rural, break out in the second half of the fourteenth century?
2. It has been suggested that there was an urgency to the humanists' quest to rescue classical manuscripts from the monasteries. What could have caused this?

Matching Exercises

In each set, match the terms on the left with those on the right.

Set A

_____ 1. Francesco Petrarch
_____ 2. Giovanni Boccaccio
_____ 3. Geoffrey Chaucer
_____ 4. Marsilius of Padua
_____ 5. John Wycliff
_____ 6. Jean Froissart

a. *On the Church*
b. *Canzoniere*
c. *Defender of the Peace*
d. *Chronicles*
e. *Decameron*
f. *Canterbury Tales*

Set B

_____ 1. Jacques van Arteveld
_____ 2. Étienne Marcel
_____ 3. John Hus
_____ 4. Cola di Rienzo
_____ 5. John Ball

a. estates leader in Paris
b. Bohemian leader
c. tribune of the Roman people
d. leader of the Peasant Rebellion (in England)
e. leader of the revolt in Flanders

Set C

_____ 1. Lollards
_____ 2. Hussites
_____ 3. Fraticelli
_____ 4. Armagnacs
_____ 5. Ciompi

a. utraquists
b. supporters of the *dauphin*
c. followers of John Wycliff
d. Florentine rebels
e. heretics who encouraged poverty as a condition of salvation

Set D

____ 1. John XXII
____ 2. Gregory XI
____ 3. John XXIII
____ 4. Martin V
____ 5. Urban VI

a. the pope named at the Council of Constance
b. the pope named at the Council of Pisa
c. the first Roman pope of the Great Schism
d. influential pope of the early Avignon period
e. pope whose death immediately preceded the Great Schism

Set E

____ 1. Charles VII
____ 2. Philip the Bold
____ 3. The Black Prince
____ 4. Edward III
____ 5. Charles IV

a. brother of John of Gaunt, victor at Poitiers
b. crowned at Reims, thanks to Joan of Arc
c. powerful Duke of Burgundy
d. ruler who signed the Golden Bull
e. ruler whose claim to the French throne touched off the Hundred Years' War

Multiple-Choice Questions

1. The Bardi, Peruzzi, and Acciaiuoli were
   a. bankers.
   b. heretics.
   c. scholars.
   d. chancellors of Florence.

2. The famous silver mines that enriched the state of Bohemia were located at
   a. Kossovo.
   b. Kutná Hora.
   c. Prague.
   d. Yeni Çeri.

3. Joan of Arc contributed to the French victory at
   a. Orléans.
   b. Crécy.
   c. Rouen.
   d. Agincourt.

4. *The Book of the City of Ladies* was a pioneering work by
   a. William of Ockham.
   b. Christine de Pizan.
   c. John Wycliffe.
   d. Giovanni Boccaccio.

5. Those who advocated the distribution of both bread and wine at communion were the
   a. Burgundians.
   b. Armagnacs.
   c. Free Spirits.
   d. utraquists.

6. The humanists were
   a. heretics who denied the divinity of Christ.
   b. opponents of clerical wealth and privilege, in the Waldensian tradition.
   c. proponents of classical scholarship.
   d. opponents of feudal tax privileges after the Black Death.

7. The Turkish empire greatly expanded its holdings in Europe under the leadership of the
   a. Jagiellonian dynasty.
   b. Ottoman dynasty.
   c. Hanseatic League.
   d. Swiss Confederation.

8. The translation of the Bible into the vernacular was a project favored by
   a. Bertrand du Guesclin.
   b. John Wycliff.
   c. Joan of Arc.
   d. John Hawkwood.

9. As a result of the Black Death,
    a. the income of rural property owners increased.
    b. the income of urban artisans and merchants increased.
    c. the population of the monasteries increased.
    d. the population of European cities decreased by an average of ten percent.

10. Beguines and beghards were
    a. not officially affiliated with the church.   c. Taborites.
    b. peasant rebels.   d. urban rebels.

Essay Questions

Using material from this and previous chapters, write an essay on each of the following topics. Include dates and detailed examples, when appropriate, to support your arguments.

1. Discuss the economic and social consequences of the Black Death.

2. Discuss the religious ferment in western Europe in the fourteenth and early fifteenth centuries. How did the Avignon papacy and Schism contribute to this ferment? What other factors were involved?

3. Trace the history of the Hundred Years' War, describing its major phases, decisive battles, and turning points. What effects did the war have on political, social, and economic life?

4. The fourteenth century was a century of popular rebellions. Name the principal rural uprisings and discuss their causes. Discuss the principal urban rebellions, emphasizing their causes and results.

Skill Building: Maps

Locate the following regions and states on the map of medieval Europe (some may not have definite boundaries). Why was each significant in this chapter? Even if you have located these on maps in earlier chapters, carefully examine the maps in this chapter; borders are not permanent. Certain states, such as Poland and Burgundy, suffered drastic adjustments of their frontiers throughout history.

a. Normandy

b. Gascony

c. Burgundy

d. Bohemia

e. Lithuania

f. Poland

g. Serbia

h. Sicily

i. Catalonia

j. Aragon

k. Castile

l. Portugal

1. Which regions supported the French cause in the Hundred Years' War? Which regions supported the English? Why did the Flemish cities tend to ally with England and resist the French during this period?

2. Which regions supported the Avignon popes? To what extent was support for the Avignon papacy related to political and commercial alliance with France? After the Schism of 1378, which regions tended to support the Roman pope against the one in Avignon?

3. Which regions experienced the most anticlerical and heretical activity in the fourteenth and fifteenth centuries? Why do you suppose these regions often conformed closely to anti-French and anti-Avignon affiliations?

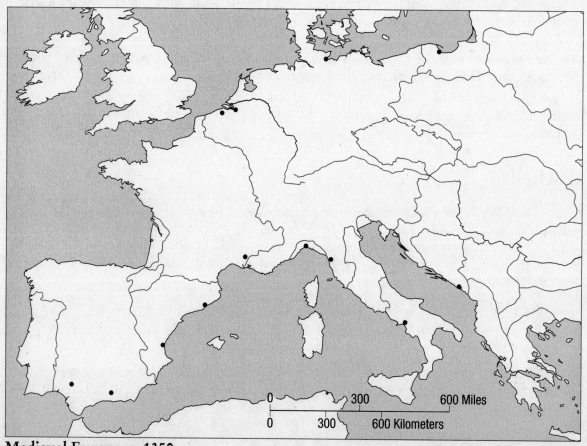

Medieval Europe, c. 1350

Locate the following cities on the map of medieval Europe. Why was each significant in this chapter?

    a. Avignon

    b. Rome

    c. Venice

    d. Florence

    e. Genoa

    f. Ragusa

    g. Pisa

    h. Naples

    i. Bruges

    j. Antwerp

    k. Ghent

    l. Lübeck

    m. Danzig

    n. Valencia

    o. Seville

    p. Barcelona

    q. Granada

1. How many of the above cities are seaports? Why do you suppose so many seaports seem to take on new historical significance in this chapter? What were the consequences of these developments?

Enrichment Exercise

Shakespeare's play Henry V *was an award-winning film in 1989, starring Kenneth Branagh. The film vividly depicts the Battle of Agincourt, which, although it had little impact on the ultimate outcome of the war, was greeted with patriotic delirium and became the occasion for a national holiday. After reading the play or watching the film, write a brief essay on the similarities and differences between the actual event and its later artistic expression. For example, did Shakespeare, nearly two centuries later, share the delirium that followed the battle in 1415?*

Document Analysis

DOCUMENT 1

Boccaccio's Decameron

The impact of the plague is vividly recounted in Boccaccio's collection of tales, The Decameron. *Using the voice of the young noblewoman Pampinea, Boccaccio describes the breakdown of social and moral order in Florence. Upon meeting six other young women in the church of Santa Maria Novella, Pampinea urges them to retire to her country estate to escape the death and disorder in Florence. There the women, joined by three young men, told tales to pass their days.*

> *Pampinea:* Dear ladies . . . here we tarry, as if, I think, for no other purpose than to bear witness to the number of the corpses that are brought here for interment. . . . And if we quit the church, we see dead or sick folk carried about, or we see those, who for their crimes were of late condemned to exile . . . but who, now . . . well knowing that their magistrates are a prey to death or disease, have returned, and traverse the city in packs, making it hideous with their riotous antics; or else we see the refuse of the people, fostered on our blood, becchini, as they call themselves, who for our torment go prancing about . . . making mock of our miseries in scurrilous songs. . . . Or go we home, what see we there? . . . where once were servants in plenty, I find none left but my maid, and shudder with terror, and feel the very hairs of my head to stand on end; and turn or tarry where I may, I encounter the ghosts of the departed. . . . None . . . having means and place of retirement as we have, stays here . . . or if any such there be, they are of those . . . who make no distinction between things honorable and their opposites, so they but answer the cravings of appetite, and, alone or in company, do daily and nightly what things soever give promise of most gratification. Nor are these secular persons alone, but such as live recluse in monasteries break their rule, and give themselves up to carnal pleasures, persuading themselves that they are permissible to them, and only forbidden to others, and, thereby thinking to escape, are become unchaste and dissolute.

Source: Giovanni Boccaccio, *The Decameron,* edited by Edward Hutton (Tudor Translations, 1955), Vol. 1, pp. 13–14.

Question

1. Pampinea observes that those fearing imminent death, even monks, give themselves over to the pleasures of the flesh. What about the numerous anecdotes about deathbed conversions and the fear of death causing people to see "the error of their ways"? What is different here?

DOCUMENT 2

Joan of Arc

Besieged by the English on October 12, 1428, the city of Orléans was saved on May 8, 1429, in a campaign that won glory for the seventeen-year-old peasant girl Joan of Arc. After capture by the English, Joan testified to her sense of divine calling before her inquisitors. Two men who knew her spoke at the trial about the bravery and religious calling of this extraordinary young woman, who called herself "The Maid." Nevertheless, Joan was convicted of heresy and burned at the stake in 1431.

JOAN [to her inquisitors]: When I was thirteen years old, I had a voice from God to help me govern my conduct. And the first time I was very fearful. And came this voice, about the hour of noon, in the summer-time, in my father's garden. . . . I heard the voice on the right-hand side . . . and rarely do I hear it without a brightness. . . . It has taught me to conduct myself well, to go habitually to church. . . . The voice told me that I should raise the siege laid to the city of Orléans. . . . And me, I answered it that I was a poor girl who knew not how to ride nor lead in war.

JEAN PASQUEREL [priest, Joan's confessor]: On the morrow, Saturday, I rose early and celebrated mass. And Joan went out against the fortress of the bridge where was the Englishman Classidas. And the assault lasted there from morning until sunset. In this assault . . . Joan . . . was struck by an arrow above the breast, and when she felt herself wounded she was afraid and wept. . . . And some soldiers, seeing her so wounded, wanted to apply a charm to her wound, but she would not have it, saying: "I would rather die than do a thing which I know to be a sin or against the will of God.". . . . But if to her wound could be applied a remedy without sin, she was very willing to be cured. And they put on to her wound olive oil and lard. And after that had been applied, Joan made her confession to me, weeping and lamenting.

COUNT DUNOIS: The assault lasted from the morning until eight . . . so that there was hardly hope of victory that day. So that I was going to break off and . . . withdraw. . . . Then the Maid came to me and required me to wait yet a while. She . . . mounted her horse and retired alone into a vineyard. . . . And in this vineyard she remained at prayer. . . . Then she came back . . . at once seized her standard in hand and placed herself on the parapet of the trench, and the moment she was there the English trembled and were terrified. The king's soldiers regained courage and began to go up, charging against the boulevard without meeting the least resistance.

JEAN PASQUEREL: Joan returned to the charge, crying and saying: "Classidas, Classidas, yield thee, yield thee to the King of Heaven; thou hast called me 'whore'; I take great pity on thy soul and thy people's!" Then Classidas, armed from head to foot, fell into the river of Loire and was drowned. And Joan, moved by pity, began to weep much for the soul of Classidas and the others who were drowned in great numbers. . . .

Source: Régine Pernoud, *Joan of Arc: By Herself and Her Witnesses* (Scarborough House, 1966), pp. 30, 90–92.

Question

1. It has been said that the entire story of Joan of Arc is preposterous; and the most preposterous fact of all is that the entire story is apparently true. What elements of the story seem to defy belief? Why do these two witnesses believe them?

DOCUMENT 3

The Founding of Tabor, 1419–1420

Master Laurence of Brezová was secretary of the city council of Prague and an early follower of Hus. In the 1420s, he composed a history of the Hussite movement. He represented a moderate faction of the movement, and in the following account of the origins of the Taborite community, he expresses both sympathy for the persecuted and rejection of the social and religious radicalism of the millenarians.

In these times therefore the faithful Czechs, both clergy and laity, who favored communion in both kinds and devotedly promoted it, and who grieved at the unjust death of Master John Hus . . . suffered very great difficulties, tribulations, anguish, and torment throughout the Kingdom of Bohemia, at the hands of the enemies and blasphemers of the Truth. . . . For these enemies of the Truth hunted down priests and laymen who ardently supported the chalice in various parts of the realm and brought them to the men of Kutná Hora, to whom they sold some for money. The Kutná Horans—Germans and cruel persecutors and enemies of the Czech—afflicted them with various blasphemies and diverse punishments, and inhumanly threw them—some alive, some first decapitated—into deep mine shafts, especially into the mine shaft near the church of St. Martin near the Kourim gate, which shaft the Kutná Horans called "Tabor.". . . In a short time more than 1,600 Utraquists [those who took communion in both kinds] were killed . . . the executioners often being exhausted by the fatigue of slaughter.

During this time certain Taborite priests were preaching to the people a new coming of Christ, in which all evil men and enemies of the Truth would perish and be exterminated, while the good would be preserved in five cities. . . . They urged that all those desiring to be saved from the wrath of Almighty God, which in their view was about to be visited on the whole globe, should leave their cities, castles, villages, and towns, as Lot left Sodom, and should go to the five cities of refuge. . . . And many simple folk . . . sold their property, taking even a low price, and flocked to these priests from various parts of the Kingdom of Bohemia and . . . Moravia, with their wives and children, and they threw their money at the feet of the priests.

Source: Howard Kaminsky, *A History of the Hussite Revolution* (Berkeley, 1967), pp. 310–312.

Questions

1. To what extent did the vicious repression of the Hussites tend to encourage the formation of the Taborites?

2. Do the Taborite beliefs described here contain echoes of other religious movements of the era, as described in the text?

DOCUMENT 4

Marsilius of Padua, The Defender of the Peace

Marsilius was one of the leading critics of papal power in the fourteenth century. In this famous treatise, he argued that the church's proper realm is spiritual, not political, and that it should be governed by the will of the faithful. Princes have authority in the political realm, and this authority should come from laws created by an assembly of the "whole body of citizens." These arguments struck directly at the church's medieval claim that all power comes from God to the church (that is, to the pope), and from there to princes, and finally to ordinary people.

The primary necessity of the law is as follows: It is necessary to establish in the polity that without which civil judgments cannot be made without complete rightness, and through which civil judgments are properly made and preserved from defect as far as it is humanly possible. . . . The judge or ruler is directed to make judgments according to the laws, because the law lacks all perverted emotions; for it is not made useful for friend or harmful for foe, but universally for all those who perform civil acts well or badly.

. . . [The] legislator, or the primary and proper efficient cause of the law, is the people or the whole body of citizens, or the weightier part thereof, through its election or will expressed by words in the general assembly of the citizens, commanding or determining that something be done or omitted with regard to human civil acts. . . .

But since the ruler is a human being, he has understanding and appetite . . . like false opinion or perverted desire or both, as a result of which he comes to do the contraries of the things determined by the law. Because of these actions, the ruler is rendered measurable by someone else who has the authority to measure or regulate him . . . in accordance with the law. For otherwise every government would become despotic, and the life of the citizens slavish and insufficient.

As for the question of who has the authority to establish this leadership [of the church], the answer must be that this authority belongs to the general council or the faithful human legislator . . . to whom it also pertains to designate the clerical college or group which shall hold this leadership. . . .

[On the pope and bishops]: Moreover, believing that they may do anything they like through the plenitude of power which they assert belongs to them, they have issued and are still issuing certain oligarchic ordinances called "decretals," wherein they command the observance of whatever measures they consider favorable to their own temporal welfare. . . . And so the Roman bishops with their clerical coteries have the firm desire and determination to maintain and defend these outrages which . . . they have perpetrated against all rulers and peoples, although most extensively and flagrantly against the Italian peoples and the Roman rulers.

Source: Marsilius of Padua, *The Defender of Peace*, Vol. 2, trans. Alan Gewirth (Ayer, 1956), pp. 37–38, 45, 87–88, 305, 341.

Questions

1. Marsilius wrote in Latin, and his word for "the church" was *ecclesia,* the same word the Athenians used to refer to their popular assembly. How might knowledge of the ancient Greeks and Romans have inspired Marsilius's arguments in favor of representative church government?

2. How might he have been influenced by recent political developments in western Europe—the creation of the Estates General in France, the Parliament in England, the Cortes in Spain? What clues do you find in these quotations and in the textbook?

CHAPTER

14

Renaissance Europe, 1430–1493

Chapter Outline

ON THE THRESHOLD OF WORLD HISTORY
The Hanseatic "Lake"
The Divided Mediterranean
New Geographical Horizons
The Voyages of Columbus

Chapter Summary

By the fifteenth century, the Italian city-states had become the economic and cultural leaders of Europe. Trade and the growth of cities created vigorous, dynamic mercantile states, unrestrained by feudalism, that controlled the capital wealth of Europe and laid the foundations of the intellectual and artistic revolution called the Renaissance. This movement was in part an extension and expansion of humanism, the tradition of classical scholarship that dated back to Petrarch. The spread of information and literacy would be accelerated by the mid-century invention of movable metal type by the Mainz jeweler Johann Gutenberg, although its impact would take decades to be fully felt. Music and the visual arts were given enormous encouragement, especially in Italy, by financial support from merchant princes and the church. Buoyed by higher wages and enhanced prestige, the artists explored new techniques, new effects, and new subjects.

Venice, built on islands in an Adriatic lagoon, was already Europe's principal gateway to the Middle East. In the fifteenth century, the Venetians also controlled significant territories on the mainland of northeastern Italy. The fall of Constantinople in 1453 eliminated her traditional trading partner and left Venice face to face with the Turks, who wanted to expand still further west. In spite of such challenges, Venice survived as a stable republic governed by aristocratic families

Milan, the largest city in Italy and probably in Europe, was ruled from the fourteenth century by the Visconti family. Their ambitions to expand Milan's territory brought frequent conflicts with their neighbors, especially Venice, but they managed to carve out a sizable north Italian empire. In 1447 Milan briefly became a republic, then fell under the control of the Sforza family, who built the famous fortress known as the Castello Sforzesca in the heart of the city; they also became notable patrons of the arts.

Florence was already an important center of banking and wool manufacture when Cosimo de Medici assumed control of the city in 1434. Cosimo preserved the façade of the republic, lavished his enormous wealth on civic projects, and gave financial support to artists and humanists. He was succeeded briefly by his sickly son Piero, and then by his brilliant grandson Lorenzo "the Magnificent," who was himself a learned and cultured patron of the arts.

The papacy, only recently delivered from the Great Schism, had to struggle briefly for authority against the conciliarists themselves; by mid-century, however, the popes were firmly in control. Nicholas V and Pius II were both scholars and humanists, but Sixtus IV and Innocent VIII were ambitious and worldly aristocrats, extravagant and ruthless in their leadership. Distrust of the papacy as an institution continued, especially in those parts of Europe most disillusioned by the Avignon years and by the Schism. Groups such as the Brethren of the Common Life, by emphasizing individual conscience and inner, lay piety, foreshadowed the Reformation.

Naples, which dominated virtually the entire southern third of the Italian peninsula, was ruled by the House of Aragon. Less urban and more feudal, this kingdom played only a small part in the culture of the Renaissance, but it was an important player in Italian war and diplomacy. In 1495, the city fell to Charles VIII of France, ushering in an age when most of the Italian city-states would fall under the control of foreign nation-states.

The only rival of the Italian peninsula for thriving cities, wealth, and cultural brilliance was the Duchy of Burgundy. Traditionally based in the Saône and upper Rhône valleys, the Burgundian dukes had acquired the wealthy cities of Flanders during the Hundred Years' War. The resulting state lacked clear borders or national identity, however, and in 1477 it was split between the Valois and the Habsburgs.

The English traditionally took great interest in the fate of Flanders, for both economic and strategic reasons. In this century, however, they were preoccupied by dynastic strife—that is, the question of who should be king—in the War of the Roses. The traditional rules of inheritance were not always followed in England, although when they were not, the consent of Parliament was usually sought (thereby setting important precedents). In 1399 the Lancasters had seized the throne; in 1461, the house of York took it back from the weak and unstable Henry VI. Civil warfare followed off and on for a quarter century. In 1483 Richard III took the crown from his twelve-year-old nephew, with Parliament's approval, but he provoked a new rebellion. Two years later he was killed at Bosworth Field by a cousin of the Lancasters who became Henry VII, founder of the Tudor dynasty.

While the Tudor and Valois dynasties were establishing their authority over emerging nation-states, the marriage of Ferdinand of Aragon with Isabella of Castile was creating the modern Spanish state. Born of the Reconquista, the Spanish state distrusted its Muslim and Jewish minorities. In 1492, Spain's rulers drove the last Moorish prince from Granada, annexed the remainder of Andalucia to the crown, and gave the Jews of Spain an ultimatum—to convert or leave. That same year, the Genoese sailor Christopher Columbus, sailing under the Spanish flag, crossed the Atlantic searching for the East Indies; his discovery would profoundly influence the histories of three continents.

On the eastern fringes of Europe, still another major new state was born. With the collapse of the Mongol empire in central Asia, the princes of Muscovy were able to assert control over a vast region. Ivan III married a Byzantine princess, assumed the imperial title *Tsar*, and even annexed the Hansa city of Novgorod, thus laying the foundations of the Russian state.

Vocabulary

auto da fé	Literally, "act of faith"; the formal sentencing ceremony of the Inquisition. Upon conviction, a person judged guilty would be turned over to civil authorities for punishment or execution.
khanates	Territories ruled by a khan. *Khan*, a word of central Asian origin, is used to refer to early Chinese and later Iranian rulers and to the chieftains of Mongol and Turkish tribes.
pederast	A molester of young boys.
fresco	A technique of painting pictures directly on wet plaster walls; also, the painting thus created.
condottieri	Mercenary (hired) soldiers or the leaders of mercenary bands, especially those employed by Renaissance city-states.
dowry	The money or valuable goods that a woman brings to her husband (or his family) at the time of marriage.
steppes	The arid, grassy plains of central Asia and southeastern Russia, inhabited by nomadic tribes.
tsar	Imperial title (the Russian word for *caesar*) assumed by the princes of Muscovy after Ivan III married a Byzantine princess. *Czar* is the Polish spelling of the same word.
nuncio	A papal representative of high rank.

florin   A gold coin first issued in Florence in 1252; it became a standard medium of exchange. Other countries later struck similar coins called *florins.*

Amerindian   An American Indian.

Self-Testing and Review Questions

Identification

After reading Chapter 14, identify and explain the historical significance of each of the following:

1. gallicanism

2. Ivan III

3. Francesco Sforza

4. Cosimo de Medici

5. War of the Roses

6. Eugenius IV

7. *studia humanitas*

8. Leonardo da Vinci

9. Marsilio Ficino

10. Hansa

11. Ferante of Naples

12. Josquin des Prés

13. Pius II

14. *Hermandad*

15. Arawaks

16. Lorenzo de Medici

17. Andrea Mantegna

18. Nicholas V

19. diaspora

20. Sixtus IV

Chronology

Indicate the events or issues associated with the following dates. Some dates may be significant for more than one reason. After you finish, answer the questions that follow.

1427

1434

1438

1453

1477

1478

1485

1492

1494

The fifteenth century saw the birth of several new states, the age of colonialism, and important technology; it also saw several noteworthy European states come to an end. What are the great watershed dates of the century and why is each important? How are the endings related to the beginnings? For example, in what ways did the fall of Constantinople encourage Atlantic exploration? How did it stimulate the Renaissance?

Matching Exercises

In each set, match the terms on the left with those on the right.

Set A

____ 1. Gonzaga
____ 2. Visconti
____ 3. Sforza
____ 4. Medici
____ 5. Aragon

a. Florence
b. Naples
c. Milan
d. Mantua
(Use one of these twice.)

Set B

____ 1. Leonardo da Vinci
____ 2. Andrea Mantegna
____ 3. Filippo Brunelleschi
____ 4. Marsilio Ficino
____ 5. Leon Battista Alberti

a. painted the Camera degli sposi
b. designed the Ospitale degl' Innocenti
c. wrote *On Architecture*
d. was a versatile Florentine painter
e. was a founder of the Platonic Academy

Set C

____ 1. Alfonso I   a. the Navigator
____ 2. Lorenzo   b. the Conqueror
____ 3. Prince Henry   c. the Magnanimous
____ 4. Mehmed II   d. the Bold
____ 5. Charles of Burgundy   e. the Magnificent

Set D

____ 1. Bartolomeu Diás   a. a famous doge
____ 2. Gert Groote   b. polyphony
____ 3. Guillaume Dufay   c. *On the Dignity of Man*
____ 4. Pietro Mocenigo   d. Florentine painter
____ 5. Pico della Mirandola   e. Brethren of the Common Life
____ 6. Filippino Lippi   f. the Cape of Good Hope

Set E

____ 1. Isabella   a. the last Byzantine ruler
____ 2. Constantine Paleologus   b. ruler who evicted the Jews
____ 3. Henry VII   c. Hungarian ruler
____ 4. Philip the Good   d. Burgundian ruler
____ 5. Matthias Corvinus   e. founder of the Tudor dynasty

Multiple-Choice Questions

1. After 1453, Hagia Sophia
   a. was settled by Sephardic Jews fleeing from Spain.
   b. was converted into a mosque.
   c. led the Mongol armies against the Tartars.
   d. introduced printing technology to eastern Europe.

2. The War of the Roses involved
   a. Anjou and Aragon.
   b. the Yorks and Lancasters.
   c. the supporters and opponents of Cosimo de Medici.
   d. Louis XI and Charles the Bold.

3. Nicholas Cusa is remembered for his
   a. conciliarism.   c. motets.
   b. movable type.   d. diplomacy.

4. The first European to round the Cape of Good Hope was
   a. Bartolomeu Diás.   c. Vasco da Gama.
   b. Christopher Columbus.   d. Nuñez de Balboa.

5. The battle of Bosworth Field resulted in the death of
   a. Charles the Bold.   c. Henry VII.
   b. Edward IV.   d. Richard III.

6. The Spanish and Portuguese divided their colonial possessions in the
   a. Pragmatic Sanction of Bourges.   c. Treaty of Lodi.
   b. Treaty of Tordesillas.   d. Council of Basel.

7. The *conversos* were distrusted by the
   a. Jagiellonians.   c. Ashkenazim.
   b. conciliarists.   d. Inquisition.

8. Johannes Gutenberg invented
   a. books.   c. movable metal type.
   b. printing.   d. the rotary press.

9. The "most serene republic" was
   a. Venice.   c. Milan.
   b. Florence.   d. Siena.

10. The fall of Constantinople resulted in all of these *except*
    a. an influx of Greek scholars into Renaissance Italy.
    b. the expulsion of the Ashkenazim.
    c. the division of the Mediterranean into Muslim and Christian sectors.
    d. new wars between Venice and the Turks.

Essay Questions

Using material from this and previous chapters, write an essay on each of the following topics. Include dates and detailed examples, when appropriate, to support your arguments.

1. Both the French and English monarchies experienced civil wars in the fifteenth century. How were these wars parallel and how were they different? Did the outcome of the Hundred Years' War help lead to the War of the Roses?

2. What developments in Europe in the fifteenth century encouraged Atlantic exploration?

3. From the time of Giotto, Italian artists placed increasingly greater emphasis on the imitation of nature. Is that a radical departure from the world view of medieval thinkers? If so, what factors led to the change?

4. What features of Italian society in the fourteenth century caused the artistic revolution to occur there first?

5. Discuss the papacy in fifteenth-century Europe. To what extent were conciliarism and the Modern Devotion after-effects of the Avignon papacy and the Schism? How was the role of the papacy changing?

Skill Building: Maps

Locate the following on the map of Europe at the end of the fifteenth century. For some of these, you may need to refer to Chapter 13. Why was each significant in this chapter?

a. Antwerp

b. Lisbon

c. Nancy

d. Prague

e. Bruges

f. Mainz

g. Strasbourg

h. Nuremberg

i. Cologne

j. Augsburg

k. Basel

l. Vienna

m. Hamburg

n. Frankfurt-am-Main

o. Lübeck

p. Rostock

q. Danzig

r. Novgorod

s. Lodi

t. Stralsund

u. Moscow

v. Volga River

w. Constantinople

1. Circle the cities of the Hansa. How were the principal trading areas of northern Europe connected to southern Europe? Why was north-south trade important?

2. Shade in the areas of Europe under Turkish control by the end of the fifteenth century. Which states were then threatened by the Ottomans? How were events in Italy and Spain affected by Ottoman expansion?

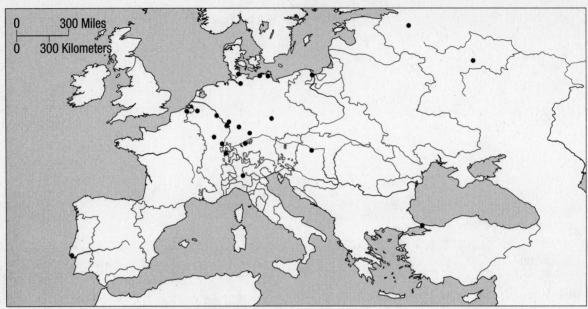

Europe at End of the Fifteenth Century

Locate the following on the map of fifteenth-century Italy. Why was each significant in this chapter?

   a. Milan

   b. Rome

   c. Venice

   d. Florence

   e. Bologna

   f. Siena

   g. Ferrara

   h. Genoa

   i. Mantua

   j. Naples

Shade in the areas of the Papal States and the Kingdom of Naples. What geographical factors led to wars between Milan and Venice and between Florence and Rome but to relative peace between Florence and Milan in the second half of the fifteenth century?

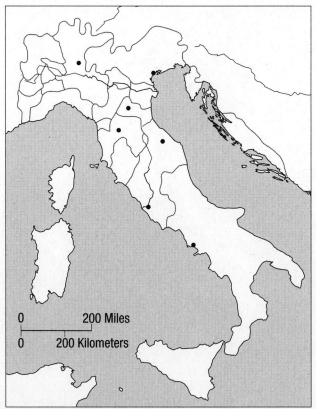

Fifteenth Century Italy

Locate the following on the map of European exploration. Why was each significant in the history of exploration?

    a. Ceuta

    b. Guinea

    c. Canary Islands

    d. Madeira

    e. Cape of Good Hope

    f. Calicut

    g. Cape Verdes Islands

    h. Bahamas

    i. Hispaniola

    j. Cadiz

Exploring New Worlds

1. The Portuguese were trying to find a new route to India, and Columbus was trying to find a new route to China. What goods were they hoping to trade? Why were the old routes no longer attractive?

2. What was the significance of the Line of Demarcation in South America? Mark it on the map.

Enrichment Exercises

1. In his play *Richard III,* Shakespeare created an enduring portrait of "Richard Crookback," the last Yorkist king of England. The greatest playwright of the Elizabethan era, Shakespeare followed certain historians of the period and depicted Richard as an ogre and thus made a saviour of Henry VII, the grandfather of Elizabeth I. Sir Laurence Olivier's unforgettable portrayal of the title role was captured on film in 1956 and remains one of the best. As you watch the film, consider the characters. Does Richard really need to murder his nephews in order to be king? What motives would Henry have had to lie after Richard's death? Are other explanations of the motives and deeds of Richard and Henry possible? Whatever conjecture you make, it has probably already been made by one of the literally dozens of historians who have examined the events of 1485. Many argue that the records of these events were intentionally falsified. Just how reliable are historical records and chronicles, especially those intended for later generations?

2. In art books look carefully at the works at Masaccio, Lorenzo Ghiberti, Donatello, Sandro Botticelli, Leonardo da Vinci, Andrea Mantegna, and Jan van Eyck. Select one of these artists and write a brief report on his life, his ideals, his patrons, and the society of his time. If you have an art museum nearby, visit it, study the artworks from the fifteenth century, and consider the same questions.

Document Analysis

Document 1

How Leonardo da Vinci Painted The Last Supper

In 1550, the Florentine painter Giorgio Vasari (*1574) published a bestseller, The Lives of the Artists, *that records for later generations the biographies of leading painters of the Italian Renaissance. A landmark in the social history of art, the very appearance of the book reflected the higher social status of Renaissance painters. A medieval painter was only a guild artisan, but the Renaissance artist was a creative genius. Like his medieval counterpart, however, the Renaissance artist started out as an apprentice in a workshop and depended on assignments from wealthy patrons. Vasari's story of Leonardo da Vinci shows the significance of patronage in artistic creation, especially patrons from the church and princely courts.*

> Leonardo also executed in Milan, for the Dominicans of Santa Maria delle Grazie, a marvellous and beautiful painting of the Last Supper. Having depicted the heads of the apostles full of splendor and majesty, he deliberately left the head of Christ unfinished, convinced he would fail to give it the divine spirituality it demands. . . . It is said that the prior used to keep pressing Leonardo, in the most importunate way, to hurry up and finish the work, because he was puzzled by Leonardo's habit of sometimes spending half a day at a time contemplating what he had done so far; if the prior had had his way, Leonardo would have toiled like one of the laborers hoeing in the garden and never put his brush down

for a moment. Not satisfied with this, the prior then complained to the duke [Ludovico Sforza], making such a fuss that the duke was constrained to send for Leonardo. . . . Leonardo, knowing he was dealing with a prince of acute and discerning intelligence, was willing (as he never had been with the prior) to explain his mind at length. . . . He explained that men of genius sometimes accomplish most when they work the least. . . . Leonardo then said that he still had two heads to paint: the head of Christ was one, and for this he was unwilling to look for any human model. . . . Then, he said, he had yet to do the head of Judas, and this troubled him since he did not think he could imagine the features that would form the countenance of a man who, despite all the blessings he had been given, could so cruelly steel his will to betray his own master and the creator of the world. However, added Leonardo, he would try to find a model for Judas, and if he did not succeed in doing so, why then he was not without the head of that tactless and importunate prior. The duke roared with laughter at this and said that Leonardo had every reason in the world for saying so.

Source: Giorgio Vasari, *Artists of the Renaissance: A Selection from Lives of the Artists,* trans. George Bull (Penguin Books, 1978), pp. 187–188.

Question

1. The *Last Supper* has not survived well because Leonardo chose to put oil paint on the wall rather than the traditional method of fresco, which was to work with water-based paints. What work habits of Leonardo, illustrated in this anecdote, may explain why Leonardo disliked fresco?

DOCUMENT 2

Marriage Negotiations: The Strozzi, 1464–1465

For upper-class Florentines, marriages represented family alliances negotiated by heads of households. In the following letters, the Florentine widow Alessandra Strozzi assumed the role normally reserved for the family patriarch in arranging a bride for her son, Filippo, who was in political exile in Naples. However, the actual negotiations were arranged by males, and the interests of the Strozzi were represented by Alessandra's son-in-law, Marco Parenti. The prospective bridegroom was only one actor in this courting game, and the prospective bride had no voice regarding her future happiness.

[April 20, 1464] . . . Concerning the matter of a wife [for Filippo], it appears to me that if Francesco di Messer Guglielmino Tanagli wishes to give his daughter, that it would be a fine marriage. . . . Now I will speak with Marco, to see if there are other prospects that would be better. . . . Francesco Tanagli has a good reputation, and he has held office—not the highest, but still he has been in office. You may ask: "Why should he give her to someone in exile?" There are three reasons. First, there aren't many young men of good family who have both virtue and property. Secondly, she has only a small dowry, 1,000 florins, which is the dowry of an artisan. . . . Third, I believe that he will give her away, because he has a large family and he will need help to settle them. . . .

[August 17, 1465] . . . Sunday morning I went to the first mass at S. Reparata . . . to see the Adimari girl, who customarily goes to that mass, and I found the

Tanagli girl there. Not knowing who she was, I stood beside her. . . . She is very attractive, well-proportioned, as large or larger than Caterina [Alessandra's daughter]. . . . She has a long face, and her features are not very delicate, but they aren't like a peasant's. From her demeanor, she does not appear to me to be indolent. . . . I walked behind her as we left the church, and thus I realized that she was one of the Tanagli. . . .

[September 13, 1465] . . . Marco came to me and said that he had met with Francesco Tanagli, who had spoken very coldly, so that I understand that he had changed his mind. . . . I believe that this is the result of the long delay in our replying to him, both yours and Marco's. Now that this delay has angered him, and he has at hand some prospect that is more attractive. . . . I am very annoyed by this business. . . .

[Filippo Strozzi eventually married Fiametta di Donato Adimari, in 1466.]

Source: Gene Brucker, ed., *The Society of Renaissance Florence: A Documentary Study* (Harper & Row, 1971), pp. 37–40.

Question

1. The text, in the section entitled "Family Alliances," offers further information on the Strozzi family and its marriage negotiations. How would you explain Alessandra Strozzi's attitude toward the dowry of 1,000 florins from a prospective daughter-in-law, compared to the size of her own daughter's dowry seventeen years earlier?

DOCUMENT 3

Infanticide in Florence

Unlike the powerful, who arranged marriage alliances on the basis of wealth and social advantage, the common people, particularly the women, faced limited options. Deceived by promises of marriage in exchange for sexual intimacy, many poorer women abandoned their illegitimate infants to escape social shame. In the following document, a pregnant woman, Monna Francesca, was deserted by the father of her child and married another man. But after the birth of her child, she feared for her own safety if her husband should discover the fact and she drowned the baby. She incurred the severity of the judicial machinery and was condemned to a horrible death.

. . . We [the magistrates] condemn . . . Monna Francesca, the daughter of Cristofano Ciuti of Villa Caso . . . , the wife of Cecco Arrighi of Ponte Boccio. . . . During the months of April, May, and June of the past year, Francesca lived at Montemurlo . . . on a farm belonging to Buonaccorso Strozzi. There she had conversations with a certain Jacopo of Romagna, Buonaccorso's servant, who told her that he wanted to take her for his wife. So Francesca, persuaded by his words and his arguments, allowed herself to become intimate with him on several occasions . . . so that she became pregnant by Jacopo. . . .

Then Francesca, knowing herself to be pregnant . . . promised to marry . . . Cecco Arrighi of Ponte Boccio . . . in the month of October. . . . Cecco did not realize that Francesca was pregnant by Jacopo . . . although she had been questioned by Cecco and his brothers about her swollen stomach. . . .

In the month of March of the present year, Francesca . . . gave birth to a healthy male child. . . . But inspired by an evil spirit and so that no one would know that she had given birth to that child, she threw him in the river . . . and as a result, this son and creature of God was drowned.

[Francesca confessed. She was led through the streets of Pistoia on a donkey, with the corpse of her child tied to her neck, and was then burned to death.]

Source: Gene Brucker, ed., *The Society of Renaissance Florence: A Documentary Study* (Harper & Row, 1971), pp. 146–147.

Questions

1. Who had more control over whom she would marry—the peasant Monna Francesca or the aristocratic women discussed in Document 2? Why?

2. Would a daughter of the Strozzi family be likely to have had the personal freedom (from supervision) to make the tragic decisions that Monna Francesca made? Why or why not?

DOCUMENT 4

Columbus Reaches Land

On October 11, 1492, after sailing for sixty-eight days across the Atlantic, Christopher Columbus reached land. He mistook the islands, later called the West Indies, for regions off the coast of China. For three months, Columbus sailed and explored the islands, describing encounters with Indians in the ship's log. Although the initial contact between Europeans and Indians was peaceful, the future fate of the Indians is suggested by Columbus's design to turn them into docile Christians and workers. The following description of Indians in Cuba was entered in the ship's log for November 11, 1492.

It appears to me that it would be well to take some of these people . . . to the Sovereigns, in order that they might learn our language and we might learn what there is in this country. Upon return they may speak the language of the Christians and take our customs and Faith to their people. I see and know that these people have no religion whatever, nor are they idolaters, but rather, they are very meek and know no evil. They do not kill or capture others and are without weapons. They are so timid that a hundred of them flee from one of us. . . .They are very trusting; they believe that there is a God in Heaven, and they firmly believe that we come from Heaven. . . . Therefore, Your Highnesses must resolve to make them Christians. I believe that if this effort commences, in a short time a multitude of peoples will be converted to our Holy Faith, and Spain will acquire great domains and riches and all of their villages. Beyond doubt there is a very great amount of gold in this country. . . ."

Source: *The Log of Christopher Columbus*, trans. Robert H. Fuson (International Marine, 1987), pp. 106–107.

Questions

1. Some recent studies of Columbus have described him as fanatic, cruel, greedy, rapacious, racist, and deliberately genocidal. Given what you have learned in the text about the European experience of the Crusades, the Spanish experience of the Reconquista, the treatment of heretics by the Inquisition, and the treatment of Jews in Spain under Ferdinand and Isabella, how many of these adjectives seem appropriate? Is Columbus an unusually despicable representative of Western culture?

2. How much authority should we give to this single quotation in evaluating Columbus's character and future behavior?

3. How does Western culture—if we assume that Columbus was typical—manage to admire gentleness and at the same time cultivate military power?

CHAPTER

15

The Struggle for Faith and Power,
1494–1560

Chapter Outline

Chapter Summary

At the end of the fifteenth century, Italian society was torn apart by wars among the city-states, civil strife, and foreign invasion. Even the Papal States were involved in the wars and conspiracies of the age. As a result, military and diplomatic skill was generally preferred to piety when selecting men for the highest church offices. Popes such as Alexander VI scandalized even the most cynical observers of the day. His successor, Julius II, famed as the patron of Michelangelo and the High Renaissance, was not especially immoral, but he was no less the warrior. Worldly and cultured church leaders such as these tolerated many immoral practices by the clergy. These practices included simony (buying or selling church offices), absenteeism, sexual immorality, nepotism (appointing one's relatives to church jobs), and extortion of money. The materialism of the papal court repelled many, including non-Italians, the otherworldly, and the naive. A general distrust of the church hierarchy had long persisted in northern Europe, and the excesses of the early sixteenth century would turn disillusionment into open revolt.

Martin Luther was a German monk trained in law and theology, a talented scholar, and a popular teacher at the new University of Wittenberg. His ideas stemmed from many sources—his study of the Scriptures and of the early church fathers, his visit to Rome (a city that he found appalling), and probably the ideas of Wycliff and Hus that had spread to his native Saxony. In 1517 he reacted against an aggressive new campaign by the church to sell indulgences. He composed (and published) his famous Ninety-five Theses, which questioned, among other things, the validity of indulgences. The reaction from Rome was more contemptuous than angry, so in 1520 Luther published three treatises that more openly and fundamentally attacked the church, the papacy, and the role of the clergy. He argued that according to Scripture, baptism and faith were necessary for salvation but "good works"—including most sacraments and indulgences—were not. He also appealed to German national feelings to rally against Rome when he called on the German princes to make the lead in reform. These treatises, like the Ninety-five Theses, were widely disseminated, thanks to the new printing technology. Luther soon had the full attention of the authorities. In 1521, when he defended his ideas at the Imperial Diet, he earned the condemnation of Charles V. He also publicly burned the papal bull that excommunicated him. Under the protection of the Elector of Saxony, Luther began his famous translation of the New Testament into German, and perhaps to dramatize his break with the clergy he married a nun.

Luther was not the only reformer of his generation. In 1520, Huldrych Zwingli of Zürich also broke with the church, and Desiderius Erasmus, a Dutch scholar and theologian, was expected to do the same, but he did not. On several issues, especially the sacraments, Luther and Zwingli did not agree, and a group called the Anabaptists challenged Zwingli's authority in Zürich. Elsewhere, peasant rebels led by Thomas Müntzer demanded social justice in the name of religion and refused Luther's orders to disperse. Finally Luther, like Zwingli with the Anabaptists, called on the civil authorities to strike down the rebels. The new religious movement, which had set out to reform the church, was now splitting into fragments in a chain reaction that seemed to have no end. Over the next few decades, the French reformer John Calvin constructed an elaborate new theology and transformed the city of Geneva to conform to his ideas. His disciples spread Calvinist ideas throughout Europe, from France to Poland, from Holland to Bavaria.

Protestantism also developed in England, but under peculiar circumstances. In 1527, Henry VIII decided to divorce his wife, Catherine of Aragon. A decade and a half of marriage had produced only a daughter, whereas a recent affair had resulted in an illegitimate son. After his request for divorce was rejected by Pope Clement VII, Henry rejected papal authority over such matters and declared himself Supreme Head of the Church of England. He then divorced Catherine and married Anne Boleyn. Although Henry probably had no intention of introducing Protestant theology into his new church, he was opposed by loyal Catholics and therefore relied on royal ministers with reformist inclinations. His second wife gave him another daughter, Elizabeth, and was executed for adultery; his third wife gave him a sickly son, Edward. After Henry died in 1547, his teenaged son became Edward VI and the Anglican church became openly Protestant. When Edward died in 1553, the throne passed to the eldest daughter, Mary, who restored the Catholic church, persecuted the Protestants, and married King Philip II of Spain. When Mary died after a bloody five-year reign, Elizabeth succeeded her. Because the Catholics considered her illegitimate, Elizabeth naturally reaffirmed the Anglican church and suppressed those who objected.

The Catholic response to Protestantism varied. Initial attempts to suppress the movement failed, and efforts to make peace with it were rejected. Pope Paul III promoted reform and renewal within the Catholic church, convened the Council of Trent, which further defined Catholic dogma, and approved the founding of the Society of Jesus, which soon became known for its vigorous defense of papal authority.

In Germany, Charles V tried but failed to crush the Protestant Schmalkaldic League, and was forced to accept the Peace of Augsburg, a treaty that recognized the Lutheran princes' rights within their own states. Charles might have been the greatest monarch in European history, ruling a domain that included Germany, Flanders, Spain, parts of Italy and Burgundy, and most of the New World, as a result of the success of *conquistadores* such as Cortés and Pizarro. Instead, he spent his reign first fighting the Turkish advance under Suleiman the Magnificent and then opposing the Lutherans in Germany. After Augsburg, he resigned in disgust and entered a monastery. His empire was divided between his brother and his son, creating two Habsburg dynasties, one in Spain and one in Austria.

The late Renaissance was also the age during which the elder Michelangelo adorned Rome, Titian led the brilliant Venetian school, and the seeds of the scientific revolution were planted by Copernicus, Vesalius, and others. Learning was especially important in Protestant Europe, where elementary schools were set up to teach ordinary people how to read—a prerequisite for Bible reading and salvation. Some of the traditional responsibilities of the clergy, such as caring for the poor, were taken over by local government.

Vocabulary

theocracy   Literally, government by God; in practice, government by clergy who claim to speak for God. Papal Rome, Calvin's Geneva, and contemporary Iran are all examples of theocracies.

sacrament   A practice or ritual believed to convey divine grace and therefore to have a significant role in achieving salvation.

pedagogic   Pertaining to teaching or to the educational process.

predestination	The theological belief that, given an all-powerful and all-knowing God, each individual's spiritual fate is preordained.
Vulgate	St. Jerome's translation of the Bible into Latin; the official version of the Bible for the western Church in the Middle Ages.
mestizo	The Spanish word for "mixed"; in the New World, a person of mixed European and Amerindian ancestry.
mulatto	The child of a European and an African. The child of a mulatto and a European was called a "quadroon" (indicating one-fourth African). The child of a quadroon and a European was called an "octoroon."

Self-Testing and Review Questions

Identification

After reading Chapter 15, identify and explain the historical significance of each of the following:

1. Suleiman the Magnificent

2. Michelangelo Buonarroti

3. Christian humanism

4. Huguenots

5. Schmalkaldic League

6. *The Prince*

7. Mohács

8. Frederick the Wise

9. Anabaptists

10. Council of Trent

11. Affair of the Placards

12. Diet of Worms

13. Guillaume Briçonnet

14. *Gymnasium*

15. Bartolomé de Las Casas

16. Hernando Cortés

17. Albrecht Dürer

18. Incas

19. Alexander VI

20. Edward VI

21. Huldrych Zwingli

22. predestination

23. Peace of Augsburg

24. Nicholas Copernicus

25. Battle of Pavia

Chronology

Indicate the events or issues associated with the following dates. Some dates may be significant for more than one reason. After you finish, answer the questions that follow.

1494

1517

1525

1527

1534

1541

1543

1545

1555

1558

1. Which years saw the careers of Luther? of Michelangelo? of Calvin? When were the reigns of Charles V? of Henry VIII? How much influence do you suppose Michelangelo had on the art of England? Why?

2. Many of Luther's ideas differed little from those of Wycliff or Hus. Study the significant events of the previous century (see Chapter 14) and explain why Luther was so much more effective at broadcasting his message.

Matching Exercises

In each set, match the terms on the left with those on the right.

Set A

____ 1. Thomas More   a. *On the Support of the Poor*

____ 2. Desiderius Erasmus   b. *To the Nobility of the German Nation*

____ 3. Juan Luis Vives   c. *Colloquies, Adages*

____ 4. Niccolò Machiavelli   d. *Utopia*

____ 5. Martin Luther   e. *Discourses*

Set B

____ 1. Girolamo Savonarola   a. Wittenberg

____ 2. John Calvin   b. Geneva

____ 3. Martin Luther   c. Augsburg

____ 4. Jakob Fugger   d. Venice

____ 5. Titian   e. Florence

Set C

____ 1. Nicholas Copernicus   a. *Handbook for a Christian Knight*

____ 2. Desiderius Erasmus   b. *Institutes of the Christian Religion*

____ 3. Martin Luther   c. *The Freedom of a Christian*

____ 4. John Calvin   d. *The First Blast of the Trumpet Against the Monstrous Regiment of Women*

____ 5. John Knox   e. *On the Revolutions of Heavenly Spheres*

Set D

____ 1. Michael Servetus   a. Condemned by Charles V

____ 2. Thomas Wolsey   b. Condemned by Alexander VI

____ 3. Martin Luther   c. Condemned by Henry VIII

____ 4. Thomas More   d. Condemned by John Calvin

____ 5. Girolamo Savonarola   (Use one of these twice.)

Set E

____ 1. *The Prince*   a. Ludovico Ariosto

____ 2. *The Courtier*   b. Baldassare Castiglione

____ 3. *De Fabrica*   c. Andreas Vesalius

____ 4. *The Praise of Folly*   d. Niccolò Machiavelli

____ 5. *Orlando furioso*   e. Desiderius Erasmus

Set F

____ 1. Mary Stuart

____ 2. Mary Tudor

____ 3. Mary of Guise

____ 4. Anne Boleyn

____ 5. Elizabeth

a. mother of Mary Stuart

b. queen of France

c. wife of Henry VIII

d. Catholic daughter of Henry VIII

e. Protestant daughter of Henry VIII

Multiple-Choice Questions

1. What did Luther, Erasmus, Tyndale, and Jacques Lefèvre d'Étaples have in common?
   a. They all broke with the papacy and founded Protestant movements.
   b. They all lived for a time in John Knox's Edinburgh.
   c. Their early careers were financially supported by the Emperor Maximilian.
   d. They all translated the Bible.

2. Which of these was the Borgia pope?
   a. Leo X
   b. Alexander VI
   c. Julius II
   d. Paul III

3. Orlando de Lassus was
   a. a composer.
   b. a printer.
   c. a humanist.
   d. the subject of a famous poem.

4. The Peasant Rebellion in Germany was led by
   a. Jakob Fugger.
   b. Huldrych Zwingli.
   c. Thomas Müntzer.
   d. Albrecht Dürer.

5. The German prince who protected Luther was
   a. Maximilian of Bavaria.
   b. Frederick of Saxony.
   c. Charles V.
   d. Christian IV.

6. The Catholics and Lutherans in Germany reached a settlement by means of
   a. the Diet of Worms.
   b. the Peace of Augsburg.
   c. the Council of Trent.
   d. the Treaty of Câteau-Cambrésis.

7. A famous study of human anatomy was the principal achievement of
   a. Palestrina.
   b. Paracelsus.
   c. Aldus Manutius.
   d. Andreas Vesalius.

8. The Jesuits were founded by
   a. Michael Servetus.
   b. Teresa of Ávila.
   c. Ignatius Loyola.
   d. Cesare Borgia.

9. Michelangelo painted the ceiling of the Sistine chapel for
   a. Alexander VI.
   b. Julius II.
   c. Leo X.
   d. Clement VII.

10. The shocking sack of Rome was the work of
    a. Henry VIII.
    b. Suleiman.
    c. Charles V.
    d. Charles VIII.

Essay Questions

Using material from this and previous chapters, write an essay on each of the following topics. Include dates and detailed examples, when appropriate, to support your arguments.

1. You have read that Luther was an Augustinian friar who placed great emphasis on the writings of St. Paul and St. Augustine. How did Luther's thought reflect Augustine's thought? (How had Christian theology been modified in the intervening centuries, and by whom?)

2. Trace the Habsburg-Valois wars; did they end the Renaissance? Why or why not? Consider changes in military technology, the cost (to rulers and their subjects) of warfare, and the political outcome of the wars.

3. Was Luther a "medieval" or a "modern" man, and why?

4. How did the religious leaders of the sixteenth century justify their intolerance?

5. How was the exploration and colonization of the non-Western world a logical extension of Renaissance society and principles? To what extent did the "discovery" of "the New World" change the mental world of Europeans in the late fifteenth and sixteenth centuries?

Skill Building: Maps

Locate the following on the map of Europe. Why was each significant in this chapter?

a. Venice

b. Nice

c. Toulon

d. Vienna

e. Geneva

f. Rome

g. Zürich

h. Strasbourg

i. Marignano

j. Nuremberg

k. Allstedt

l. Florence

m. Wittenberg

n. Freiburg

o. Mainz

p. Trent

1. It has been argued that the Reformation was, in part, an anti-Italian movement. In which areas of Europe was Protestantism most successful?

2. Of the Protestant areas, which became predominantly Lutheran? Calvinist? Which of these two became an international movement, and which was largely confined to a single area? Why?

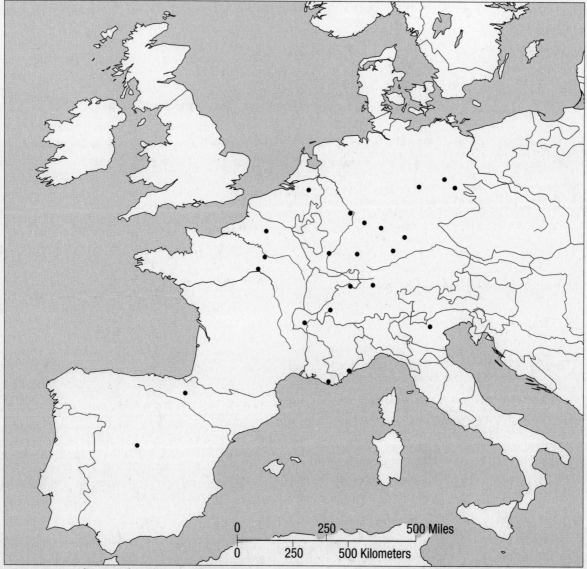

Europe in the Early Sixteenth Century

Locate the following on the map of European settlement. Why was each significant in this chapter?

a. Mozambique

b. Guinea

c. Newfoundland

d. Brazil

e. Montréal

f. Potosí

g. Yucatán

h. Tenochtitlán

i. Lima

j. Spain

k. Colombo

l. Portugal

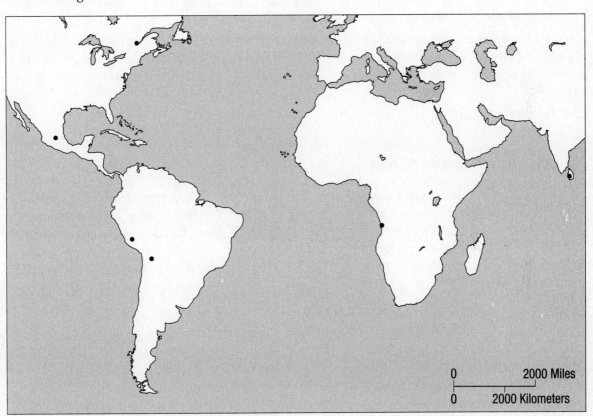

European Settlement in the New Worlds

Enrichment Exercises

1. Some historical figures led lives more fascinating than the best fiction. Several dozen clever, passionate, strong-willed, ambitious people intriguing among themselves, with the fate of nations in their hands, are as dramatic as any novel. This is why the story of Henry VIII, his wives and his children, has been retold, and filmed, so many times. Here are some of the good films about the Tudors:

A Man for All Seasons (1966) with an outstanding cast, won Academy Awards for Best Picture, Best Director, Best Actor, Best Screenplay, and cinematography. It dramatizes the falling out between Thomas More and Henry VIII.

Anne of a Thousand Days (1969) is based on Maxwell Anderson's play about Henry VIII and Anne Boleyn; Richard Burton plays Henry VIII.

The Six Wives of Henry VIII was a critically acclaimed series for television created by the BBC and broadcast in the United States as part of the PBS Masterpiece Theater series. Each of the six episodes is ninety minutes long.

Watch one of these films and write a two-page essay about it. How faithful is it to the historical facts reported in the text?

2. In art books, look carefully at the works of Raphaël, Michelangelo, Titian, Dürer, Holbein, and El Greco. What do the artworks tell you about the artists? their patrons? their ideals? their milieu? If you have an art museum nearby, visit it, study the artworks from the sixteenth century, and consider the same questions. Then write a brief report on the artist whose works you enjoy the most.

3. Read the book of Romans in the New Testament. Why do you think Martin Luther found it so compelling? What parts of it seem to have affected his thinking most strongly? Write a one- or two-page essay about Romans and its influence on Luther and the sixteenth century.

Document Analysis

DOCUMENT 1

Hernan Cortés on the Aztecs

In Mexico, the Spaniards met a sophisticated civilization. The Aztec empire, with its capital at Tenochtitlán (the site of Mexico City today), ruled over many subject Indian populations, partly through frightening rituals of human sacrifice and cannibalism. Cortés's letters to Charles V reporting on the progress of the Spanish conquest reflect both his admiration for the grandeur of Aztec cities and his disgust with cannibalism. The letters represent a fascinating source of early information about "foreign" cultures. They also provide reasons for imperial and colonial domination.

> This great city of Tenochtitlán is built on the salt lake. . . . It has four approaches by means of artificial causeways. . . . The city is as large as Seville or Cordoba. Its streets . . . are very broad and straight, some of these, and all the others, are one half land, and the other half water on which they go about in canoes. . . . There are bridges, very large, strong, and well constructed, so that, over many, ten horsemen can ride abreast. . . . The city has many squares where markets are held. . . . There is one square, twice as large as that of Salamanca, all surrounded by arcades, where there are daily more than sixty thousand souls, buying and selling. . . . In the service and manners of its people, their fashion of living was almost the same as in Spain, with just as much harmony and order; and considering that these people were barbarous, so cut off from the knowledge of God and other civilized peoples, it is admirable to see to what they attained in every respect. [From the second letter]
>
> It happened . . . that a Spaniard saw an Indian . . . eating a piece of flesh taken from the body of an Indian who had been killed. . . . I had the culprit burned,

explaining that the cause was his having killed that Indian and eaten him which was prohibited by Your Majesty, and by me in Your Royal name. I further made the chief understand that all the people . . . must abstain from this custom. . . . I came . . . to protect their lives as well as their property, and to teach them that they were to adore but one God . . . that they must turn from their idols, and the rites they had practised until then, for these were lies and deceptions which the devil . . . had invented. . . . I, likewise, had come to teach them that Your Majesty, by the will of Divine Providence, rules the universe, and that they also must submit themselves to the imperial yoke, and do all that we who are Your Majesty's ministers here might order them. . . . (From the fifth letter)

Source: *Letters of Cortés: The Five Letters of Relation from Fernando Cortés to the Emperor Charles V,* trans. Francis A. MacNutt (Rio Grande, 1908), Vol. 1, pp. 256–257, 263; Vol. 2, pp. 244–245.

Question

1. Even more disgusting to the Spaniards than the actual human sacrifice was the fact that one of its purposes was to obtain flesh forcannibalism. Much has been written about the crimes of the Spanish *conquistadores* in destroying Aztec culture, and of their greed and cruelty. Yet, since the Spanish had the power to stop human sacrifice and cannibalism, were they not obligated to do so? Why or why not?

DOCUMENT 2

Martin Luther on "The Freedom of a Christian"

"The Freedom of a Christian", composed and published in 1520, was one of Luther's three most popular pamphlets sounding the "battle cry" of the Reformation. Unlike the usual Latin theological treatises, which were restricted to academic circles, Luther's essay, written in German and mass produced as cheap pamphlets, reached a wide public. This work sets out the reformer's idea of justification by faith: namely, that salvation consisted in reading the Gospels and in believing. At one stroke, Luther undermined the entire structure of the Catholic church, making the clergy, their sacraments, their rules and good works irrelevant to salvation.

One thing, and only one thing, is necessary for Christian life, righteousness, and freedom. That one thing is the most holy Word of God, the gospel of Christ. . . . It is easy to see from what source faith derives such great power and why a good work or all good works together cannot equal it. No good work can rely upon the Word of God or live in the soul, for faith alone and the Word of God rule in the soul. Just as the heated iron glows like fire because of the union of fire with it, so the Word imparts its qualities to the soul. It is clear, then, that a Christian has all that he needs in faith and needs no works to justify him; and if he has no need of works, he has no need of the law; and if he has no need of the law, surely he is free from the law. . . . This is that Christian liberty, our faith, which does not induce us to live in idleness or wickedness but makes the law and works unnecessary for any man's righteousness and salvation.

Source: *Luther's Works,* American Edition, Vol. 31 (Concordia, 1957), pp. 345, 349–350.

Questions

1. The emphasis on the Scriptures as the sole reliable source of revelation, as expressed earlier by Wycliff and here by Luther, appeared at the same time as the spread of literacy and the rise of the middle class in Europe. Is this a coincidence?

2. Why were vernacular translations of the Bible (for instance, into German and English) important to the reformers but distrusted by the Catholic clergy?

DOCUMENT 3

Violence and Honor Between the Sexes

In Marguerite de Navarre's Heptameron, *the fourth story of the first day was told by Ennasuite, a noblewoman. The story tells of the obsession of a gentleman at the Flemish court for the princess, a woman of great beauty and virtue. When his attentions caused her to be friendly to him, the gentleman invited the princess to stay at his castle. During the night, he stole into her room, professed his love, and when rejected, attempted to rape her. Fighting him off, the princess was saved by her lady-in-waiting. After the story, the male and female characters in* Heptameron *commented on their conduct: Hircan claimed that male honor justified even murder, to which Nomerfide, a noblewoman, responded in horror.*

> "And that, Ladies, is a story that should strike fear into the hearts of any man who thinks he can help himself to what doesn't belong to him. The Princess's virtue and the good sense of her lady-in-waiting should inspire courage in the hearts of all women. . . ."
>
> "In my opinion," said Hircan, "the tall lord of your story lacked nerve, and didn't deserve to have his memory preserved. What an opportunity he had! He should never have been content to eat or sleep till he'd succeeded. And one really can't say that his love was very great, if there was still room in his heart for the fear of death and dishonor."
>
> "And what," asked Nomerfide, "could the poor man have done with two women against him?"
>
> "He should have killed the old one, and when the young one realized there was no one to help her, he'd have been half-way there!"
>
> "Kill her!" Nomerfide cried. "You wouldn't mind him being a murderer as well, then? If that's what you think, we'd better watch out we don't fall into your clutches!"
>
> "If I'd gone that far," he replied, "I'd consider my honor ruined if I didn't go through with it!"

Source: Marguerite de Navarre, *The Heptameron*, trans. P. A. Chilton (Penguin Books, 1984), pp. 96–97.

Questions

1. Was a nobleman's "honor" actually challenged when rebuffed in the act of rape, or is Marguerite de Navarre exaggerating to make a point?

2. What is "honor," and who had it? What affronts to "honor" could actually justify violence? With what consequences?

DOCUMENT 4

Pope Julius Excluded from Heaven

This wonderfully wicked scene appears in a short Latin dialogue, Julius Excluded, *published anonymously in early 1517. The book enjoyed a huge success, much to the anger of the church.* Julius Excluded *was written by Desiderius Erasmus, a Dutchman who enjoyed an international reputation as a leading humanist. When he traveled to Italy in 1506, Erasmus saw for himself the corruption of the Italian clergy, the power and pomp of the papacy, and the destruction of warfare partly caused by the politics of Julius II.*

Published on the eve of the Reformation, this delightful satire appeared only a few years before the open challenge to papal authority by Martin Luther, who also observed Julius's papal court during his 1510 journey to Rome. Later, in confrontations between the opponents and defenders of the Catholic church, Luther and Erasmus found themselves on opposite sides.

In this opening scene, Pope Julius finds that heaven's gate is locked and St. Peter, the gatekeeper, is less than friendly:

JULIUS: How about opening the door, you, right away! If you wanted to do your job right you would have come to meet me—with the whole parade of angels, in fact.

PETER: Pretty bossy, all right. But first, you tell me who you are. . . .

JULIUS: Cut out the foolishness, if you have any sense. For your information, I am the famous Julius the Ligurian, and I trust you recognize the letters P.M., unless you have forgotten the alphabet altogether.

PETER: I take it they stand for Pestilential Maximum. . . .

JULIUS: Oh, come on—they stand for Pontifex Maximus, the supreme Pontiff. . . .

JULIUS: Why don't you cut out the nonsense and open the door, unless you would rather have it battered down? In a word—do you see what a retinue I have?

PETER: To be sure, I see thoroughly hardened brigands. But in case you don't know it, these doors you must storm with other weapons.

JULIUS: Enough talk, I say! Unless you obey right away, I shall hurl—even against you—the thunderbolt of excommunication, with which I once terrified the mightiest of kings, or for that matter whole kingdoms. You see the Bull already prepared for this purpose?

PETER: What damned thunderbolt, what thunder, what Bulls, what bombast are you talking to me about, pray? We never heard anything [about] those matters from Christ.

Source: *The Julius exclusus of Erasmus,* trans. Paul Pascal (Bloomington, Ind., 1968), pp. 45–49.

Questions

1. Who was pope in 1517, when this satire was published? How did this pope feel about Julius II? How did this pope react to Martin Luther's challenges?
2. Speculate on whether Erasmus would have published this satire five years earlier.

Practice Questions for Examinations
for Part II (Chapters 13–15)

1. Discuss the changing relationship between the Islamic world and the Christian West from the age of the caliphs to the Battle of Lepanto. What factors caused conflict? What factors promoted cultural exchange?

2. Discuss the revival of long-range trade and the growth of cities during the High Middle Ages and the Renaissance. What developments stimulated the growth of commerce?

3. In what ways were the Renaissance and Reformation culminations of intellectual and cultural movements that had begun during the Middle Ages? In what ways were they unique and different from what had come before?

PART

III

The Take-Off of the West,
1560–1894

CHAPTER

16

Religious Warfare and Crises of Authority, 1560–1640

Chapter Outline

STATE POWER AND RELIGIOUS CONFLICT

French Religious Wars
A New Relationship Between State and Religion: The Politiques
English Protestantism
Spanish Imperial and Religious Power
Oligarchy and Religious Toleration in the Dutch Republic

RELIGIOUS CONFLICT AND THE INTERNATIONAL BALANCE OF POWER

Conflict Between England and Spain
Eastern Europe: The Clash of Faiths and Empires
The Thirty Years' War, 1618–1648
The Consequences of Constant War

ECONOMIC CRISIS AND REALIGNMENT

The Causes of Economic Crisis
Famine and Disease
Patterns of Landholding and Family Life
The Changing Economic Balance in Europe

THE SCRAMBLE FOR POLITICAL AUTHORITY
Monarchical Authority
Constitutional Resistance in England
Settlements in the New World

ALL COHERENCE GONE: A CLASH OF WORLD VIEWS
New Relations Expressed in the Arts
The Mechanical Universe
Scientific Method
Magic and Witchcraft

Chapter Summary

The expanding wealth of many sixteenth-century European states, linked by trade to the New World and to the East, was offset in the seventeenth century by harsh weather, disease, and war. The new warfare, typified by the Thirty Years' War (1618–1648), brought unprecedented destruction to human life (both military and civilian) and to the economies of the lands through which the armies passed. The causes of wars, and the natures of the states that waged them, changed subtly in the years from 1560 to 1640. Religion was an important factor in justifying violence and inflaming the masses, but religious motives for war were often linked to political motives. The eventual waning of religion as a factor in international conflict can be seen in the policies of Louis XIII's France, a Catholic country guided by a chief minister who was himself a cardinal. France used every means to prevent the triumph of the Catholic Habsburgs over their Protestant enemies in Germany for the simple reason that it was in the best interests of the French state to do so.

In France, the religious conflicts were stirred up by families—Valois, Guise, Bourbon—competing for the throne. Catherine de Medicis, the Florentine widow of Henry II, served as regent and tried to preserve the throne for her weak sons. She was opposed by various factions who wanted the crown for themselves. The Bourbons had the best claim, but they were burdened by association with the Huguenots, a fact that the Catholic Guise family, along with the Catholic nobility and the Spanish Habsburgs, tried to exploit. The Saint Bartholomew's Day massacre was perhaps the bloodiest of many incidents that took place. An unpredictable series of events followed: the Valois Henry III murdered his Guise allies, then was himself assassinated. The Bourbon who remained, crowned Henry IV, converted to Catholicism to help calm the country, but he also ended the persecution of his former coreligionists, the Huguenots, with the Edict of Nantes. The Bourbons came to represent a new political settlement for France, one which transcended religious differences in the name of national unity. Henry IV rebuilt the war-torn economy and began to focus his attention on the Habsburg forces that encircled the country. His successor Louis XIII, ably advised by Richelieu, would continue to build a strong central monarchy and a flourishing mercantilist economy, and to probe for weaknesses in the Habsburg empire.

The Thirty Years' War, the last great religious conflict in central Europe, was also touched off by a dynastic struggle. The Peace of Augsburg (1555) had failed to prevent the spread of Protestant sects not stipulated in the original agreement, and after 1600 the Protestant and Catholic German states sorted themselves into opposing militant leagues. In 1618 the Bohemians tried to prevent the succession of the Catholic Habsburg Archduke Ferdinand, and invited the Protestant (Wittelsbach) Count Palatine to be their king. This defiance threatened to tip the balance in the entire Holy Roman Empire, and so the leagues went to war. The Count Palatine was soon dispatched (he was called "the Winter King"), but others came forward to prevent a Catholic triumph—first the King of Denmark, then the powerful Gustavus Adolphus of Sweden. Finally the French, who had financed Gustavus' campaigns, openly entered the war, and the Habsburgs, weakened by decades of fighting, consented to the *status quo.* In effect, they agreed to a permanent state of religious disunity in the empire. The decline of Habsburg power in central Europe, along with that of Spain, was a triumph for the French Bourbons.

Another important source of conflict was the threat to the traditional partnership between church and state, which had been upheld by theories such as divine right. Such relationships broke down when the throne and the people came to embrace different religious beliefs. In England and the Netherlands, for example, the desire for independence in ritual caused religious leaders to challenge royal authority in general. The Dutch had commercial as well as religious motives for demanding independence from Spain, and their revolt was supported, for different reasons, by both England and France. In England, the rulers seemed unable to coordinate their political attitudes with the fluid religious situation in the country. Henry VIII and his son Edward VI had created a moderately Protestant country, but Mary I's efforts to reimpose Catholicism left a legacy of bitterness. Elizabeth I, who was considered technically illegitimate by the Catholics, had little choice but to return to Anglicanism, but her aims seem to have been to maintain order and preserve her political position, rather than to express any sort of theological zeal. Like her contemporary Henry IV, she was a *politique,* and England flourished under her rule as France did under his. After her death, the English throne passed to the Stuarts of Scotland. James VI of Scotland became James I of England, but his reign was marred by constant bickering over the structure and liturgy of the Church of England and the privileges of Parliament. His son Charles I was even less in harmony with Parliament, so that a variety of forces, some of them religious, began to build toward a constitutional crisis.

The success of moderation and tolerance in some countries, and the disaster wrought by war and intolerance in others, was not lost on the intellectuals of the day. The need for new ways to acquire and evaluate knowledge, and to solve disputes, was obvious. Copernicus used mathematics rather than Scripture to explain the solar system. René Descartes advocated deductive reasoning, the same sort he used in his geometry. Francis Bacon preferred induction and what would become scientific thought; Galileo agreed, and made dramatic discoveries. Yet such systems were not controlled by either human law or theology, and thus seemed to constitute a threat to authority. Some intellectuals received royal support and patronage, but Galileo was bullied into denying his discoveries and was placed under house arrest by the Inquisition. In spite of such setbacks, a scientific and philosophical revolution had begun.

Vocabulary

absolutism	The belief that total and unconditional power should be vested in the monarch for the good of the state or nation. Such a doctrine is usually opposed by groups or classes that enjoy traditional privileges or liberties, such as nobles, independent clergy, or assemblies with more than advisory powers.
billeting	Boarding soldiers in civilian homes. Kings have used billeting at various times to avoid asking for new taxes or to intimidate or punish rebellious citizens.
boyars	Russian nobles.
defenestration	From the Latin word for window, *fenestra.* Therefore, to defenestrate something is to throw it out of a window, and the use of this word to describe the incident at Prague in 1618 is irreverently humorous.

harpsichord	A musical instrument in which a harplike array of strings is plucked by mechanisms operated from a keyboard. The harpsichord became the standard harmony instrument of the Baroque era.
mercantilism	An economic system in which the government tried to increase the monetary wealth of the nation by carefully regulating the economy, (usually) encouraging the development of domestic industry and agriculture, promoting a favorable balance of trade, and accumulating gold and silver bullion. Overseas colonies were useful in attaining mercantilist goals.
mannerism	An artistic style, particularly associated with sixteenth-century Italy, that forms a bridge between the earlier Renaissance and the later Baroque styles.
politiques	Those who believed that national unity was more important than the triumph of one religious faction over another; to that end, they favored compromise and, if necessary, toleration.
presbytery	An assembly of ministers and elders who governed the Scottish Reformed church. The Scottish *kirk* thus became "Presbyterian," and the English church, governed by bishops, was "Episcopal."
puritans	Members of the Church of England who, inspired by Calvinist ideas, favored "purifying" the liturgy by eliminating Roman Catholic ritual and paraphernalia.

Self-Testing and Review Questions

Identification

After reading Chapter 16, identify and explain the historical significance of each of the following:

1. Gaspard de Coligny

2. Edict of Nantes

3. nobility of the robe

4. Philip II

5. King James version

6. William of Orange

7. Ivan IV the Terrible

8. *Don Quixote*

9. Albrecht von Wallenstein

10. Richelieu

11. Giordano Bruno

12. Defenestration of Prague

13. Catherine de Medicis

14. El Greco

15. United Provinces

16. Duke of Alba

17. Michael Romanov

18. *paulette*

19. Peter Paul Rubens

20. Lepanto

Chronology

Indicate the events or issues associated with the following dates. Some of the dates may be significant for more than one reason. After you finish, answer the questions that follow.

1558

1566

1572

1577

1588

1593

1603

1613

1618

1632

1. When did Calvinism spread to England? to Scotland? to Germany? What developments—social, economic, political—enabled it to spread so rapidly?

2. Scientists from Copernicus to Galileo created a revolution in European thought. What dates marked landmarks in this revolution? How did the ideas spread so rapidly? Why were authorities unable to contain "dangerous" new ideas?

Matching Exercises

In each set, match the terms on the left with those on the right.

Set A

_____ 1. "No bishop, no king."   a. Elizabeth I

_____ 2. "Paris is worth a mass."   b. Olivares

_____ 3. "God blew and they were scattered."   c. Henry IV

_____ 4. "One king, one law, one coinage."   d. James I

Set B

_____ 1. Petition of Right   a. ended the Dutch revolt (1576)

_____ 2. Edict of Nantes   b. ended the French wars of religion (1598)

_____ 3. Edict of Restitution   c. restricted the powers of English kings (1628)

_____ 4. Pacification of Ghent   d. defined Elizabethan Anglicanism (1563)

_____ 5. Thirty-Nine Articles   e. outlawed Calvinism in Germany (1629)

Set C

_____ 1. Sully   a. minister of Henry IV

_____ 2. Richelieu   b. minister of Louis XIII

_____ 3. Olivares   c. minister of Philip IV

_____ 4. Oxenstierna   d. minister of Gustavus Adolphus

_____ 5. Alba   e. minister of Charles I

_____ 6. Strafford   f. led the armies of Philip II

Set D

_____ 1. Albrecht von Wallenstein   a. Holy Roman Emperor

_____ 2. Christian IV   b. king of Sweden

_____ 3. Frederick V   c. king of Denmark

_____ 4. Gustavus II Adolphus   d. Count Palatine of the Rhine

_____ 5. Ferdinand II   e. ambitious mercenary general

Set E

_____ 1. Nicolaus Copernicus   a. the author of *Discourse on Method*

_____ 2. Galileo Galilei   b. the author of *The Advancement of Learning*

_____ 3. Johannes Kepler   c. silenced by order of the Inquisition

_____ 4. Francis Bacon   d. described the functioning of the heart

_____ 5. William Harvey   e. the first to say the sun is the center of the solar
                       system

_____ 6. René Descartes   f. argued that the orbits of planets are elliptical

Multiple-Choice Questions

1. Catherine de Medicis' policies included
   a. urging that her son, Henry de Bourbon, convert to Catholicism.
   b. supporting the Dutch rebellion, even though it meant a war with Spain.
   c. playing factions off against each other to preserve her sons' thrones.
   d. marrying Gaspard de Coligny and making him her co-ruler.

2. Philip II's greatest success may well have been
   a. the Spanish Armada.   c. the Dutch revolt.
   b. the Battle of Lepanto.   d. his marriage to Mary I of England.

3. Philip II's famous palace—part fortress, part monastery—was
   a. Buen Retiro.   c. El Escorial.
   b. Aranjuez.   d. The Alhambra.

4. The population of Europe in the seventeenth century
   a. doubled.   c. increased slowly.
   b. generally declined.   d. remained about the same.

5. Elizabeth I's reign was threatened by Catholic plots centered around her cousin and heir
   a. Mary Stuart, Queen of Scots.   c. Catherine de Medicis.
   b. Mary Tudor.   d. Mary of Guise.

6. English Puritans felt threatened by
   a. the Inquisition.   c. the Spanish Fury.
   b. the Spanish Inquisition.   d. the Court of the Star Chamber.

7. One of the greatest of the early composers of opera, and the author of *Orfeo*, was
   a. Lope de Vega.   c. Jean Bodin.
   b. Diego Velázquez.   d. Claudio Monteverdi.

8. The spread of Protestantism among the French nobility was encouraged by the conversion of Henry IV's mother,
   a. Jeanne d'Albret.   c. Catherine de Medicis.
   b. Charlotte de Bourbon.   d. Mary Stuart.

9. The Time of Troubles was ended by the succession of
   a. Boris Godunov.   c. Ivan IV the Terrible.
   b. Michael Romanov.   d. Ivan III the Great.

10. That the Thirty Years' War had ceased to be a religious war was made clear by the intervention of
    a. France.   c. Denmark.
    b. Spain.   d. Norway.

Essay Questions

Using material from this and previous chapters, write an essay on each of the following topics. Include dates and present detailed examples, when appropriate, to support your arguments.

1. Compare and contrast the reigns of Elizabeth I and Henry IV. How were the challenges they faced, and the solutions they offered, similar or different?
2. What factors caused the Peace of Augsburg (1555) to unravel? With what consequences?

3. To what extent were the experiences of western monarchs (England, France, Spain) mirrored by those in the east, especially Russia?

4. An unprecedented number of women governed major states in the period 1560–1640. Do you think the experiences of women of all classes, as described in this chapter, are related to this phenomenon? How?

5. Was the period from 1560 to 1648 one of success or failure for the Habsburg states? Why?

Skill Building: Maps

Locate the following regions on the map of Europe. Why was each significant in this chapter?

a. Lützen

b. Prague

c. Poland-Lithuania

d. London

e. Antwerp

f. Amsterdam

g. Novgorod

h. White Mountain

i. Dutch Republic

j. Spain

k. the Palatinate

l. Bohemia

1. Catholicism remained strong in a few states, such as Ireland and Poland, that were geographically isolated from the southern European strongholds of Catholicism. Why?

2. Which European states emerged as colonial powers by the mid-seventeenth century? What did these states have in common? In what ways were they different?

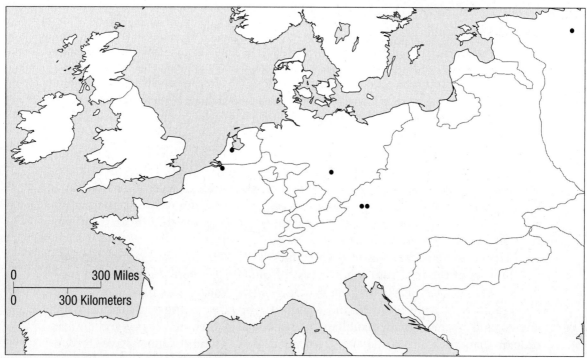

Europe in the Seventeenth Century

Enrichment Exercise

1. Numerous films depict the reign of Elizabeth, but the British-made television series *Elizabeth R* (1976) is probably the best. The life of the queen is presented in six dramatic episodes, each ninety minutes long. An alternative to this series is the grim and disturbing film *The Last Valley* (1971), set during the Thirty Years' War. This production, with a fine cast, vividly demonstrates the pillaging of the armies and the reaction of the peasants. Write a short essay relating *The Last Valley* or one of the episodes of *Elizabeth R* to the information presented in the text.

Document Analysis

DOCUMENT 1

The Saint Bartholomew's Day Massacre

Charlotte de Mornay (1550–1606) was the wife of Philippe de Mornay, one of the Protestant leaders during the French wars of religion. She was an example of the many educated and intellectually sophisticated Huguenot noblewomen who strongly influenced the religious choices of their families and friends. In the following passage, she describes her experience during the Saint Bartholomew's Day Massacre. At the time, she was a young widow (her first husband died in the religious wars before she was twenty), and she was planning to leave to spend the winter with her sister.

While I was still in bed, one of my kitchen servants, who was of the religion [Huguenot] and was coming from the city, came very terrified to find me. She told me that people were being killed everywhere. . . . Looking from my windows into Saint Antoine Street where I lived, I saw that everyone was very agitated, and several guards were wearing white crosses in their hats [to identify themselves as Catholics]. . . . I sent my daughter, who was then three and a half years old, in the arms of a servant to Mister de Perreuze . . . one of my closest relatives and friends, who let her in the back gate, received her, and sent word to ask if I would come, saying I would be welcome. I accepted his offer and left myself. . . . There was sedition all over the city. It was then eight in the morning, and I had no sooner left my lodgings than the servants of the Duke of Guise came in, called my host to find me, and looked for me everywhere. Finally, they sent to my mother telling her that if I wanted to bring them 100 *écus*, they would spare my life and my goods. . . . After having thought a little, I decided it was not a good idea to let it be known where I was or to go to find them, but I begged my mother to let them know that she did not know where I was and to offer them the sum that they were demanding. Having heard nothing from me, they pillaged my lodgings. . . .

[Mister de Perreuze] was obliged to hide us . . . me with one of my servants in a hollow of the roof vaulting; the rest of our people were disguised and hidden as well as possible. Inside the vaulting, at the top of the attic, I heard the strange cries of men, women, and children who were being massacred in the streets, and having left my daughter below, I was in such perplexity and almost despair that, without fearing that I offended God, I would sooner have thrown myself out the window than to fall alive into the hands of the populace and see my daughter massacred—something I feared more than my death. . . . [After fleeing from one house to another, she hid for five days in the home of a grain merchant, then took a boat out of Paris, where she was stopped because she did not have a passport. She narrowly escaped capture and certain death by posing as a servant and hiding in the house of a vineyard worker. Throughout the ordeal, she steadfastly refused to go to mass in order to save herself.]

Source: *Mémoires de Madame de Mornay*, 2 vols. (J. Renouard, 1868–1869), Vol. 1, pp. 59–62.

Question

1. What basic assumptions of the sixteenth century caused Mme de Mornay's persecutors to feel justified in their deeds? Were their attitudes related to the assumptions that caused Mme de Mornay to prefer capture and death to saying a mass?

DOCUMENT 2

Sir John Hayward Describes the Young Queen Elizabeth

In the following passages, notice how the observer attributes the best of all qualities to Elizabeth. Like other monarchs of the time, she is described as all-seeing—as well as beautiful and brilliant.

Now, if ever any person had either the gift or the style to win the hearts of people, it was this Queen. . . . Every motion seemed a well guided action; her eye was set upon one, her ear listened to another, her judgment ran upon a third, to a fourth she addressed her speech; her spirit seemed to be everywhere, and yet so entire in her self, as it seemed to be nowhere else.

. . . She was a Lady, upon whom nature had bestowed, and well placed, many of her fairest favors; of stature average, slender, straight, and amiably composed; of such state in her carriage, as every motion of her seemed to bear majesty.

. . . In life, she was most innocent; in desire, moderate; in purpose, just; of spirit, above credit and almost capacity of her sex; of divine wit, as well for depth of judgment, as for quick conceit and speedy expedition; of eloquence, as sweet in the utterance, so ready and easy to come to the utterance; of wonderful knowledge both in learning and affairs; skillful not only in Latin and Greek, but also in diverse other foreign languages: none knew better the hardest art of all others, that is, of commanding men.

Source: *Gloriana's Glass,* Alan Glover, ed. (Nonesuch Press, 1953), pp. 57–58.

Question

1. Hayward (1560–1627) was a classical scholar. His first work, *The Life and Reign of King Henry IV* (1599), which probably influenced Shakespeare, resulted in his imprisonment at the end of Elizabeth's reign. Do the words above, published posthumously, sound like those of a dangerous radical? What does this excerpt indicate about the fears and suspicions that prevailed in the royal courts of the period?

DOCUMENT 3

Galileo Before the Inquisition

After the formal interrogation was ordered (first paragraph below), Galileo had to appear in the white robe of a penitent to hear his sentence. He was condemned to prison (which in reality was a kind of house arrest) and forced to make a public statement (second paragraph below). (Contrary to the often-told story, Galileo did not leave his sentencing muttering, "But it still moves." The story was invented around 1640, but it does capture his spirit of resistance.)

Sanctissimus [This Most Holy Tribunal] decreed that said Galileo is to be interrogated on his intention, even with the threat of torture, and, if he sustains [the test], he is to abjure [vehement suspicion of heresy] in a plenary assembly of the Congregation of the Holy Office, then is to be condemned to imprisonment at the pleasure of the Holy Congregation, and ordered not to treat further, in whatever manner, either in words or in writing, of the mobility of the Earth and the stability of the Sun; otherwise he will incur the penalties of relapse.

I, Galileo, son of the late Vincenzo Galilei, Florentine, aged seventy years . . . have been pronounced by the Holy Office [of the Inquisition] to be vehemently suspected of heresy, that is to say, of having held and believed that the Sun is the center of the world and immovable and that the Earth is not the center and moves: . . . with sincere heart and unfeigned faith I abjure, curse, and detest the aforesaid errors and heresies.

Source: Giorgio de Santillana, *The Crime of Galileo* (University of Chicago Press, 1955, reprint London, 1961), pp. 292–293, 312.

Question

1. The Inquisition's notions about the location and movement of earth and sun were based only vaguely on Scripture, but very specifically on the ideas of Claudius Ptolemy, which had been canonized in the works of medieval theologians such as Thomas Aquinas. What, then, were Galileo's real crimes?

DOCUMENT 4

Confessions of a Witch

Witch-persecutions gained credibility from confessions of the accused, which were often extracted under torture. An old, illiterate Frenchwoman, Suzanne Gaudry, was tortured to obtain a confession and then burnt at the stake in 1652. Her confession includes many of the typical elements: the witch's sabbath, sexual love of the devil, flying at night.

> Asked how long she has been in subjugation to the devil.—Says that it has been about twenty-five or twenty-six years, that her lover also then made her renounce God, Lent, baptism, that he has known her carnally three or four times, and that he has given her satisfaction. . . .
>
> Asked if the devil did not advise her to steal from Elisabeth Dehan and to do harm to her. —Said that he advised her to steal from her and promised that he would help her; but urged her not to do harm to her; and that is because she [Elisabeth Dehan] had cut the wood in her [Suzanne Gaudry's] fence and stirred up the seeds in her garden, saying that her lover told her that she would avenge herself by beating her.

Source: From J. Français, *L'Eglise et la Sorcellerie* (Paris, 1910), pp. 236–251. Quoted in Alan C. Kors and Edward Peters, *Witchcraft in Europe, 1100–1700* (University of Pennsylvania Press, 1972), pp. 266–275.

Question

1. Given the absurd charges to which Gaudry and others in this era confessed, it is hardly surprising that the U.S. founding fathers later insisted on constitutional guarantees against the extraction of confession under duress. Would the legal officials of 1652 have argued that such protections unduly hindered them in carrying out their duties?

CHAPTER

17

Rebellion and State Building, 1640–1690

Chapter Outline

ABSOLUTISM VERSUS ARISTOCRATIC CONSTITUTIONALISM IN CENTRAL AND EASTERN EUROPE

Poland-Lithuania Overwhelmed
An Uneasy Balance: Habsburgs and Ottoman Turks
Brandenburg-Prussia and Sweden: Militaristic Absolutism
Russia: Foundations of Bureaucratic Absolutism

WEST EUROPEAN AND NORTH AMERICAN CONSTITUTIONAL MODELS

The Merchant Republics
England's Glorious Revolution of 1688
New World Echoes

COHERENCE REGAINED: ELITE AND POPULAR CULTURE

The Scientific Revolution Consolidated
Order and Power in the Arts
The Cultivation of Manners
Piety and Witchcraft

Chapter Summary

The French entry into the Thirty Years' War hastened the conclusion of that bloody conflict but did not bring peace to Europe. The Treaty of Westphalia signaled the rise of France, the decline of Spain, and a period of rebuilding in central and eastern Europe. The Spanish had lost Portugal and finally admitted the loss of the Dutch provinces. The decline of Austrian influence in northern Germany permitted the rise of new, powerful states such as Brandenburg-Prussia. The Ottoman Turks continued their westward expansion, reaching the gates of Vienna and laying siege to that city. In the north, the much-enlarged Polish-Lithuanian state was challenged by a Cossack revolt that raged for decades. This "Deluge" eventually drew Russia, Sweden, and other neighboring states into a northern war. The "Great Elector" Frederick William of Brandenburg-Prussia was probably the greatest beneficiary of this conflict, and Poland the greatest loser. Even so, the Polish King John Sobieski was able to send a force to relieve Vienna from the Turks in 1681. The Habsburgs pursued the retreating Turks down the Danube valley over the next decades, carving a new empire out of former Ottoman domains. The new Habsburg empire was more ethnically diverse than the German states, and more willing to accept Viennese rule.

France was the real winner of the Thirty Years' War, but neither Richelieu nor Louis XIII, the authors of the successful strategy, lived to see it. The new ruler of France was Louis XIII's son Louis XIV, a child when he inherited the crown. His claim to the throne was preserved only by the efforts of his minister Mazarin, who managed to suppress an aristocratic rebellion and steer the war to its conclusion. Later, Mazarin's policies would end the war with Spain and secure a marriage alliance between the two states. After assuming control of France in 1661, Louis XIV became the very personification of absolute monarchy, ruling a rich state from a sumptuous palace, expanding an overseas colonial empire, and imprinting his own individual taste on the fashion, art, music, architecture, and literature of his age. Nevertheless, even his extraordinarily successful reign was marred by some poor judgments (he revived the French religious controversies, persecuting Huguenots and Jansenists) and by incessant wars of aggression against his neighbors.

While the continental Europeans experimented with absolute monarchy, England struck out in an entirely different direction. There, Charles I's unpopular religious policies—insisting on conformity to the Anglican ritual and persecuting dissenters—and contempt for Parliament brought him into open conflict with its leaders. In 1642, Charles tried to arrest his fiercest critics in Parliament and thus touched off the English Civil War. Parliament organized its own army, a force dominated by the Puritan Oliver Cromwell, and within a few years had defeated the royalists and captured the king. The enemies of the crown were hardly unified; some favored religious toleration, others wished to impose a new state religion (Presbyterianism), and many groups combined their religious convictions with their aspirations for expanded political rights and social justice. Parliamentary leaders, who were invariably members of the propertied classes, were alarmed by the social radicalism that they saw emerging. In 1649, the Parliament, purged of its Presbyterian members, abolished the House of Lords, tried and executed the king, and declared England a commonwealth. For several years, England was dominated by Oliver Cromwell, who was given the title "Lord Protector." After his death, the leaders of England could agree on no alternative but to restore the monarchy, putting the son of Charles I on the throne.

Charles II's reign was generally popular. He ended the state-imposed moral austerity of Cromwell's Puritan rule, subsidized science and the arts much as the French kings did, and encouraged the rebuilding of the city of London (made necessary by the tragic fire of 1666). But he also reimposed Anglican services and irritated many by his friendship with Louis XIV (who had sheltered him during the Commonwealth) and by his toleration of Catholics. Many Puritans, when they were treated precisely as they had treated the Anglicans, left England in disgust. Only reluctantly did Parliament agree to the succession of Charles II's Catholic brother James, and then only because he had several Protestant daughters who would be his heirs. Soon after he became king, however, James II had a son. The members of Parliament were outraged at this affront to their "liberties," and evicted both the king and his heir. They invited James' daughter Mary and her husband William of Orange, the Dutch stadholder, to rule jointly. This sequence of events soon became known as the Glorious Revolution. Thus the reign of William and Mary did not introduce a new ruling family but did represent a direct interference in the normal pattern of succession.

Parliament's assertion of its right to interfere in the succession and, for that matter, its right to try and execute Charles I, contradicted the traditional concepts of divine-right monarchy still exercised on the continent. Louis XIV claimed to be king by God's will, but such a claim was increasingly difficult to defend in a Europe that tolerated religious diversity in international treaties. If kings did not rule by divine right, then by what right? Thomas Hobbes, who had tutored Charles II during his exile, argued that governments were necessary to maintain law and order, and that their power, derived indirectly from the consent of the governed, was absolute. This argument preserved absolutism while refuting divine right and thus became widely accepted. But Hobbes' theory would never have justified the Glorious Revolution, so the Whig philosopher John Locke proposed that governments exist to protect the natural rights of the governed; thus their authority is not absolute, and they should be replaced when they no longer carry out their basic responsibilities. Locke also argued in favor of inductive reason and scientific method. His arguments seemed particularly persuasive when coupled with the prodigious achievements of his contemporaries such as Isaac Newton and other members of the Royal Society.

Vocabulary

catechism	A religious instruction book in the form of questions and answers.
frondeur	A participant in the Fronde; the term evokes a schoolboy who uses a slingshot (*fronde*) when the teacher's back is turned.
intendants	French regional officials, directly accountable to the king, who usurped some of the traditional powers of the nobility and helped to create a centralized, absolute monarchy.

parlement	French courts, staffed by professional lawyers who had become nobles. The word shares the same origins (the French word *parler,* to talk) with the English word Parliament, but the institutions were very different.
pejorative	Disparaging.
protégé	In French, the past participle of "to protect"; therefore, a protected person, a client, a political favorite.
schismatic	A religious dissenter or heretic.
serf	A laborer legally attached to the land but not actually the property of the landowner. The institution of serfdom is legally distinct from slavery, in which one human being owns another, but in actual practice the two are similar.
stadholder	Originally, a viceroy of the Spanish king in the Netherlands. After the United Provinces gained their independence, the title was adopted by the head of the Dutch state.
tariff	A tax, especially on imports.

Self-Testing and Review Questions

Identification

After reading Chapter 17, identify and explain the historical significance of each of the following:

1. Rembrandt van Rijn

2. William and Mary

3. *Augustinus*

4. Gian Lorenzo Bernini

5. Aphra Behn

6. the Deluge

7. Declaration of Indulgence

8. congregationalism

9. Lord Protector

10. Stenka Razin

11. *shtetl*

12. the Fronde

13. Jean-Baptiste Colbert

14. Commonwealth

15. Treaty of Karlowitz

16. Jean-Baptiste Lully

17. John Sobieski

18. *Areopagitica*

19. Bill of Rights

20. Treaty of Westphalia

21. Mazarin

22. Leopold I

23. Zemskii Sobor

24. Old Believers

25. Jan Vermeer

Chronology

Identify the events or issues associated with the following dates. Some of these dates may be significant for more than one reason. After you finish, answer the questions that follow.

1648

1649

1654

1659

1660

1666

1670

1683

1685

1688

1699

1. What were the dates of Locke's important works? of Newton's? How were the two men and their works similar?

2. How long was Louis XIV king (after his father died) before he actually assumed power? What important events during that time influenced the policies and events of his rule?

3. Many studies of European history consider the years 1648–1649 or 1688–1689 to have been major turning points. Why?

Matching Exercises

In each set, match the terms on the left with those on the right.

Set A

_____ 1. ruling family of Spain

_____ 2. ruling family of Portugal

_____ 3. ruling family of France

_____ 4. ruling family of Brandenburg-Prussia

_____ 5. ruling family of Russia

_____ 6. ruling family of England and Scotland

_____ 7. ruling family of the Holy Roman Empire

a. Stuart

b. Habsburg

c. Bourbon

d. Hohenzollern

e. Romanov

f. Braganza

(Use one of these twice)

Set B

_____ 1. *Principia Mathematica*

_____ 2. *Provincial Letters*

_____ 3. *Two Treatises of Government*

_____ 4. *Paradise Lost*

_____ 5. *Essay Concerning Human Understanding*

_____ 6. *Leviathan*

a. John Milton

b. John Locke

c. Blaise Pascal

d. Thomas Hobbes

e. Isaac Newton

(Use one of these twice)

Set C

_____ 1. Mme de Sévigné

_____ 2. Mme de Lafayette

_____ 3. Mme de Maintenon

_____ 4. Anne of Austria

_____ 5. Christina

a. Louis XIV's mistress and second wife

b. French novelist, author of *The Princess of Clèves*

c. author of revealing letters about life at Versailles

d. Queen of Sweden who abdicated her throne

e. Louis XIII's wife, Louis XIV's mother

Set D

____ 1. William III
____ 2. James II
____ 3. Charles I
____ 4. Charles II
____ 5. Oliver Cromwell

a. was tried and executed for treason
b. took power as a result of the Glorious Revolution
c. was overthrown because of his Catholicism
d. organized the New Model Army
e. rebuilt London after the Great Fire

Set E

____ 1. Pascal
____ 2. Poussin
____ 3. Le Nôtre
____ 4. Lully
____ 5. Molière

a. French playwright, author of *The Middle-Class Gentleman*
b. French philosopher, author of *Pensées*
c. Louis XIV's favorite composer
d. painter at the French court
e. landscape architect at Versailles

Multiple-Choice Questions

1. Thomas Hobbes believed that
   a. left to their own devices, humans are selfish and require firm government.
   b. Charles II was too poorly educated to rule.
   c. all men are born with the rights of life, liberty, and property.
   d. God is a natural force, uninfluenced by faith or prayers.

2. The factions in Parliament debating the succession of James II were
   a. Cavaliers and Roundheads.
   b. Diggers and Levellers.
   c. Seekers and Ranters.
   d. Whigs and Tories.

3. Which of these is *not* associated with Louis XIV?
   a. *L'état, c'est moi.*
   b. the Sun King
   c. the Great Elector
   d. Versailles

4. The Rump Parliament resulted directly from
   a. the Navigation Act.
   b. Pride's Purge.
   c. the Declaration of Indulgence.
   d. the Glorious Revolution.

5. The Edict of Nantes was eventually revoked by
   a. Richelieu.
   b. Mazarin.
   c. Louis XIV.
   d. Bishop Bossuet.

6. The French religious faction that criticized the Jesuits and admired Augustine and Calvin was called the
   a. Old Believers.
   b. Junkers.
   c. Quakers.
   d. Jansenists.

7. The royal palace that best demonstrates absolute royal power in the seventeenth century is
   a. Versailles.
   b. Schönbrunn.
   c. Whitehall.
   d. El Escorial.

8. Frederick William was the famous ruler of
   a. Alsace and Lorraine.
   b. Brandenburg and Prussia.
   c. Lithuania and Poland.
   d. Hungary and Bohemia.

9. John Locke argued that
   a. this is the best of all possible worlds.
   b. absolutism is natural and based on Scripture.
   c. humans are born with minds that are "blank slates," and we learn through experience.
   d. the action and reaction between two objects are equal and opposite.

10. Corneille and Racine were famous
    a. heretics.   c. painters.
    b. playwrights.   d. scientists.

Essay Questions

Using material from this and earlier chapters, write an essay on each of the following topics. When appropriate, include dates and detailed examples to support your arguments.

1. Many admirers of Cromwell consider him an advocate of liberty, religious toleration, and representative government in the face of Anglican and Catholic tyranny. Based on the information presented in this chapter, write an essay arguing for or against this position.

2. To what extent are today's reputations of western European states as cultural meccas the result of policies of seventeenth-century monarchs?

3. What was so "glorious" about the Glorious Revolution?

4. How did the policies of Henry IV, Richelieu, and Mazarin prepare the way for the absolutism of Louis XIV?

5. Which states were growing in wealth and power in the late seventeenth century, which were in decline, and why?

Skill Building: Maps

Locate the following regions on the map of Europe. Why was each significant in the present chapter?

a. Kiev

b. Spanish Netherlands

c. Brandenburg-Prussia

d. Ottoman empire

e. Berlin

f. Transylvania

g. Russia

h. Vienna

i. Danube River

j. Catalonia

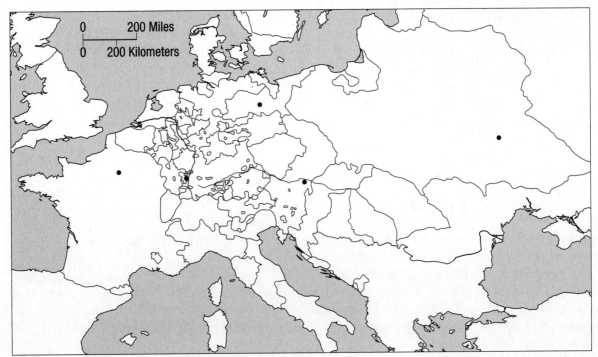

Europe, c. 1648

k. Lorraine

l. Prussia

m. Bavaria

n. Strasbourg

o. Ukraine

p. Lithuania-Poland

q. Paris

r. Swiss Confederation

1. Mark on the map the direction of Louis XIV's military campaigns.
2. What are the disadvantages of states, such as Poland, that do not have clear and fixed borders?
3. What parts of Europe were under Turkish control at the time of the siege of Vienna? What lands had the Habsburgs recaptured by the end of the seventeenth century? What was the legacy of Turkish conquest in these countries?

Enrichment Exercise

Many single-volume abridgments are available of the great *Diary* of Samuel Pepys, a government official in the London of Charles II. Obtain one of these from a library, read it, then write a brief paper. In your essay, assess Pepys' personality, explain how this extraordinary diary managed to be preserved, and discuss the great events that Pepys witnessed.

Document Analysis

DOCUMENT 1

The Levellers' Manifesto

An Agreement of the Free People of England *was a pamphlet published May 1, 1649, as part of the dispute between the Levellers and their superiors in the army and the state. Four leaders of the Levellers had been arrested at the end of March on charges of treason for publishing seditious pamphlets. As part of their defense, the four published the pamphlet excerpted below. Although the tone is moderate, the proposals were radical for the time. They argued for virtually universal manhood suffrage, for the immediate dissolution of Parliament and election of a new one, and for religious toleration.*

> We the free People of England . . . Agree to ascertain our Government, to abolish all arbitrary Power, and to set bounds and limits both to our Supreme, and all Subordinate Authority. . . .
>
> I. That the Supreme Authority of England and the Territories therewith incorporate, shall be and reside henceforward in a Representative of the People consisting of four hundred persons, but no more; in the choice of whom (according to naturall right) all men of the age of one and twenty yeers and upwards (not being servants, or receiving alms, or having served the late King in Arms or voluntary Contributions) shall have their voices; and be capable of being elected to that Supreme Trust. . . .
>
> VIII. . . . That the next and all future Representatives, shall continue in full power for the space of one whole year: and that the people shall of course, chuse a Parliament once every year. . . .
>
> X. That we do not impower or entrust our said representatives to continue in force, or to make any Lawes, Oaths, or Covenants, whereby to compell by penalties or otherwise any person to any thing in or about matters of faith, Religion or Gods worship or to restrain any person from the profession of his faith, or exercise of Religion according to his Conscience, nothing having caused more distractions, and heart burnings in all ages, then persecution and molestation for matters of Conscience in and about Religion.

Source: William Haller and Godfrey Davies, eds., *The Leveller Tracts, 1647–1653* (Columbia University Press, 1944), pp. 318–328.

Questions

1. How had the events of the Civil War caused religious and political liberty to become so closely associated in the popular mind?

2. Because these Levellers seem willing to disfranchise the supporters of Charles I, how much credence would you place in their pledge of universal religious freedom?

3. Why would members of the propertied classes fear democracy?

DOCUMENT 2

Life at the Court of Louis XIV

Elisabeth Charlotte, duchess of Orléans, was the German wife of Louis XIV's brother. She spent fifty years at the French court, apparently spending much of her time writing about forty long letters every week. In the following one, written in 1676, she describes how the king personally expressed his concern to her about a fall she took from her horse during a hunt. The letter shows how much Louis' every act influenced the behavior of the nobles at court.

> Although I had not hurt myself or fallen on my head, he would not rest until he had personally examined my head on all sides . . . he also led me back to my room and even stayed with me for a while to see whether I might become dizzy. . . . I must say that even now the King still shows me his favor every day. . . . This is also the reason that I am now very much à la mode; whatever I say or do, whether it be good or awry, is greatly admired by the courtiers, to the point that when I decided to wear my old sable in this cold weather to keep my neck warm, everyone had one made from the same pattern, and sables have become quite the rage. This makes me laugh, for five years ago the very people who now admire and wear this fashion so laughed at me and made so much fun of me with my sable that I could no longer wear it. This is what happens at this court: if the courtiers imagine that someone is in favor it does not matter what the person does, one can be certain that the courtiers approve of it; but if they imagine the contrary, they will think that person ridiculous, even if he has come straight from heaven.

Source: *A Woman's Life in the Court of the Sun King: Letters of Liselotte von der Pfalz, 1652–1722 (Elisabeth Charlotte, Duchesse d'Orléans).* Trans. Elborg Forster (Johns Hopkins University Press, 1984), pp. 17–18.

Questions

1. Is the behavior of the king, as described here, that of a cold and egotistical monarch?
2. Other than the fact that she is his sister-in-law, why might Louis XIV treat this German noblewoman with more deference than he would a French noble?
3. Does this passage help explain how the king's taste in music, art, and literature became universal in France?

DOCUMENT 3

The Advantages of Overseas Trade, 1664

This pamphlet was written by order of Colbert, Louis XIV's chief minister, to argue for the advantages of colonial trade and the foundation of a French East India Company. It describes at length the growing wealth of the Dutch based on such trade. The pamphlet was translated almost immediately into English as a warning of French ambitions—a reflection of the significance of trade in seventeenth-century international rivalries.

> Now of all commerces whatsoever throughout the whole world, that of the East Indies is one of the most rich and considerable. From thence it is (the sun being kinder to them, than to us) that we have our merchandise of greatest value and that which contributes the most not only to the pleasure of life but also to glory, and magnificence. From thence it is that we fetch our gold and precious stones

and a thousand other comodities (both of a general esteem and a certain return) to which we are so accustomed that it is impossible for us to be without them, as silk, cinnamon, pepper, ginger, nutmegs, cotton cloth, oüate (vulgarly [cotton] wadding), porcelain, woods for dyeing, ivory, frankincense, bezoar [an antidote for poisons], etc. So that having an absolute necessity upon us, to make use of all these things, why we should not rather furnish ourselves, than take them from others, and apply that profit hereafter to our own countrymen, which we have hitherto allowed to strangers, I cannot understand.

Why should the Portuguese, the Hollanders, the English, the Danes, trade daily to the East Indies possessing there, their magazines, and their forts, and the French neither the one nor the other? . . . To what end is it *in fine* that we pride ourselves to be subjects of the prime monarch of the universe, if being so, we dare not so much as show our heads in those places where our neighbors have established themselves with power? . . .

What has it been, but this very navigation and traffic that has enabled the Hollanders to bear up against the power of Spain, with forces so unequal, nay, and to become terrible to them and to bring them down at last to an advantageous peace? Since that time it is that this people, who had not only the Spaniards abroad, but the very sea and earth at home to struggle with, have in spite of all opposition made themselves so considerable, that they begin now to dispute power and plenty with the greatest part of their neighbors. This observation is no more than truth, their East India Company being known to be the principal support of their state and the most sensible cause of their greatness.

Source: F. Charpentier, *A Discourse Written by a Faithful Subject to his Christian Majesty, Concerning the Establishment of a French Company for their Commerce of the East Indies,* trans. R. L'Estrange (London, 1664), reprinted in Geoffrey Symcox, *War, Diplomacy, and Imperialism, 1618–1763* (Walker and Co., 1974), pp. 257–260.

Question

1. The demand in France for exotic goods from the East implies a market economy within the country; yet royal permission was required for the establishment of a French East India company. What distinctions were being made between the local market economy (with little royal supervision), and world trade and capitalism, which required government approval? Why?

DOCUMENT 4

The Muscovite Code of Laws, 1649

The Tsarist code of 1649 turned the peasants of Muscovy into serfs by forbidding them to migrate to escape their debts to their lords (whether the tsar himself, nobles, or clergy). The power of the Muscovy nobles over their peasants was reinforced by provisions that allowed the landowners to capture and bring back any escaped peasants. The legal and administrative system was used to keep track of all the peasants.

1. Any peasants of the Sovereign and labourers of the crown villages and black volosts [administrative areas] who have fled from the Sovereign's crown villages and from the black volosts . . . are to be brought to the crown villages of the Sovereign and to the black volosts to their old lots according to the registers of inquisition with wives and children and with all their peasant property without term of years.

2. Also should there be any lords holding an estate by inheritance of service who start to petition the Sovereign about their fugitive peasants and labourers and say that their peasants and labourers who have fled from them live in the crown villages of the Sovereign and in black volosts or among the artisans in the artisan quarters of towns or among the musketeers, cossacks or among the gunners, or among any other serving men in the towns ... [there follows a long list of all the possible places to which fugitives might have fled] then those peasants and labourers in accordance with law and the [right of] search are to be handed over according to the inquisition registers which the officers handed in to the Service Tenure Department.

20. But if any people come to anyone in an estate held by inheritance or service and say that they are free and those people want to live under them as peasants or as labourers, then those people to whom they come are to question them: who are those free people, and where is their birthplace and under whom did they live and where have they come from, and are they not somebody's runaway people, peasants and labourers, and whether they have charters of manumission. And if any say they do not have charters of manumission on them, those holding estates by service and inheritance are to get to know genuinely about such people, are they really free people; and after genuinely getting to know, to take them the same year to be registered. . . .

22. And if any peasants' children deny their fathers and mothers they are to be tortured.

Source: Thomas G. Barnes and Gerald D. Feldman, eds., *Renaissance, Reformation, and Absolutism, 1400–1660* (University of California Press, 1972), pp. 148–151.

Questions

1. What problems did the tsar seek to solve by means of the 1649 Code?

2. Why did the Russian government continue to restrict travel even after the abolition of serfdom?

CHAPTER

18

New Societies and the Early Enlightenment, 1690–1740

Chapter Outline

THE BIRTH OF A CRITICAL SPIRIT

Rise of the New Skepticism
Popularization of Science
Travel Literature and Relativism in Morals
Raising "The Woman Question"
The Ideal of Progress

Chapter Summary

Cash crops—particularly sugar, coffee, and tobacco—assumed major importance in the European economy in the first half of the eighteenth century. Sugar, which required a tropical climate, had always been a motive for colonialism, and the arduous work of growing, harvesting, and refining the product served to encourage the slave trade. Coffee, originally obtained from the Middle East, could be grown in both Asia and South America, whereas tobacco was raised from Virginia to the Caribbean and beyond. As Europeans prowled the globe looking for new products and markets, the trade in spices, dyes, cotton cloth, furs, and precious metals increased. Slaves became a commodity. Typically purchased from African slave merchants and transported under filthy conditions to the New World, they often outnumbered the Europeans—a fact that contributed to their brutal treatment.

European society was also undergoing monumental changes. The climate had become more moderate, and agricultural production, here and there improved by new practices or stimulated by new crops, increased. From Britain to eastern Europe there was a general tendency toward larger estates and entrepreneurial agriculture, fewer subsistence farms, and therefore fewer peasants. The consequent increase in urban populations may have contributed to the general increase in population throughout Europe, because there was no significant improvement in medicine or sanitation. Larger cities had their amenities—the new middle-class culture of the cafés and pubs; the proliferation of newspapers, journals, and popular literature (the novel); and the popularization of art. An example of the latter is the rise of opera as a popular diversion. In previous centuries, professionally produced music had been a luxury affordable only by aristocratic patrons and the church. In England, politics became a sort of national diversion.

France continued to dominate the continent. The aging Louis XIV fought his last two, and biggest, wars. In the War of the League of Augsburg, he continued trying to expand his domains toward the Rhine River, but now he was opposed by a coalition headed by his old nemesis, William III. During the Dutch War, William had opened the dikes and inundated the French army, and now he was king of England. Discouraged and graying, Louis might not have fought any more wars, but the offer of the Spanish crown to his grandson was too extraordinary to resist. In the War of the Spanish Succession, this prize was achieved at the cost of many key colonial possessions. Upon the death of Louis XIV, the French throne passed to the infant Louis XV, who was dominated by an aristocratic regency. The government virtually bankrupted itself with speculative investments, and the reputation of French arms failed to prevent Russia and Austria from trying to strip the young king's father-in-law of Poland's crown. The traditional dominance of the king over the nobility was no longer an accepted fact, nor was the superiority of the French economy or the French military.

In England, William III and Mary II were popular and successful rulers, and William was an effective military leader in the War of the League of Augsburg. Upon his death in 1702 (Mary had died in 1696), the throne passed to Mary's sister, Anne, the last Protestant offspring of James II. To guarantee that neither James nor his Catholic children would ever return, Parliament merged the two Stuart kingdoms of England and Scotland into one—Great Britain—and fixed the line of succession, after Anne, upon the Protestant Electors of Hanover. Thus when Anne died in 1715, although there had been an unsuccessful uprising by James' son and his Catholic and Tory supporters, the new king of Great Britain was George I. George had grown up in Germany and spoke little English. Moreover, he was dominated by the House of Commons, which was in turn dominated by the brilliant politician Robert Walpole, who in effect invented an early form of the cabinet system that governs Great Britain today. Parliament, controlled by powerful merchant interests, led Britain through several wars against its colonial archrivals, France and Spain. After these wars, Britain emerged as the leading colonial power in the world.

The successes of the western colonial powers were not lost on Tsar Peter I (known as the Great) who made numerous reforms in a Russia that was rapidly emerging as the dominant power in eastern Europe. Peter wanted to "westernize" his state, and he did succeed in founding a new seaport capital and in building up the navy, but the depth to which his other reforms penetrated Russian society is debatable. The rise of Russia was enhanced by the steady decline of its rivals—Poland, Sweden, and the Ottoman empire. The Habsburgs consolidated their power in southeastern Europe, and on the Baltic the Prussian state grew stronger and more militaristic.

The eighteenth century was the age of the Enlightenment, an intellectual movement inspired by the achievements of rational philosophers and scientists such as Newton, Locke, and Bayle. Leaders of the new movement included Montesquieu, who gave up his career as a magistrate to pursue his irreverent and speculative writing, and Voltaire, the brilliant writer and wit who popularized the ideas of Newton on the continent. None of the ready assumptions of the past, even those involving the relationships of the sexes, were safe from the probing rationalism of Enlightenment thinkers.

Vocabulary

attaché   An official diplomatic assistant, often with some special expertise, to a minister or ambassador.

cameralism   An economic reform program, related to mercantilism, whose ultimate goal was to enhance the power of the crown. A "cameralist" is an economic advisor who makes political considerations a high priority.

cantata   An extended musical composition featuring, in Bach's time, vocal soloists with instrumental and sometimes choral accompaniment. In other eras, the word may refer to different sorts of compositions.

conspicuous consumption   Extravagant spending motivated more by a desire to demonstrate wealth than to satisfy any actual needs. Although this behavior was typical of court society of this era, the term was coined by American economist Thorstein Veblen in 1899.

Covent Garden   An area west of the city of London that became a desirable address in the eighteenth century. It was the site of a famous market, an Italianate *piazza*, coffee houses, and the Royal Opera House, with which it became synonymous.

Creole   A word with many meanings, including: (1) a person born in the colonies but of European descent; (2) an American, white or of mixed race, with French or Spanish ancestry; (3) anything resulting from a mixture of European, African, and American influences, such as the language of Haiti or the cuisine of New Orleans.

fakir	Originally a Muslim who chose a life of poverty and austerity; later a wandering holy man of India.
fête galante	In painting, a scene showing a group of stylish aristocrats in an idyllic, outdoor setting such as a formal garden or park, enjoying games, music, or casual flirtation. This genre of painting celebrates the elegance and indolence of eighteenth-century nobility.
fugue	A musical composition in which the theme is presented by a succession of "voices" that imitate, echo, or answer each other.
indigo	A popular blue dye made from the plants of the *Indigofera* species.
Jacobite	A supporter of King James II, from the Latin form of his name. Not to be confused with "Jacobean," which refers to the culture of the age of James I, or with "Jacobin," which refers either to Dominican friars or to a political faction during the French Revolution.
oratorio	A baroque composition similar to an opera but based on a religious subject. The name is derived from the Oratorio of S. Filippo Neri in Rome, where the first such productions were given around 1600.

Self-Testing and Review Questions

Identification

After reading Chapter 18, identify and explain the historical significance of each of the following:

1. War of Jenkins' Ear

2. Mary Astell

3. Johann Sebastian Bach

4. Ferenc Rákóczi

5. Daniel Defoe

6. Treaty of Utrecht

7. Fleury

8. Enlightenment

9. St. Petersburg

10. *The Messiah*

11. rococo

12. Sir Robert Walpole

13. Act of Union

14. *The Spectator*

15. League of Augsburg

16. John Law

17. Great Northern War

18. enclosure movement

19. Eliza Heywood

Chronology

Identify the events or issues associated with the following dates. Some of these dates may be significant for more than one reason. After you finish, answer the questions that follow.

1686

1694

1697

1701

1709

1713

1715

1721

1738

1. How did European rulers of the early eighteenth century mimic the court, palace, and army of Louis XIV?
2. Many studies of European history consider the year 1715 to be a major turning point. Why?

Matching Exercises

In each set, match the terms on the left with those on the right.

Set A

_____ 1. *Conversation on the Plurality of Worlds*	a. Bayle
_____ 2. *News from the Republic of Letters*	b. Voltaire
_____ 3. *Letters Concerning the English Nation*	c. Fontanelle
_____ 4. *A Historical and Critical Dictionary*	d. Montesquieu
_____ 5. *Fable of the Bees*	e. Mandeville
_____ 6. *Persian Letters*	(May be used more than once)
_____ 7. *Elements of the Philosophy of Newton*	

Set B

____ 1. George II
____ 2. Augustus III
____ 3. Queen Anne
____ 4. Philip V
____ 5. Charles XII
____ 6. Charles II
____ 7. Frederick William I

a. ruler of Prussia
b. ruler of Sweden
c. ruler of Hanover and Britain
d. ruler of Saxony and Poland
e. last Habsburg ruler of Spain
f. first Bourbon ruler of Spain
g. last Stuart ruler of England and Scotland

Set C

____ 1. Fénélon
____ 2. Antoine Watteau
____ 3. François de Callière
____ 4. Montesquieu
____ 5. Jeanne-Marie Guyon

a. *On the Manner of Negotiating with Sovereigns*
b. Quietism
c. an archbishop
d. a judge
e. a rococo painter

Set D

____ 1. Angola
____ 2. Java
____ 3. Florida
____ 4. Carolinas
____ 5. Brazil
____ 6. Jamaica

a. Spain
b. Great Britain
c. Netherlands
d. Portugal
(May be used more than once)

Set E

____ 1. William Petty
____ 2. John Law
____ 3. Daniel Defoe
____ 4. Robert Walpole
____ 5. Addison and Steele

a. published *The Spectator*
b. created the Mississippi Bubble
c. was the first "prime minister"
d. studied population changes
e. wrote *Moll Flanders*

Multiple-Choice Questions

1. Rivalry between Great Britain and Spain over colonial trade resulted in
   a. the enclosure movement.
   b. the Mississippi Bubble.
   c. the War of Jenkins' Ear.
   d. the Treaty of Nystad.

2. The Philadelphians were
   a. a tribe of American Indians in what is today Pennsylvania.
   b. a Pietistic sect founded by Jane Leade.
   c. pioneers of the novel.
   d. a school of painters, followers of Boucher.

3. Inoculation against smallpox was pioneered in the early eighteenth century by
   a. Lady Mary Wortley Montagu.
   b. François Poullain de La Barre.
   c. Jeanne-Marie Guyon.
   d. Edward Jenner.

4. The Jacobites tried to prevent the coronation of
   a. Philip of Anjou in Spain.
   b. George of Hanover in Britain.
   c. Augustus III of Saxony in Poland.
   d. Louis XV in France.

5. The "Pretenders" were
   a. speculators encouraged by John Law.
   b. the Catholic Stuart descendants of James II.
   c. Russian nobles who feigned enthusiasm for Peter I's reforms.
   d. Russians who opposed Alexei's religious reforms.

6. Robert Walpole was a
   a. Catholic.
   b. Quietist.
   c. Jacobite.
   d. Whig.

7. The reforms of Peter the Great were designed to
   a. drive the Turks from the Black Sea and take possession of the Straits.
   b. insulate Russia from Western influences.
   c. introduce Western technology and culture to Russia.
   d. turn Russia into a constitutional monarchy.

8. Frederick William I is perhaps best remembered for
   a. his encouragement of art and music.
   b. his colonial acquisitions in Canada.
   c. his obsession with the military.
   d. being a model father.

9. Bayle argued that
   a. successful negotiations harmonize the real interests of both parties.
   b. the desire to enrich oneself could promote economic prosperity.
   c. a separation of governmental powers is the best insurance against tyranny.
   d. truth is obtained through rational investigation, not blind faith.

10. A *quilombo* was
    a. a hide-out for escaped slaves.
    b. a coffee plantation.
    c. a swashbuckling novel.
    d. a slave ship.

Essay Questions

Using material from this and earlier chapters, write an essay on each of the following topics. When appropriate, include dates and detailed examples to support your arguments.

1. The textbook notes that Europeans believed Africans and American Indians to be intellectually inferior. Given their limited knowledge of human history and their complete ignorance of modern subjects such as anthropology, what other possible reasons were available to Europeans to explain entire cultures without cities, literacy, and so on? As Europeans learned more about the rest of the world, did their confidence in their own superiority become stronger or weaker?

2. Explain why travelers and travel literature were so popular in Europe after 1690–1700. What factors had inhibited travel before this time?

3. Coffee, sugar, tobacco, and tea, like spices in the Middle Ages, were all nutritionally unnecessary and also difficult to produce and obtain. Yet they seem to have had more impact on European cash economies than staples did, and they were major factors in stimulating national economies, colonialism, and the spread of slavery. Why were they so important? Can you think of any parallels in the modern world?

4. Many of the authors and thinkers mentioned in this chapter are French. Why was French culture so influential in the eighteenth century?

5. Discuss the relations, cultural as well as political, between Great Britain and France in the years 1690–1740. Why do two countries with so much in common always seem to be on opposite sides in the wars?

Skill Building: Maps

A. *Locate the following on the map of the world. (You may need to consult maps in earlier chapters or in an atlas.) Why was each location significant in this or the previous chapter?*

a. Cape of Good Hope

b. thirteen colonies

c. Bombay

d. Peru

e. Calcutta

f. Russian empire

g. Florida

h. Canada

i. Pondicherry

j. Angola

k. Java

l. India

m. Brazil

n. Caribbean islands

o. Cuba

1. What European power (if any) was particularly associated with each of the places above? Choose a color for each major colonial power and shade in the areas that each one influenced.

2. What insights into early 1990s events in the former Soviet Union can be gained by studying the expansion of Russia in the seventeenth century?

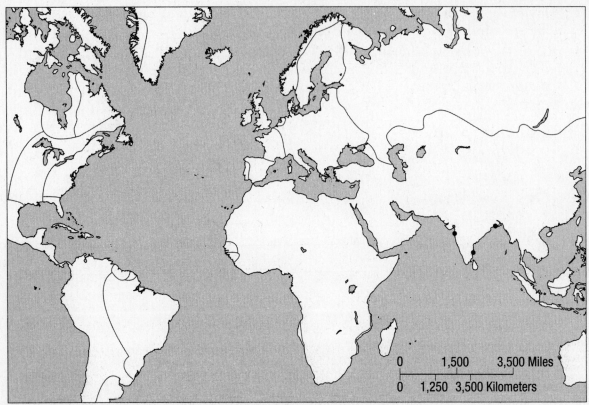

European Colonialism in the Early Eighteenth Century

B. *Locate the following on the map of Europe. How was each significant in the present chapter?*
   a. Scotland

   b. Warsaw

   c. Gibraltar

   d. Vienna

   e. Austrian Netherlands*

   f. Madrid

   g. St. Petersburg

   h. Hanover

---

*These are the same as the Spanish Netherlands, discussed in previous chapters. They were ceded to the Austrian Habsburgs at the Treaty of Utrecht.

i. Berlin

j. Dutch Republic

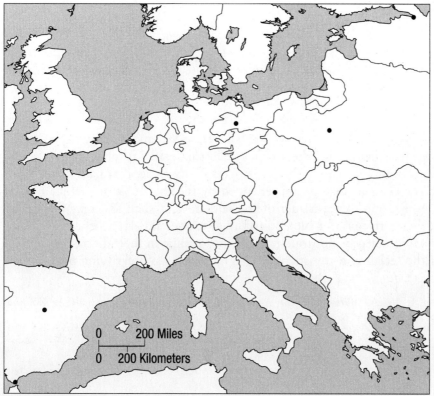

Europe in 1715

1. Why do you suppose that the Spanish Netherlands and Gibraltar, as well as other territories, were taken from Spain at the Treaty of Utrecht?

2. Which of the participants at the conference would you imagine insisted on this?

3. If one counts Spain as a dynastic acquisition of the Bourbons, do you think Louis XIV considered the treaty a net loss or gain?

Enrichment Exercise

Henry Fielding's most famous novel, *Tom Jones,* became an Academy Award winning film in 1963, and the same author's *Joseph Andrews* was made into a film in 1977. See one or both of these, and write an essay that includes answers to the following questions: Who was the probable audience for stories of this sort in the eighteenth century? Why did eighteenth-century English novels frequently feature such themes as lost children, rustic innocents menaced by urban corruption, and struggles over inheritances? How are cities depicted?

Document Analysis

DOCUMENT 1

Slave Laws in Virginia

In 1705, the House of Burgesses of the colony of Virginia passed a comprehensive act defining the status of black, mulatto, and Indian slaves. According to the law, two justices of the peace could authorize sheriffs to search for runaway slaves. Proclamations to this effect were to be published on Sundays and nailed to church doors. The law also outlined the rights of the pursuers over slaves, who legally had no rights at all.

> It shall be lawful for any person or persons whatsoever, to kill and destroy such slaves by such ways and means as he, she, or they shall think fit, without accusation or impeachment of any crime for the same: And if any slave, that hath run away and lain out as aforesaid, shall be apprehended by the sheriff, or any other person, upon the application of the owner of the said slave, it shall and may be lawful for the county court, to order such punishment to the said slave, either *by dismembering,* or any other way, not touching his life, as they in their discretion shall think fit, for the reclaiming any such incorrigible slave, and terrifying others from the like practices.

Source: A. Leon Higginbotham, Jr., *In the Matter of Color: Race and the American Legal Process (The Colonial Period)* (Oxford University Press, 1978), p. 56.

Questions

1. How common was the death penalty? maiming? Were the penalties unusually cruel for the era?
2. Where might a runaway slave escape to from Virginia in 1705?
3. What conditions described in the text might give rise to such a harsh law?

DOCUMENT 2

Peter the Great and Western Customs

In this selection from his diary, Johann-Georg Korb, secretary to the Austrian ambassador to Moscow, describes Peter's influence on dress at court. Peter had returned not long before from his famous western journey, and in earlier passages, Korb had described the horrible torture and execution of conspirators against the tsar.

> February 22, 1699—
> The representatives as well as the magnates of Muscovy, by invitation in the name of his Majesty the Czar, went to a banquet of regal magnificence and most sumptuous festivities to last two days, in the new palace which was dedicated with yesterday's rites to Bacchus. Prince Szeremetow, as a Knight of Malta, with the cross of the order on his breast, imitated most happily the German manners, and wore the German dress; by which, though he found favour with his prince, and was held in especial honour, he won the envy of the Boyars [high-ranking nobles], who feared that he would, by help of his Majesty's favour, work his way up to great and eminent power. . . . The Czar perceiving some of his military officers hankering after new fashions, wearing very loose coats, cut off the cuffs

that hung down too low, and thus addressed them: "See these things are in your way; you are safe nowhere with them; at one moment you upset a glass; then you forgetfully dip them in the sauce; get gaiters made of them."

Source: Johann-Georg Korb, *Diary of An Austrian Secretary of Legation at the Court of Czar Peter the Great*, trans. The Count MacDonnell. Reprint edition (Da Capo Press, 1968), pp. 256–257.

Questions

1. In your opinion, was Peter's influence on manners at his court a parody of Louis XIV's at Versailles?

2. In what other areas, according to the text, did Peter westernize Russian life and culture?

DOCUMENT 3

Montesquieu's Persian Letters (1721)

In this selection from Montesquieu's Persian Letters, *the fictional Persian traveler Rica writes to a friend at home describing the court of Louis XIV. In a harsh aside, he also expresses amazement at the powers of the pope in Rome. This excerpt is typical of Montesquieu's literary style: instead of describing foreign customs from the European point of view, he portrays foreign characters who are surprised at French customs. In this way, he demonstrates that there is no natural or inevitable quality to European ways of life; in fact, he makes them seem hilariously funny. The* Persian Letters *is an example of the rococo in literature because of its constant variation of themes and its often erotic and playful subject matter.*

The King of France is the most powerful ruler in Europe. . . . He has been known to undertake or sustain major wars with no other funds but what he gets from selling honorific titles, and by a miracle of human vanity, his troops are paid, his fortresses supplied, and his fleets equipped.

Moreover, this king is a great magician. He exerts authority even over the minds of his subjects; he makes them think what he wants. If there are only a million crowns in the exchequer, and he needs two million, all he has to do is persuade them that one crown is worth two, and they believe it [Montesquieu is referring to currency debasement]. . . .

You must not be amazed at what I tell you about this prince: there is another magician, stronger than he, who controls his mind as completely as he controls other people's. This magician is called the Pope. He will make the king believe that three are only one [the doctrine of the trinity], or else that the bread one eats is not bread, or that the wine one drinks not wine [the sacrament of communion], and a thousand other things of the same kind.

Source: From Montesquieu, *Persian Letters*. Trans. C. J. Betts (Penguin, 1973), pp. 72–73.

Questions

1. Given the fact that Montesquieu inherited and later sold his own position on a provincial parlement, why does he seem resentful of the fact that such offices could be bought and sold?

2. From the text description of French court life, what do you suppose was the reaction of the French nobility to Montesquieu's satire?

DOCUMENT 4

Mary Astell's Views on Marriage

In recent years, Mary Astell has attracted considerable attention as the first English feminist. She argued with wit and passion against doctrines of the natural inferiority of women. In addition to her feminist writings on marriage and women's education, Astell also participated in many of the political debates of the day. She was a devout Anglican and Tory sympathizer who believed in the divine right of kings at a time when such views were increasingly considered old-fashioned, yet her feminist writings were far ahead of their time. In her Reflections upon Marriage *(first published anonymously in 1700), Astell suggested that remaining single was a real alternative to marriage, because it could give upper-class women at least some measure of independence. In the following selection, Astell replies to her critics.*

Tis true, thro' Want of Learning, and of that Superior Genius which Men as Men lay claim to, she was ignorant of the *Natural Inferiority* of our Sex, which our Masters lay down as a Self-Evident and Fundamental Truth. She saw nothing in the Reason of Things, to make this either a Principle or a Conclusion, but much to the contrary. . . .

That the Custom of the World has put Women, generally speaking, into a State of Subjection, is not deny'd; but the Right can no more be prov'd from the Fact, than the Predominancy of Vice can justifie it. . . .

The Domestic Sovereign [husband] is without Dispute Elected, and the Stipulations and Contract are mutual, is it not then partial in Men to the last degree, to contend for, and practise that Arbitrary Dominion in their Families, which they abhor and exclaim against in the State? For if Arbitrary Power is evil in itself, and an improper Method of Governing Rational and Free Agents, it ought not to be Practis'd any where; Nor is it less, but rather more mischievous in Families than in Kingdoms, by how much 100,000 Tyrants are worse than one.

Source: Mary Astell, *Reflections upon Marriage*, 3rd ed. (R. Wilkin, 1706), as reprinted in Bridget Hill, ed., *The First English Feminist: Reflections upon Marriage and other Writings by Mary Astell* (St. Martin's Press, 1986), pp. 71, 72, 76.

Questions

1. From your study of the textbook, how do you suppose Astell's opinions would have been received by various readers of the period?

2. Are the philosophical and political assumptions of Astell's arguments, as presented here, consistent with her political beliefs?

CHAPTER

19

The Promise of a New Order, 1740–1787

Chapter Outline

OPPOSITION AND REBELLION AGAINST STATE POWER
Food Riots and Peasant Uprisings
Public Opinion and Political Opposition
Revolution in North America

Chapter Summary

The Enlightenment reached its high tide during the last half of the eighteenth century, when the ideas and ideals of the movement penetrated other lands and were even reflected in the policies of the rulers, some of whom were appalled by its lack of respect for tradition, others fascinated by its potential to reform their states and enhance their wealth and power. The Enlightenment dominated literature, the arts, and conversation at fashionable salons and Masonic lodges. It was naturally opposed by the religious establishment, because it considered religion irrelevant at best and the clergy to be the fount of superstition and intolerance. The *philosophes,* the spokesmen of the new movement, included a variety of writers whose works ranged from metaphysical philosophy to sentimental novels. They were most effective as popularizers, and the principles of the Enlightenment were presented in histories, plays, and the ambitious *Encyclopedia.* The search for natural laws caused them to question accepted beliefs in economics, education, the treatment of criminals, and the relationship between the sexes. The *philosophes* also questioned each other and quarrelled among themselves, debating the limits of reason. The same era witnessed a revival of religion, a new emotionalism in some novels, and a renewed interest in the supernatural and the unexplained.

Enlightenment ideals were reflected in the policies of several European rulers who became known as "enlightened despots," but the degree of their enlightenment is questionable. Catherine II the Great of Russia and Frederick II the Great of Prussia both corresponded with *philosophes* and reformed education, but they also waged cynical wars and expanded the power of the nobility. Holy Roman Emperor Joseph II, the son of Maria Theresa, seems to have been more genuinely motivated by the new principles, but many of his reforms met resistance from the many special interests in his diverse lands. The French kings also attempted a few reforms, but the French nobility, which grew stronger in the eighteenth century, was entrenched in its *parlements* and privileges, and adept at turning the language of the Enlightenment back upon the reformers. The result was a nobility that thwarted the most important innovations, and was militant in its determination to fight "tyranny." The court was polarized, and the *bourgeoisie* was frustrated by the failure of government reform in the state that was the very center of the Enlightenment.

Another frustration that the French faced in this period was the virtual destruction of their overseas empire. The French fought in all of the European wars of the age, and fared badly. In 1740, Frederick II demanded compensation for the succession of Maria Theresa as empress and invaded Silesia, thus setting off the War of Austrian Succession. When France and Spain joined Prussia, Great Britain, already at war with Spain over Jenkins' Ear, backed Austria. Maria Theresa managed to keep her throne but had to accept the loss of Silesia; the British gained no significant new colonial territories but did develop a naval superiority that would serve them well in the next war. With the coming of peace, Austria set about gaining new allies against the formidable new state of Prussia. When Austria and France gave up their traditional rivalry and became allies, it constituted a diplomatic revolution; they were also joined by Russia. Great Britain, perhaps to protect the crown territories of Hanover, and to continue her colonial rivalry with France, became the ally of Prussia. The Seven Years' War proved a disaster for France, which lost her claims to Canada and India; Britain emerged from this war the unquestioned colonial leader. Russia dropped out of the war in 1762, and Maria Theresa failed to regain Silesia.

An indirect result of the war was a new settlement in eastern Europe, where Russia made war on the Turks while reaching compromises with Austria and Prussia. One of these agreements was the First Partition of Poland.

The British suffered a serious blow to their colonial ambitions toward the end of the eighteenth century when their thirteen mid-Atlantic colonies rebelled. The colonies claimed mistreatment, arguing in the Whig rhetoric of the British ruling class. Assisted by the French, the Spanish, and the Dutch, the Americans managed to win their revolt and created an independent regime based on a mixture of Whig and Enlightenment principles. This outcome astonished many, but to others seemed the natural culmination of a century of progress and reason.

Vocabulary

classical	Having originality, balanced proportions, enduring appeal; thus Greece and Rome were "classical" civilizations. In the eighteenth century, the word was applied to certain styles of art and music thought to have the same qualities of proportion and restraint as ancient art; the term is still applied to the musical style of Haydn, Mozart, and some of their contemporaries.
corvée	Unpaid labor, often repairing the roads, that medieval tenants owed their masters as a sort of tax. Such feudal dues were still collected in the eighteenth century, but they inspired increasing resentment.
Deism	A sort of religion based on the idea that God created the universe and the laws that govern it, but that supernatural intervention in earthly matters ceased at that point; consequently, there is no need for clergy, ritual, or organized religion.
empiricism	The belief that all knowledge derives from experience rather than from innate ideas. The concept, which is particularly associated with Locke and Hume, derives its name from Sextus Empiricus, an ancient Skeptic.
flintlock	A firing mechanism for small arms. In the late seventeenth century, the flintlock system replaced the earlier, clumsier firelock and matchlock systems, revolutionizing eighteenth-century firearms and warfare.
laissez-faire	Literally "leave it alone" or "let it be." The term was coined by the French physiocrat François Quesnay to sum up his advice on how government should deal with the economy. Louis XV once asked Quesnay what he would do if he were king, and Quesnay replied, "Nothing." Thus, *laissez-faire* economics at that time was the opposite of mercantilism.
philosophe	The French word for "philosopher," often used to differentiate the intellectuals of the Enlightenment from philosophers in other periods; *philosophes* were often more publicists and popularizers than metaphysicists.
physiocrat	A *philosophe* concerned with economics.
neoclassical	Having to do with a movement in art, architecture, and poetry in the eighteenth century that advocated scrupulous fidelity to the aesthetic rules and principles of Greco-Roman (classical) art. The style was inspired by new scholarship into ancient art and literature and by archeological discoveries.

Self-Testing and Review Questions

Identification

After reading Chapter 19, identify and explain the historical significance of each of the following:

1. Abbé Raynal

2. *The Critique of Pure Reason*

3. spinning jenny

4. Partition of Poland

5. Boston Tea Party

6. Denis Diderot

7. Articles of Confederation

8. Pragmatic Sanction

9. Jean Calas

10. Silesia

11. Cesare Beccaria

12. Jean-Baptiste Greuze

13. Battle of Rossbach

14. Pugachev

15. *Confessions*

16. Treaty of Utrecht

17. George III

18. Adam Smith

19. "putting out" system

20. *The Marriage of Figaro*

Chronology

Identify the events or issues associated with the following dates. Some of these dates may be significant for more than one reason. After you finish, answer the questions that follow.

1740

1748

1756

1763

1765

1773

1776

1780

1783

1. The year 1776 is significant in several different contexts. How are the several "unrelated" events of 1776 actually interconnected?
2. How did the Seven Years' War relate to other events (and dates) of this period?

Matching Exercises

In each set, match the terms on the left with those on the right.

Set A

____ 1. Samuel Richardson   a. Scottish economist, author of *The Wealth of Nations*

____ 2. William Hogarth   b. founder of Methodism

____ 3. John Wesley   c. controversial member of Parliament

____ 4. John Wilkes   d. popular artist

____ 5. Adam Smith   e. English novelist, author of *Clarissa Harlowe*

Set B

____ 1. *The New Heloise*   a. Montesquieu

____ 2. *The Critique of Pure Reason*   b. Voltaire

____ 3. *Spirit of the Laws*   c. Rousseau

____ 4. *Natural History of Religion*   d. Hume

____ 5. *The Philosophical Dictionary*   e. Kant

____ 6. *The Social Contract*   (Use one of these twice)

Set C

_____ 1. Cesare Beccaria   a. hostess of a fashionable Paris salon

_____ 2. Mme Vigée Lebrun   b. reformer who advocated abolition of torture and the death penalty

_____ 3. Mme Geoffrin   c. aristocratic female _philosophe_

_____ 4. Mme du Châtelet   d. fashionable court painter

_____ 5. Jacques Turgot   e. economic advisor to Louis XVI

Set D

_____ 1. _Emile_   a. Beaumarchais

_____ 2. _The Marriage of Figaro_   b. Voltaire

_____ 3. _The Sorrows of Young Werther_   c. Rousseau

_____ 4. _The Age of Louis XIV_   d. Raynal

_____ 5. _Philosophical and Political History of European Colonies and Commerce in the Two Indies_   e. Goethe

Set E

_____ 1. Voltaire   a. "the first citizen of a free people"

_____ 2. Gustavus III   b. "the first servant of the state"

_____ 3. Joseph II   c. "_Écrasez l'infâme_"

_____ 4. Frederick II   d. "unfortunate in all his enterprises"

Multiple-Choice Questions

1. The _Encyclopedia_ was
   a. a witty survey of English usage by Samuel Johnson.
   b. a monumental compendium of human knowledge, edited by Diderot.
   c. a collection of essays on all subjects, commissioned by Pope Clement XIV.
   d. a portable version of Bayle's _Dictionnaire_, written by Voltaire.

2. John Kay, James Watt, and Edmund Cartwright were
   a. inventors.
   b. economists.
   c. Irish rebels.
   d. novelists.

3. The Hasidic movement was founded by
   a. Moses Mendelssohn.
   b. Gotthold Lessing.
   c. Emelyan Pugachev.
   d. Ba'al Shem Tov.

4. The French and Indian War was another name for
   a. the War of Austrian Succession.
   b. the Seven Years' War.
   c. the Great Northern War.
   d. the War of Bavarian Succession.

5. Catherine II's greatest successes were achieved
   a. in foreign affairs.
   b. by abolishing serfdom.
   c. through her fortunate marriage.
   d. by granting a constitution.

6. The classical style in music is perhaps best represented by
   a. Bach and Handel.
   b. Beethoven and Schubert.
   c. Haydn and Mozart.
   d. Liszt and Wagner.

7. Rousseau did *not* believe that
   a. the revival of science and the arts had contributed to moral decline.
   b. individual interests must be subordinated to the "general will" of the community.
   c. the education of women should differ significantly from the education of men.
   d. women should be encouraged to pursue public careers, as in the salons.

8. The Gordon Riots began as protests against
   a. American independence.
   b. the toleration of Catholicism.
   c. the annexation of Ireland.
   d. a new tax on sheep.

9. Jacques Turgot
   a. launched the Great Awakening.
   b. attempted economic reforms in France.
   c. is famous for his *Confessions*.
   d. abolished the rotten boroughs.

10. The Pragmatic Sanction was intended to guarantee a smooth succession for
    a. Catherine II.
    b. Elizabeth II.
    c. Louis XV.
    d. Maria Theresa.

Essay Questions

Using material from this and earlier chapters, write an essay on each of the following topics. When appropriate, include dates and detailed examples to support your arguments.

1. Discuss in detail the achievements of Frederick II of Prussia. Does he deserve to be called "the Great"?

2. Some historians have argued that the wars of the late seventeenth and eighteenth centuries constituted a "second Hundred Years' War" between France and England. Do you agree? Who won?

3. Who were the principal "enlightened despots" and what did they do? To what extent was each enlightened? despotic?

4. Was Jean-Jacques Rousseau a daring and original thinker, or was he a provocative but mainstream thinker?

5. Trace the influence of Enlightenment ideas on the origins and outcomes of the American Revolution.

Skill Building: Maps

Locate the following cities or regions on the map of Europe. Why was each significant in the present chapter?

a. Austria

b. Rossbach

c. Poland (before 1772)

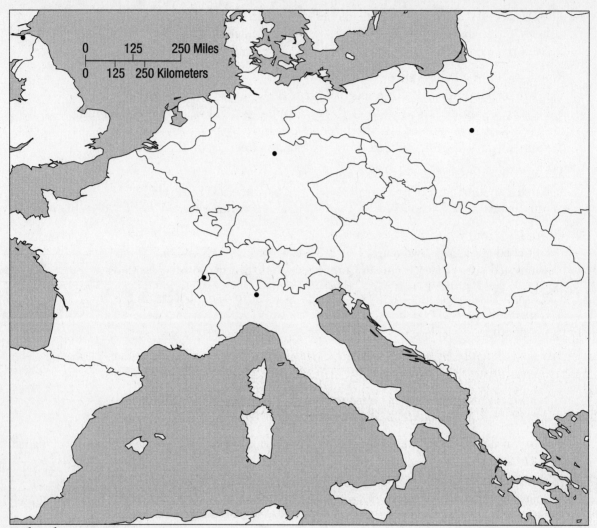

Poland, c. 1750

    d. Geneva

    e. Milan

    f. Silesia

    g. Edinburgh

    h. Warsaw

1. On the map, show the borders of Poland-Lithuania before and after the First Partition (1772). What conclusions can you draw about the shift of power in central and eastern Europe?

2. From what you have learned about the Seven Years' War and other colonial wars, was the "First World War" (1914–1918) misnamed? Discuss.

Enrichment Exercise

In 1782, the French author François Choderlos de Laclos, a soldier and secretary to Louis XVI's cousin, the duc d'Orléans, wrote a troubling novel entitled *Les Liaisons dangéreuses*. In this century, it has inspired two stunning films: the stylish and award-winning *Dangerous Liaisons* (1988)* and the less celebrated but also worthwhile *Valmont* (1989), directed by Milos Forman. Read the novel or see one of the films, and write a short essay describing Choderlos' vision of the French nobility on the eve of the French Revolution. Did novels such as this affect public opinion? In what way?

Document Analysis

DOCUMENT 1

The Manifesto of the Enlightenment

The Encyclopedia or Rational Dictionary of the Sciences, Arts, and Crafts *(1752–1772), edited chiefly by Denis Diderot, was published originally in seventeen volumes, with eleven accompanying volumes of illustrations. In hundreds of articles written by the leading intellectuals of the time, the* Encyclopedia *gave its readers detailed information about every conceivable aspect of knowledge from science to religion. The King's Council and the pope both condemned it as harmful to established authority. Recent studies have shown that it was bought by thousands of readers when it appeared in cheaper editions. In this selection, one of the chief targets of the Enlightenment, "fanaticism," is explained and criticized.*

> FANATICISM, noun (Philosophy) is blind and passionate zeal born of superstitious opinions, causing people to commit ridiculous, unjust, and cruel actions, not only without any shame or remorse, but even with a kind of joy and comfort. *Fanaticism,* therefore, is only superstition put into practice. . . . The particular causes of *fanaticism* are to be found:
>
> 1) In the nature of dogmas. If they are contrary to reason, they overthrow sound judgment and subject everything to imagination whose abuses are the greatest of all evils. . . . Obscure dogmas produce a multitude of interpretations thereby creating the dissension of the sects. Truth does not make any *fanatics.* It is so clear that it hardly allows any contradiction; it so penetrates the mind that the most demented people cannot diminish its enjoyment. . . .
>
> 5) In the intolerance of one religion in regard to others, or of one sect among several of the same religion, because all hands join forces against the common enemy. . . .
>
> 6) In persecution, which arises essentially from intolerance. . . .
>
> *Fanaticism* has done much more harm to the world than impiety. What do impious people claim? To free themselves of a yoke, while *fanatics* want to extend their chains over all the earth. Infernal zealomania! Have we ever seen sects of unbelievers gather into mobs and march with weapons against the Divinity? Their souls are too weak to spill human blood.

Source: From *Denis Diderot's The Encyclopedia: Selections,* ed. and trans. Stephen J. Gendzier (Harper and Row, 1967), pp. 104–106.

---

* Do not confuse this with Roger Vadim's 1960 film, which also happens to be named *Les Liaisons dangéreuses!*

Questions

1. Which of the *philosophes* and enlightened despots described in the textbook do you think would agree with the ideas in this selection? Why?

2. In our age, those who are considered "tolerant" usually try to avoid offending the sensibilities of others. The historian Carl Becker once noted ironically that Voltaire believed in toleration but couldn't abide priests. What does the author of this article think about "tolerating" fanaticism?

DOCUMENT 2

A Woman from Salon Society Writes to a King

Marie Thérèse Geoffrin, the salon hostess, carried on an extensive correspondence with writers and political leaders all over Europe. One of her most faithful correspondents was the king of Poland, to whom she wrote long letters at least once a month between 1765 and 1777. The king called her "my dear Mama" in his letters; she called him "my dear son, my dear king." Excerpts from Mme Geoffrin's letter to King Stanislaus August Poniatowski of Poland, dated August 7, 1765, show the range of concerns that she wrote about.

> I am sending to you a banker named Claudel who is returning to Warsaw. He will have with him a printed memoir on a new kind of mill. The more I have learned about it, the more I see that this machine is very well-known. Your Majesty is best advised to invite a miller to come from France; he will know how to set it up and show how to use it, and use of it can spread from there.
>
> Prince Sulkowski [a Polish nobleman] met Mr. Hennin at my salon. Mr. Hennin had been for a long time in Warsaw, and they talked together about Poland. I see with pain that it has a very bad government [Stanislaus was elected king only in 1764]; it seems almost impossible to make it better. . . .
>
> I sent you the catalogue of the diamonds of Madame de Pompadour [King Louis XV's mistress had died recently and her diamonds were auctioned off] . . .
>
> Do not forget, my dear son, to send the memoir on commerce to Mr. Riancourt when he returns. . . .
>
> I cannot report any news yet on your project for paintings; I am very sad about the death of poor Carle Vanloo [a leading French painter who died in July 1765]. It was a horrible loss for the arts.

Source: *Correspondence inédite du roi Stanislas-Auguste Poniatowski et de Madame Geoffrin (1764–1777)*, ed. Charles de Mouy (Slatkine, 1970, reprint of 1875 edition), pp. 164–168. English translation by Lynn Hunt.

Questions

1. The fact that Marie-Thérèse Geoffrin was a *bourgeoise* does not seem to have interfered with her friendship with the king of Poland. What role in the relationship is played by the fact that she was French?

2. What did each gain from the relationship?

DOCUMENT 3

The Emancipation of the Jews in Austria

Like the Jews in most European countries, the Jews in Austria were subject to various forms of discrimination. Emperor Joseph II removed the worst impositions in a series of ordinances released in 1781 and 1782. The following excerpts from them show the influence of the Enlightenment, but they also show how deep the feelings of antisemitism went in the Austrian population.

In order to make the Jews more useful, the discrimination hitherto observed in relation to their clothing is abolished in its entirety. Consequently the obligation for the men to wear yellow armbands and the women to wear yellow ribbons is abolished. If they behave quietly and decently, then no one has the right to dictate to them on matters of dress.

Within two years the Jews must abandon their own language. . . . Consequently the Jews may use their own language only during religious services.

Those Jews who do not have the opportunity to send their children to Jewish schools are to be compelled to send them to Christian schools, to learn reading, writing, arithmetic and other subjects.

Jewish youths will also be allowed to attend the imperial universities.

To prevent the Jewish children and the Jews in general suffering as a result of the concessions granted to them, the authorities and the leaders of the local communities must instruct the subjects in a rational manner that the Jews are to be regarded like any other fellow human-beings and that there must be an end to the prejudice and contempt which some subjects, particularly the unintelligent, have shown towards the Jewish nation and which several times in the past have led to deplorable behaviour and even criminal excesses. On the other hand the Jews must be warned to behave like decent citizens and it must be emphasised in particular that they must not allow the beneficence of His Majesty to go to their heads and indulge in wanton and licentious excesses and swindling.

Source: From T. C. W. Blanning, *Joseph II and Enlightened Despotism* (Longman, 1970), pp. 142–144.

Questions

1. Joseph's brother, the Grand Duke of Tuscany, had a prosperous independent colony of Jews in his seaport, Livorno. Does Joseph seem to expect the Jews to flourish under his new edict?
2. Does Joseph expect resistance from his own officials?
3. From what you have read in the text, why do you think Joseph waited until 1781 to issue this (and many other) decrees?

DOCUMENT 4

The American Experience and Its Lessons

Thomas Jefferson (1743–1826) was one of the leaders of the American struggle for independence. Author of the Declaration of Independence of 1776, governor of Virginia, minister to France, sec-

retary of state, vice-president, and third president of the United States, Jefferson was known as an admirer of the philosophes. *In his* Notes on the State of Virginia *(1781–1782), he demonstrated his wide range of interests, writing on everything from geology to law. The excerpts included here show his command of constitutional issues, his interest in more democratic forms of government, and his deep concern about the legacy of slavery. Himself a slaveowner, Jefferson wrote in his* Notes *about the possibility of emancipating the slaves, but only on the condition that they be sent away to establish a separate colony.*

Query XIII: Constitution

This constitution [of the state of Virginia] was formed when we were new and unexperienced in the science of government. It was the first too which was formed in the whole United States. No wonder then that time and trial have discovered very capital defects in it.

1. The majority of the men in the state, who pay and fight for its support, are unrepresented in the legislature, the roll of freeholders intitled to vote, not including generally the half of those on the roll of the militia, or of the tax-gatherers.

2. Among those who share the representation, the shares are very unequal. . . .

3. The senate, is by its constitution, too homogeneous with the house of delegates. . . .

Query XIV: Laws

In this section Jefferson advocates emancipating the slaves, educating girls of former slave families to age eighteen and boys to twenty-one, and then sending them away to unspecified colonies.

It will probably be asked, Why not retain and incorporate the blacks into the state, and thus save the expence of supplying, by importation of white settlers, the vacancies they will leave? Deep rooted prejudices entertained by the whites; ten thousand recollections, by the blacks of the injuries they have sustained; new provocations; the real distinctions which nature has made; and many other circumstances, will divide us into parties, and produce convulsions which will probably never end.

Source: *Thomas Jefferson Selected Writings,* ed. Harvey C. Mansfield, Jr. (AHM Publishing Corporation, 1979), pp. 28–29, 37.

Questions

1. From your reading of the chapter, would you say that Thomas Jefferson's ideas were typical of the *philosophes* of his day, or that they were fairly original? Discuss.

2. Would Jefferson be pleasantly surprised or pessimistic about race relations in the United States today?

CHAPTER

20

The Age of Revolutions, 1787–1799

Chapter Outline

Chapter Summary

The French Revolution, one of the seminal events in modern history, began with an unassuming fiscal crisis, a fairly common event in the eighteenth century and an increasingly frequent one in France. But this crisis occurred at a time when demands for broad popular representation and individual freedoms were being heard from Geneva to the mouth of the Rhine, and from Philadelphia to Warsaw. The French had helped the Americans win their war of independence, but the burden on the French treasury was staggering. The obvious solution was to reform the archaic tax structure, in which the wealthiest groups paid virtually no taxes at all. Louis XVI was not opposed to reforms, but the privileged classes were, and their resistance drove him to an extraordinary step: in 1789 he convened the Estates General, a medieval assembly that had not met since the monarchy had begun to move toward absolutism almost two centuries earlier.

In the new assembly, the common people (known as the Third Estate) were wealthier, more articulate, and far more politically astute than their medieval predecessors. They came already inspired by Enlightenment ideas and the examples of recent events, especially in America; furthermore, their numbers were doubled because of the king's special decree. The delegates of the Third Estate were determined to give the king his tax reforms, but they also intended to transform France into a constitutional monarchy with guarantees of individual liberties similar to those enjoyed by Englishmen and Americans. After arguing about voting procedures with the other two estates, the clergy and the nobility, they broke the deadlock by declaring themselves the National Assembly—in other words, asserting that only they truly spoke for the French people—and openly pledged that they would give France a constitution.

The king, who couldn't seem to decide which group to back, then fired the popular minister Necker, apparently signaling his opposition to the National Assembly. On July 14, 1789, a Parisian mob seized the royal fortress known as the Bastille. Seeing the people asserting themselves in this way and demonstrating their support for their representatives, the king hastily withdrew his open opposition to the reforms. In the next months, the assembly abolished feudal privilege and approved a declaration of rights. Alarmed nobles fled the country, and confused peasants rioted in the countryside. In October, as famine threatened the cities, a mob of women seconded by the National Guard forced Louis and the royal family to move from Versailles to the center of Paris. The reforms became more radical, especially with regard to the church, and open opposition broke out here and there in the country, supported by emigrant nobles. In 1791 the royal family tried to flee from France, thereby admitting their fundamental opposition to the direction of the reforms. The captured and embarrassed king signed the new constitution in 1791, and France was transformed into a constitutional monarchy.

The outbreak of war against Austria in 1792 precipitated a new crisis. Fearing defeat and the end of the reforms, the *sans-culottes* of Paris attacked the Tuileries. This new wave of violence resulted in the end of the monarchy and the declaration of a republic. Louis was tried for treason and condemned to death. But the war went badly and the republican factions quarreled. In 1793 the *sans-culottes* once again asserted themselves, driving out the more moderate delegates and creating a Jacobin regime to deal with the crisis. Robespierre, a virtual dictator, used terror to deal with his enemies while supporting a program of reforms, some significant, others silly. The Terror was a military success, but Robespierre's increasing paranoia alarmed those political allies whom he hadn't already turned upon and sent to the guillotine. In July 1794, Robespierre was overthrown, executed, and the Terror ended.

Robespierre's successors pursued a more moderate course within France, while military victories continued abroad under brilliant young officers such as Napoleon Bonaparte. A new constitution created a two chambered legislature and an executive Directory of five men to govern France. The ideals of the Revolution, spread far and wide by the government agents, publications, and the French armies, were not always successfully put into practice. The French supported the rebels in the Netherlands, but Polish patriots were crushed and their country partitioned. The Austrians were defeated in Italy, but an Irish uprising failed to evict the British from their island. Napoleon won glory but little else in his famous Egyptian campaign. By 1799 the corruption of the French government and the failure of its military efforts made its leaders vulnerable. In November the Directory was overthrown in a conspiracy that put Napoleon in charge of the French government.

Vocabulary

cisalpine From the Latin *cisalpinus*, literally "on this side of the Alps," as opposed to *transalpine*, "on the other side of the Alps."

guillotine A machine for beheading people; such devices, in use throughout Europe in the eighteenth century, were considered more efficient and therefore more humane than the axe.

nation Originally, a group of people at least distantly related to each other; a sort of extended tribe, sharing a common culture and language. One can have a nation without a state (for example, the Jews after the dispersion, or the Poles at the end of this era), but it is usually a goal of "nationalism" to assure that the nation has its own land and a common government.

patriots From the Latin word *patria* (fatherland), patriots are those who love and support their native land. In the eighteenth century, the word was used in the American colonies, the Netherlands, Poland, France, and elsewhere. Note that patriotism is *not* a synonym for nationalism, although the two are often confused.

propaganda The Latin word for "propagating" or "spreading abroad." After 1622, the Congregatio de propaganda fide (congregation for propagating the faith) coordinated the missionary efforts of the Roman Catholic Church. Because the "Propaganda" was an agency for spreading ideas and arguments on behalf of an organization, it is easy to see how the modern meaning evolved.

rump Hindquarters; a small portion of meat remaining after the larger portion has been cut off. Therefore, a small group of members who remain after the majority of an assembly or committee has been expelled. An example was the Rump Parliament in England (see Chapter 17).

sacralize To sanctify, or make holy.

sections Any of the forty-eight districts or wards of the city of Paris created by the National Assembly. As the Revolution progressed, certain sections, dominated by *sans-culottes* and "passive" citizens and with their own armed contingents, became important agents for radical political change.

seigneurial Feudal.

universal manhood suffrage A political system in which all adult males may vote. The term was used commonly in the nineteenth century to indicate elections that were not restricted to the land-owning or wealthy classes. The term was not intended to exclude women, because the concept of women voting was not yet an issue.

Self-Testing and Review Questions

Identification

After reading Chapter 20, identify and explain the historical significance of each of the following:

1. Tadeusz Kosciuszko

2. Bastille

3. Marie-Antoinette

4. Civil Constitution of the Clergy

5. September massacres

6. the Mountain

7. *La Marseillaise*

8. Jacobins

9. Cult of Reason

10. Atlantic Revolution

11. Partitions of Poland

12. Toussaint L'Ouverture

13. Cisalpine Republic

14. tricolor

15. October Days

16. Third Estate

17. Girondins

18. Reign of Terror

19. *sans-culottes*

20. Republic of Virtue

Chronology

Identify the events or issues associated with the following dates. Note that most of these dates are significant for several events or for events in different countries. After you finish, answer the questions that follow.

1787

1789

1791

1792

1793

1794

1795

1797

1798

1799

1. Many historians refer to the landmark events in modern history by the month or day on which they occurred, such as the October Days, August Days, and September Massacres during the French Revolution, or the July Revolution, June Days, March Laws, and so on in other times or places. What characteristics of modern history make this custom useful?

2. One interpretation of the French Revolution is that there were two revolutions, one in 1789, another in 1792. Do you agree with this interpretation? Why or why not?

Matching Exercises

In each set, match the terms on the left with those on the right.

Set A

_____ 1. *The Rights of Man*   a. Mary Wollstonecraft

_____ 2. *A Vindication of the Rights of Woman*   b. Edmund Burke

_____ 3. *Reflections on the Revolution in France*   c. Abbé Sieyès

_____ 4. *What Is the Third Estate?*   d. Olympe de Gouges

_____ 5. "Declaration of the Rights of Women"   e. Thomas Paine

Set B

_____ 1. October Days   a. a mob attacked the king's fortress

_____ 2. September Massacres   b. the prisons were emptied, the prisoners murdered

_____ 3. 9 Thermidor   c. the women of Paris marched to Versailles

_____ 4. 18 Brumaire   d. Napoleon overthrew the Directory

_____ 5. Bastille Day   e. Robespierre was overthrown

Set C

_____ 1. Jacques Necker   a. famous artist

_____ 2. Maximilien Robespierre   b. minister whose firing provoked the Bastille affair

_____ 3. Georges-Jacques Danton   c. someone executed during the Terror

_____ 4. C.-A. de Calonne   d. reformer who tried to establish a Republic of Virtue

_____ 5. Jacques-Louis David   e. a man whose financial reforms were rejected by the notables

Set D

_____ 1. Maximilien Robespierre   a. commander of the National Guard

_____ 2. Toussaint L'Ouverture   b. First Consul

_____ 3. Napoleon Bonaparte   c. Committee of Public Safety

_____ 4. Lucien Bonaparte   d. Governor of Sainte-Domingue

_____ 5. Lafayette   e. President of the Council of Five Hundred

Set E

_____ 1. Catherina Mulder   a. Girondist leader

_____ 2. Mme Roland   b. assassinated Marat

_____ 3. Charlotte Corday   c. disputed Rousseau's views on education

_____ 4. Olympe de Gouges   d. Dutch Orangist known as "Kaat Mossel"

_____ 5. Mary Wollstonecraft   e. confronted the National Assembly over women's rights

Multiple-Choice Questions

1. The *sans-culottes* were
   a. priests who swore the oath of the Civil Constitution of the Clergy.
   b. urban artisans and shopkeepers who played a major role in revolutionary politics.
   c. *bourgeois* dandies who intimidated Jacobins after the fall of Robespierre.
   d. prisoners sentenced to the guillotine.

2. The revolutionary leader known as "the incorruptible" was
   a. Robespierre.   c. Danton.
   b. Marat.   d. Barras.

3. The rural unrest of 1789 was called
   a. the White Terror.   c. the Great Fear.
   b. the Red Terror.   d. the Reign of Terror.

4. While in Paris, the king of France lived in
   a. Fontainbleau.   c. the Tuileries.
   b. the Hôtel de Ville.   d. the Bastille.

5. One result of the Irish uprising of 1798 was
   a. the annexation of Ireland to Great Britain.
   b. Nelson's victory at Aboukir Bay.
   c. that the French were able to invade England across the Irish Sea.
   d. Irish independence.

6. Robespierre tried to found a new religion called
   a. the Cult of Reason.   c. the Cult of the Supreme Being.
   b. the Republic of Virtue.   d. the Civil Constitution of the Clergy.

7. In August 1789, the National Assembly formulated a list of rights and guarantees known as
   a. *The Rights of Man.*
   b. the Brunswick manifesto.
   c. the Declaration of the Rights of Man and Citizen.
   d. the Estates General.

8. What was the first Estate?
   a. the nobility
   b. the clergy
   c. the press
   d. the nonclerical, nonnoble majority of the French people

9. After the fall of Robespierre, a new French constitution established an executive committee of five men called
   a. the Directory.   c. the Helvetic Republic.
   b. the Mountain.   d. the Committee of Public Safety.

10. The French army of the revolutionary period
    a. never recovered after the emigration of the noble officers.
    b. had difficulty recruiting soldiers.
    c. dramatically defeated Lord Nelson at Aboukir Bay.
    d. surpassed the achievements of even Louis XIV's armies.

Essay Questions

Using material from this and earlier chapters, write an essay on each of the following topics. When appropriate, include dates and detailed examples to support your arguments.

1. Why did so many European states declare war on revolutionary France?

2. How did the character and personality of Louis XVI affect the events of the Revolution? Could the outcome have been different?

3. How did the constitutional monarchy disintegrate into dictatorship? Was the Terror inevitable? Was it necessary?

4. What role did the nobility play in setting the stage for the French Revolution?

5. One common theory in the decades after 1789 was that the Revolution had been brought on by the pernicious ideas of the *philosophes*. Do you agree?

Skill Building: Maps

Locate the following on the map of western Europe. Why was each location significant in the present chapter?

a. Batavian Republic

b. Lyon

c. Helvetic Republic

d. Brittany

e. Vendée

f. Piedmont

g. Paris

h. Toulouse

i. Former Austrian Netherlands

j. Gironde

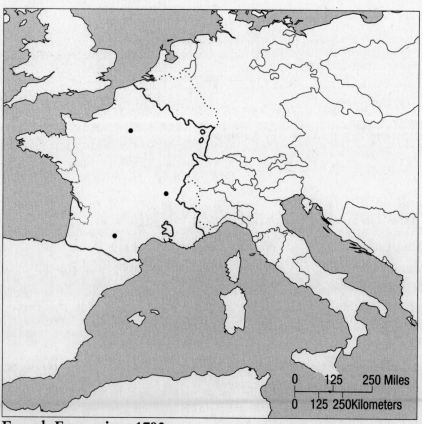

French Expansion, 1790s

k. Corsica

l. French Republic

m. Tuscany

1. What do the regions of France that actively opposed the Revolution have in common?
2. On the map, shade the areas occupied by France; with a different color, shade the areas annexed by France.
3. How were the military goals of the revolutionary armies different from those of the armies of Louis XIV? Why were they successful?

Enrichment Exercise

The most famous English novel of the Revolution, Charles Dickens's *A Tale of Two Cities,* reveals less about the actual historical events than it does about the political attitudes of Dickens and of Victorian Britain. One of the fascinating aspects of the French Revolution is that the issues it raised are forever fresh, and everyone who retells the story usually does so with certain assumptions and biases. See one of the following films and write an essay about the experience, answering the questions that follow the descriptions.

- The film *Danton* (1982) by Polish director Andrzej Wajda, explores the personal relationship between Danton and Robespierre, showing that their dispute was based as much on incompatible personalities as on political opinions. Some critics also see the film as a commentary on European politics in the last decade of the Cold War. If so, what might that message be? Are the principles of the French Revolution relevant today?

- The film *La nuit de Varennes* (1983) depicts an imaginary journey to Varennes in 1791. In the coach are several historical figures (Casanova, Thomas Paine, Rétif de la Bretonne) who debate the issues of the day, unaware that they are sharing the road with the escaping royal couple. How does this French film depict France's revolutionary tradition?

- The film commonly known as *Marat/Sade* (1966; the actual title is much longer) is based on a powerful play by Peter Weiss. In this flight of fancy, the officials of an insane asylum in Napoleonic France are entertaining important visitors with a play written for the occasion and directed by the notorious Marquis de Sade, himself one of the inmates. The play-within-a-play recounts the murder of Marat by Charlotte Corday, an event that causes the inmate-performers to relive all the disturbing emotions of the revolutionary period. Some critics believe that Weiss's play was a telling commentary on the situation in the 1960s. If so, what might that message be? Are there aspects of the French Revolution that might serve as a warning to today's political leaders?

Document Analysis

DOCUMENT 1

Contrasting Views of the Rights of "Man"

The French National Assembly adopted the Declaration of the Rights of Man and Citizen *on August 26, 1789. The Declaration served as the preamble to the Constitution of 1791 and remains influential to this day as an idealistic statement of human rights. A parallel* Declaration of the Rights of Woman and Citizen *was composed in 1791 by the early feminist Olympe de*

Gouges, who complained that rights could not be truly human unless they extended to women as well.

Declaration of the Rights of Man and Citizen

The representatives of the French people, constituted as a National Assembly, considering that ignorance, disregard or contempt of the rights of man are the sole causes of public misfortunes and governmental corruption, have resolved to set forth a solemn declaration of the natural, inalienable and sacred rights of man. . . .

1. Men are born and remain free and equal in rights. Social distinctions may be based on common utility [rather than on birth].

2. The aim of all political association is to preserve the natural and imprescriptible rights of man. These rights are liberty, property, security and resistance to oppression.

3. The principle of all sovereignty rests essentially in the nation. No body and no individual may exercise authority which does not emanate from the nation expressly [thus even the king was now subservient to the nation].

10. No one may be disturbed for his opinions, even in religion, provided that their manifestation does not trouble public order as established by law.

11. Free communication of thought and opinion is one of the most precious of the rights of man. Every citizen may therefore speak, write and print freely, on his own responsibility for abuse of this liberty in cases determined by law.

Declaration of the Rights of Woman and Citizen

The mothers, daughters, and sisters, representatives of the nation, demand to be constituted a national assembly. Considering that ignorance, disregard of or contempt for the rights of women are the only causes of public misfortune and of governmental corruption, they have resolved to set forth in a solemn declaration, the natural, inalienable and sacred rights of woman. . . .

1. Woman is born free and remains equal in rights to man. . . .

3. The principle of all sovereignty resides essentially in the Nation, which is none other than the union of Woman and Man. . . .

4. Liberty and Justice consist of rendering to persons those things that belong to them; thus, the exercise of woman's natural rights is limited only by the perpetual tyranny with which man opposes her; these limits must be changed according to the laws of nature and reason.

10. No one should be punished for their opinions. Woman has the right to mount the scaffold; she should likewise have the right to speak in public, provided that her demonstrations do not disrupt public order as established by law.

Source: Susan Groag Bell and Karen M. Offen, *Women, the Family, and Freedom: The Debate in Documents*, Vol. 1 (Stanford University Press, 1983), pp. 105–106.

Questions

1. Why do you suppose that the *Declaration of the Rights of Man and Citizen* made no mention of women?

2. How effective was Olympe de Gouges at parodying and using the arguments of the *Declaration of the Rights of Man and Citizen* for her own purposes?

DOCUMENT 2

The Definition of a Sans-Culotte

The participation of the common people in the French Revolution set the example for all future revolutions. Most of the sans-culottes *were artisans and shopkeepers, neither rich nor penniless but respectable and hardworking. They favored price controls, direct participation in their own assemblies, and harsh measures against aristocrats and presumed enemies. The newspaper article excerpted here gives an idealized portrait but one that captures a readiness to use violence in defense of the Revolution.*

A *sans-culotte,* you rogues? He is someone who always goes about on foot, who has not got the millions you would all like to have, who has no castles, no valets to wait on him, and who lives simply with his wife and children, if he has any, on the fourth or fifth story. He is useful because he knows how to till a field, to forge iron, to use a saw, to roof a house, to make shoes, and to spill his blood to the last drop for the safety of the Republic. . . .

In the evening he goes to the assembly of his Section, not powdered and perfumed and nattily booted, in the hope of being noticed by the citizenesses in the galleries, but ready to support sound proposals with all his might and ready to pulverize those which come from the despised faction of politicians.

Finally a *sans-culotte* always has his sabre well-sharpened, ready to cut off the ears of all opponents of the Revolution.

Source: D. G. Wright, *Revolution and Terror in France, 1789–1795* (Longman, 1974), p. 116.

Questions

1. The excerpt expresses high regard for the *sans-culottes,* for their simple honesty and public spirit. What qualities does it describe that do not bode well for the future of French democracy?

2. From your study of the chapter, evaluate the role played by the *sans-culottes* in the Revolution.

DOCUMENT 3

Robespierre Defines the Republic of Virtue

In a speech to the National Convention on behalf of the Committee of Public Safety, Robespierre outlined his vision of the goals of the French republic. His "Report on the Principles of Political Morality" was delivered on February 5, 1794, as part of an ongoing struggle within the convention over the direction of policy. It preceded the arrest and execution of two major groups of deputies: the so-called ultra-revolutionaries and the "indulgents" or followers of Danton.

What is the goal toward which we are heading? The peaceful enjoyment of liberty and equality; the reign of that eternal justice whose laws have been inscribed, not in marble or stone, but in the hearts of all men, even in that of the slave who forgets them and in that of the tyrant who denies them. . . .

We want, in a word, to fulfill nature's desires, accomplish the destiny of humanity, keep the promises of philosophy, absolve providence from the long reign of crime and tyranny. Let France, formerly illustrious among the enslaved lands, eclipsing the glory of all the free peoples who have existed, become the model for the nations, the terror of oppressors, the consolation of the oppressed, the ornament of the world—and let us, in sealing our work with our blood, see at least the early dawn of universal bliss—that is our ambition, that is our goal.

What kind of government can realize these wonders? Only a democratic or republican government—these two words are synonyms. . . .

If the mainspring of popular government in peacetime is virtue, amid revolution it is at the same time [both] virtue and *terror:* virtue, without which terror is fatal; terror, without which virtue is impotent. Terror is nothing but prompt, severe, inflexible justice; it is therefore an emanation of virtue. It is less a special principle than a consequence of the general principle of democracy applied to our country's most pressing needs.

Source: Keith Michael Baker, ed., *The Old Regime and the French Revolution* (University of Chicago Press, 1987), pp. 370, 374.

Questions

1. From your study of the chapter, would you say that "the early dawn of universal bliss" was a goal shared by many of the French people? Discuss.

2. What criteria, according to Robespierre, justify the use of terror and violence? Are his fears real or imaginary?

DOCUMENT 4

Mary Wollstonecraft, Vindication of the Rights of Woman *(1792)*

Mary Wollstonecraft was born in poverty in 1759. She worked as a lady's companion, a schoolteacher, and a governess while beginning her career as a self-supporting journalist and novelist. In London she became friends with many of the leading intellectuals and reformers of the day, including the writer Thomas Paine, the poet William Blake, and the Swiss painter Henry Fuseli. Her book on women's rights earned her instant notoriety as she questioned basic assumptions about women's role in society. One leading politician and writer called her a "hyena in petticoats." Wollstonecraft went to Paris in 1792, where she was horrified by the guillotine but retained her optimism about the prospects of the French Revolution. In 1797, this first prophet of feminism died of complications in childbirth. Her daughter, Mary, survived and became the novelist Mary Shelley, author of Frankenstein.

If then women are not a swarm of ephemeron triflers, why should they be kept in ignorance under the specious name of innocence? . . . As to the argument respecting the subjection in which the sex has ever been held, it retorts on man. The many have always been enthralled by the few; and monsters, who scarcely have shown any discernment of human excellence, have tyrannized over thousands of their fellow-creatures. . . . China is not the only country where a living man has been made a God. *Men* have submitted to superior strength to enjoy with impunity the pleasure of the moment; *women* have only done the same, and therefore till it is proved that the courtier, who servilely resigns the birthright of a man, is not a moral agent, it cannot be demonstrated that woman is essentially inferior to man because she has always been subjugated.

Source: Carol H. Poston, ed., *Vindication of the Rights of Woman* (W. W. Norton, 1975), p. 37.

Questions

1. Wollstonecraft would doubtless agree with Olympe de Gouges on most points. Which woman is probably the more effective debater? Discuss.

2. Why do you suppose that interest in women's rights was emerging at this time? What trends described in the text would encourage attention to the condition of women's lives?

CHAPTER
21

Napoleon, the Restoration, and the Revolutionary Legacy, 1799–1832

Chapter Outline

CHALLENGES TO THE CONSERVATIVE ORDER
  Industrial Growth in Britain
  New Social and Political Doctrines
  New Nationalist Aspirations
  Liberal and Nationalist Movements on the Periphery
  Revolution and Reform in Western Europe
  Romanticism

Chapter Summary

The First Consul dominated the new French government, wielding executive power and manipulating the legislative branch. The young Bonaparte was able to push through his own programs. Moderate and popular, they earned him widespread support from the army, the middle classes, the peasants, and the church, virtually all groups except die-hard monarchists and Jacobins. Napoleon won victories and brought peace with the Holy Roman Emperor (1801) and even with Britain (1802). In 1804 he took advantage of this popularity to crown himself Emperor of the French, thus ending the Republic and inaugurating the Empire. Napoleon continued the legal reforms begun under the Consulate, and the Napoleonic Code stands as his greatest achievement, a massive revision of French law that finally eliminated the feudal laws and privileges that had accumulated for centuries, systemized many of the reforms of the revolution, and generally modernized and centralized the state. On the other hand, the new code eliminated a number of rights that women had won under the Old Regime, making men legally responsible for the behavior of their wives and daughters and granting authority accordingly. Napoleon, like the revolutionary regimes that preceded him, advocated centralized education; at the same time, like the Bourbon monarchs, he patronized the arts and sciences.

The military domination of Europe, which had begun during the revolution, continued and even increased under Napoleon's shrewd leadership. Napoleon fought off coalition after coalition, often organized by the Austrians, who were unable to accept their loss of dominion over the Italian and German states. Although Napoleon won some striking victories, he was never able to deal successfully with the British navy; by 1806 he decided to defeat the British economically by shutting off their trade with the continent. To achieve this goal, Napoleon cynically overthrew uncooperative monarchs and replaced them with his brothers and sisters. He also heavily taxed France's allies to build his Grand Army. High-handed tactics such as these bred anti-French sentiments and open rebellion. Meanwhile, his enemies were imitating his military organization and strategy, and European armies became ever larger, the victories more difficult and costly. In 1812, Tsar Alexander I rebelled against the French blockade. To punish him, Napoleon sent over a half million troops into Russia; the campaign was a disaster, and the loss of the Grand Army made his downfall inevitable. In 1813, a growing coalition defeated the French and drove them from Germany; in 1814, with France itself being invaded, Napoleon abdicated. But even from exile on the Mediterranean island of Elba, Napoleon proved formidable. In 1815, dissatisfied with his situation and the treatment of his supporters, he invaded France with a handful of men and managed to regain control of the government. He was only narrowly defeated at Waterloo.

Shortly after Napoleon's abdication in 1814, the nations of Europe met in one of the most famous diplomatic gatherings of all time, the Congress of Vienna. The assembled nations, presided over by the Austrian Chancellor Metternich, restored the old monarchies and established a balance of power that discouraged the outbreak of major wars. It failed, nevertheless, to address the liberal and nationalist aspirations of many Europeans. Within a few years, German students staged demonstrations, and in 1819 one of them murdered a Russian agent. In spite of the repressive Karlsbad Decrees, revolutions erupted in 1820 in Spain, Portugal, and Naples. In

1821 Greek patriots, secretly backed by Russia, began a war of independence against the Ottoman Empire. After the death of the wavering Tsar Alexander in 1825 (the occasion for the ill-fated Decembrist Revolt), the new tsar, Nicholas I, was more aggressive in asserting his autocratic rule and in pursuing Russian interests in the Balkans. In 1827, public opinion and fear of Russian expansion prompted Britain and France to intervene on behalf of the Greeks. By 1829, Greece was declared an independent state, and Russian influence in the Balkans was clearly established. The success of the Greek nationalists may have inspired other revolutionary groups throughout Europe to test the conservative establishment. In 1830, the French overthrew the reactionary Charles X; the Belgians, who had been placed under the control of the Protestant Dutch at the Congress of Vienna, asserted their independence successfully, but the Polish attempt to do the same was thwarted by Russia. In Britain, the aspirations of the growing working class led to the Reform Bill of 1832, which increased the number of voters but still fell far short of democracy.

The early nineteenth century saw the rise of new philosophies or ideologies that profoundly affected political, intellectual, and artistic life. Conservatism was a reaction against revolutionary agitation for political and social change. Socialism attempted to define and prescribe solutions for the social problems resulting from industrialization. Romanticism, with origins in the previous century, became the most important influence on literature, music, and painting and other visual arts in the nineteenth century.

Vocabulary

concordat	A treaty between a secular state and the papacy.
bourgeoisie	The middle class. Prior to the nineteenth century, the word usually meant the urban merchant class, but socialist writers borrowed the word to indicate the new industrial class.
proletariat	The industrial working class; early socialists revived the old Latin word for unpropertied laborer, *proletarius,* to give this new class a name.
sinecure	An office or position that generates income but requires little or no labor; originally, a church office that did not involve direct care of the faithful—thus *sine cura* (Latin for "without care").
lycée	French secondary school, administered by the state. The word derives from the Greek Lyceum, discussed in Chapter 4.
cacophony	Loud, irritating, confusing noise, as in many people shouting at once.
nationalism	In the context of this chapter, loyalty to one's nation—that is, one's extended ethnic and linguistic family, such as Germans, Italians, or French. Nationalism might be a force for national pride, as in France; it might inspire national unification movements, as in Italy or Germany; or it might incite rebellion against foreign rule, as in Greece.
liberalism	In the context of this chapter, admiration for the ideals of the French Revolution—freedom of speech and the press, economic liberty, and representative government. The nineteenth-century liberal was typically *bourgeois,* moderate, and opposed to radical working-class movements, which appeared to present a threat to private property. The text will provide a more detailed discussion in Chapter 22.
conservatism	In the context of this chapter, a political philosophy that opposed abrupt, hasty, or drastic political or social change. Thus the conservatives of the age distrusted the revolutionary ideals of liberty, equality, and democracy, and sought order in traditional monarchy and religion.

romanticism	An intellectual, literary, and artistic movement emphasizing the role of emotion, sentiment, and passion in life and art. The romantics admired individualism, action, the exotic, and the supernatural; they distrusted science and rationalism.
coup d'état	A revolutionary act, an overthrow of the government, often by another branch of the government; for example, the military might overthrow a constitutional regime and impose a *junta*.
abolitionists	People who wish to abolish something; for the nineteenth century, the word almost always refers to opponents of slavery.
séance	In French, a meeting, assembly, or official session, with the implication that those in attendance are seated; in English, the word implies a group attempting to communicate with the spirit world.
Magyars	The people who live in Hungary; also their language.
émigrés	French nobles who went into exile during the Revolution; any political refugees living abroad.
carbonari	Members of secret societies that formed in southern Italy to oppose French rule and later became revolutionary patriotic societies throughout the Italian peninsula.

Self-Testing and Review Questions

Identification

After reading Chapter 21, identify and explain the historical significance of each of the following:

1. Ypsilanti

2. *compagnonnages*

3. Napoleonic Code

4. Talleyrand

5. Burschenschaften

6. Peterloo

7. Reform Bill of 1832

8. utilitarianism

9. Charles Fourier

10. Pius VII

11. Karlsbad Decrees

12. Simon Bolívar

13. Ludwig van Beethoven

14. Toussaint L'Ouverture

15. the Third Section

16. Confederation of the Rhine

17. Holy Alliance

18. metric system

19. Arc de Triomphe

20. Sir Walter Scott

21. Joseph Fouché

22. G. W. F. Hegel

23. Legion of Honor

24. Claude Berthollet

25. Ultras

Chronology

Identify the events or issues associated with the following dates. Some of these dates may be significant for more than one reason. After you finish, answer the questions that follow.

1799

1802

1804

1809

1812

1814

1815

1819

1820

1825

1830

1832

1. Napoleon was born in 1768. How old was he when he became First Consul? Emperor? when he divorced and remarried? when his son was born? when he went into exile? How might his age and private life have affected his public actions?
2. Why did revolutionary activity seem to occur in clusters, as in the revolutions of 1820, 1821, and 1830?

Matching Exercises

In each set, match the terms on the left with those on the right.

Set A

____ 1. Germaine de Staël a. *The Genius of Christianity*

____ 2. Friedrich Schiller b. *Corinne*

____ 3. Mary Shelley c. *Faust*

____ 4. Wolfgang van Goethe d. *The Betrothed*

____ 5. François-René de Châteaubriand e. *William Tell*

____ 6. Alessandro Manzoni f. *Frankenstein*

Set B

____ 1. Amiens a. in 1801, an important victory by Napoleon over Austria

____ 2. Tilsit b. in 1802, peace between France and Great Britain

____ 3. Adrianople c. in 1806, defeat of the legendary Prussian army by Napoleon

____ 4. Jena d. in 1807, peace between France and Russia

____ 5. Marengo e. in 1812, burning of this city

____ 6. Moscow f. in 1829, Greek independence

Set C

____ 1. Joseph Bonaparte a. ruled Italy in the name of Napoleon

____ 2. Louis Bonaparte b. ruled Sweden

____ 3. Jerome Bonaparte c. ruled Naples, then Spain

____ 4. Eugène de Beauharnais d. followed c. as ruler of Naples

____ 5. Murat e. ruled Holland

____ 6. Bernadotte f. ruled Westphalia

Set D

____ 1. Trafalgar
____ 2. Austerlitz
____ 3. Leipzig
____ 4. Borodino
____ 5. Navarino Bay
____ 6. Waterloo

a. defeat of a Turkish fleet by Britain and France, 1827
b. a difficult battle on the road to Moscow, 1812
c. Nelson's greatest victory, 1805
d. Wellington's greatest victory, 1815
e. Napoleon's greatest victory, 1805
f. the Battle of Nations, 1813

Set E

____ 1. Francis I
____ 2. Alexander I
____ 3. Charles IV
____ 4. George IV
____ 5. Frederick William III
____ 6. Nicholas I

a. tsar of Russia at the time of Napoleon
b. ruler of Russia after the Decembrist revolt
c. ruler of Spain, forced by Napoleon to abdicate
d. regent, then king of Great Britain
e. the last Holy Roman Emperor
f. king of Prussia

Multiple-Choice Questions

1. At the Congress of Vienna,
   a. the French were not welcome and their interests were unrepresented.
   b. national self-interest was discouraged, and idealism prevailed.
   c. Metternich emerged as Europe's leading statesman.
   d. all the nations agreed to join the tsar's Holy Alliance.

2. After the fall of Napoleon, the new king of France was
   a. Charles X.
   b. Louis-Philippe.
   c. Louis XVII.
   d. Louis XVIII.

3. Machinery and its impact on employment were particular concerns of the
   a. *carbonari.*
   b. Luddites.
   c. millenarians.
   d. Decembrists.

4. Napoleon died at
   a. Corsica.
   b. Elba.
   c. Waterloo.
   d. St. Helena.

5. The Continental System was
   a. the new political arrangement of Europe arranged at the Congress of Vienna.
   b. Napoleon's plan to destroy Britain by shutting off its trade with Europe.
   c. the first international railroad consortium.
   d. an alliance of socialist groups.

6. Napoleon's second wife, the mother of his son, was
   a. Josephine de Beauharnais.
   b. Julie von Krüdener.
   c. Marie-Louise.
   d. Caroline Bonaparte.

7. Romanticism was
   a. strictly a literary movement, with little influence on art or music.
   b. a logical extension of the Enlightenment, sharing the same ideals.
   c. typified by Byron, Beethoven, and Delacroix.
   d. a movement unusually unanimous on religious and political matters.

8. The Hundred Days was
   a. the disastrous campaign of the Grand Army in Russia in 1812.
   b. the eventful first phase of the Greek struggle for independence.
   c. the period beginning with Napoleon's return from Elba and ending with Waterloo.
   d. the time of sweeping reform that followed the establishment of the Consulate.

9. The British socialist who transformed his textile factory in New Lanark, Scotland, into a paternalistic community was
   a. Edmund Burke.   c. Robert Peel.
   b. Arthur Wellesley.   d. Robert Owen.

10. Alphonse de Lamartine and Alexander Pushkin were
   a. socialists.   c. diplomats.
   b. poets.   d. scientists.

Essay Questions

Using material from this and previous chapters, write an essay on each of the following topics. When appropriate, include dates and cite detailed examples to support your arguments.

1. The textbook speaks of Napoleon's "dreams of conquest," yet Napoleon claimed later that he always wanted peace and was driven to war only by the relentless, self-serving opposition of the British. Why does the history of Napoleonic Europe lend itself to differing interpretations?

2. Much literature about the life of Napoleon is "romantic"—the lone hero, the self-made man, the man of destiny, the triumph of the will. What aspects of his career instead reflect rationalism and the Age of Enlightenment?

3. How did the concepts "liberal" and "conservative" emerge from the rival ideologies of the revolutionary era? Do they mean the same today as they did then?

4. It has been argued that by 1830 nationalism was replacing liberalism and democracy as the principal cause of revolutionary disturbances in Europe. Referring to the text, construct a chronology of the disturbances from 1817 to 1832, and then test the argument.

5. In the new industrial world, the early socialists tried to establish social systems that were both rational and just. How did each of the leading socialists attempt to achieve these goals? To what extent do their goals reflect the Enlightenment? To what extent were they romantic?

Skill Building: Maps

A. Locate the following on the map of Europe. Why was each significant in the present chapter?
   a. Kingdom of Westphalia

   b. (Napoleonic) Kingdom of Italy

   c. Bavaria

   d. Paris

   e. Madrid

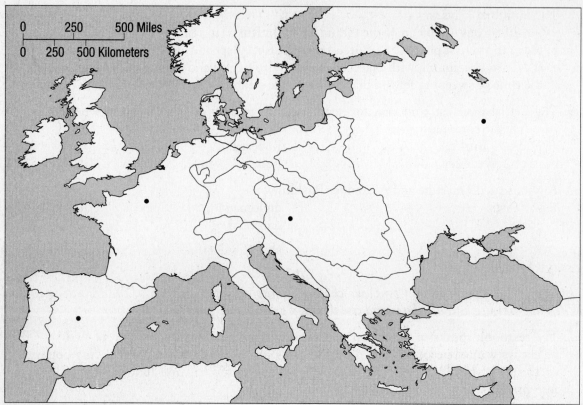

Europe in the Early Nineteenth Century

f. Elba

g. Danubian Principalities

h. Grand Duchy of Warsaw

i. Kingdom of Naples

j. Corsica

k. Moscow

l. Vienna

m. Greece

n. Kingdom of Portugal

1. How drastically was the map of Europe redrawn at the Congress of Vienna?

2. For what reasons might Russia have supported Greek independence and other such movements in the Balkans?

B. *Locate the following on the map of Latin America. Why was each significant in the present chapter?*

  a. Mexico

  b. Brazil

  c. Haiti

  d. Paraguay

  e. Venezuela

  f. United Provinces of Central America

  g. Colombia

1. Latin America had been dominated by Spain and Portugal for centuries. Then, in only one generation, most of the colonies declared their political independence. What factors contributed to this enormous change? Discuss.

Latin American Independence, 1804–1830

Enrichment Exercise

In 1831 Victor Hugo wrote his great novel *Notre-Dame de Paris,* which in English is usually called *The Hunchback of Notre-Dame.* The novel has been translated into film at least four times, the best of which is the atmospheric 1939 version with Charles Laughton and Maureen O'Hara. Also noteworthy is the 1982 version, made for television, with an all-star cast led by Anthony Hopkins and John Gielgud; in the 1957 film, famous actors fail to overcome the artificial-looking sets. Read the book or watch one of the films and write an essay commenting on the ways the plot and characters reflect the ideas and issues of the nineteenth century, such as the plight of the lower classes, the privileges of the church, the role of the poet, and nostalgia for the Middle Ages. Note that in some of the films the plot, especially the ending, is altered.

Document Analysis

DOCUMENT 1

Napoleon's Civil Code and Women

Napoleon's Civil Code made the concept of separate spheres for husbands and wives a legal reality. Men were to have all powers in the public world; women were to confine themselves to the privacy of the home. The following provisions illustrate wives' subordination to their husbands and their disadvantages in suing for divorce.

Of the Rights and Respective Duties of Husband and Wife

212. Husband and wife mutually owe to each other fidelity, succor, and assistance.
213. The husband owes protection to his wife, the wife obedience to her husband.
214. The wife is obliged to live with her husband, and to follow him wherever he may think proper to dwell; the husband is bound to receive her, and to furnish her with everything necessary for the purposes of life, according to his means and condition.
215. The wife can do no act in law without the authority of her husband. . . .

Of Causes of Divorce

229. The husband may demand divorce for cause of adultery on the part of his wife.
230. The wife may demand divorce for cause of adultery on the part of her husband, where he shall have kept his concubine in their common house.

Of the Effects of Divorce

298. In the case of divorce allowed at law for cause of adultery, the guilty party can never marry his or her accomplice. The adulterous wife shall be condemned by the same judgment, and upon the requisition of the public ministry, to confinement in a house of correction for a certain period, which shall not be less than three months, nor exceed two years.

Source: Geoffrey Bruun, *Napoleon and His Empire* (Van Nostrand, 1972), pp. 123–124.

Questions

1. The Napoleonic Code reflected the *bourgeois* values that became dominant in France as a result of the revolution. How might the laws excerpted here have been a reaction against the perceived decadence of the Old Regime nobility?

2. Rousseau's ideas about women and their place in society were described in earlier chapters. Are these reflected in the Napoleonic Code?

DOCUMENT 2

A Letter from the Yorkshire Luddites

The introduction of shearing machines into Yorkshire in 1810–1811 caused unemployment and widespread resentment among the artisans who were displaced by the machines. In 1812 gangs of Luddites wrecked many machines in a series of raids. The following letter was sent to a manufacturer in 1812. It is impossible to tell if it was genuine, but it gives a sense of the atmosphere in Britain at this critical time.

> Sir,
> Information has just been given in, that you are a holder of those detestable Shearing Frames, and I was desired by my men to write to you, and give you fair warning to pull them down, and for that purpose I desire that you will understand I am now writing to you, you will take notice that if they are not taken down by the end of next week, I shall detach one of my lieutenants with at least 300 men to destroy them, and furthermore take notice that if you give us the trouble of coming thus far, we will increase your misfortunes by burning your buildings down to ashes. . . . We hope for assistance from the French Emperor in shaking off the Yoke of the Rottenest, wickedest and most Tyrannical Government that ever existed. . . . We will never lay down our arms till the House of Commons passes an act to put down all the machinery hurtfull [sic] to the Commonality and repeal that to the Frame Breakers. . . .
> Signed by the General of the Army of Redressers,
>
> Ned Ludd, Clerk

Source: G. D. H. Cole and A. W. Filson, *British Working Class Movements: Selected Documents, 1789–1875* (Macmillan, 1951), pp. 113–115.

Questions

1. Industrialization had resulted in widespread economic dislocation in Britain in the late eighteenth century. How had the French contributed to the suffering of English artisans in the years immediately preceding this letter? Were the French or the English more to blame?
2. Why is it reasonable to distrust the authenticity of this letter?

DOCUMENT 3

Proclamation of the Decembrists in Russia, 1825

Prince Sergei Petrovich Trubetskoi was slated to be named dictator during the Decembrist revolt of 1825 in Russia. In fact, he lost his nerve and kept out of sight. He had written a proclamation setting forth the principles of the revolt as supported by the secret societies, which were largely composed of nobles and elite officers. The proclamation makes clear the liberal aims of the revolt, with the following provisions:

1. The abolition of the previous government.
2. The establishment of a temporary [government] until the formation of a permanent [one] by elected deputies.

3. Freedom of the press, and hence the abolition of censorship.
4. Freedom of worship to all faiths.
5. Abolition of property rights over persons [that is, the abolition of serfdom].
6. Equality before the law of all estates and, therefore, abolition of Military Tribunals and all types of Judicial Commissions.

Source: Marc Raeff, *The Decembrist Movement* (Prentice-Hall, 1966), p. 101.

Question

1. Are the ideals of the Decembrists based on Russian traditions? If not, what might have inspired them?

DOCUMENT 4

Romanticism

Marie Henri Beyle, known by his pen name Stendhal, wrote art criticism as well as famous novels such as The Red and the Black *(1830). In his review of the Salon, or Exhibition, of 1824, he described the impact of romanticism in painting and contrasted it explicitly with classicism.*

We are at the dawn of a revolution in the fine arts. The huge pictures composed of thirty nude figures inspired by antique statues and the heavy tragedies in verse in five acts are, without a doubt, very respectable works; but in spite of all that may be said in their favor, they have begun to be a little boring. If the painting of *The Battle of the Romans and the Sabines* [by the neoclassical painter Jacques-Louis David] were to appear today, we would find that its figures were without passion and that in any country it is absurd to march off to battle with no clothes on. . . . The romantic in all the arts is that which shows the men of today and not those who probably never existed in those heroic times so distant from us. . . . That which may console *romanticism* for the attacks of the [newspaper] *Journal des débats* is that good sense applied to the arts has made immense progress in the last four years and particularly among the leaders of society.

Source: Elizabeth Gilmore Holt, ed., *The Triumph of Art for the Public, 1785–1848: The Emerging Role of Exhibitions and Critics* (Princeton University Press, 1983), pp. 261, 279.

Questions

1. Are Stendhal's assertions that romanticism realistically depicts "the men of today" consistent with the evidence and examples in the text? Why is it not surprising that the romantics contradicted each other in describing their movement?
2. Stendhal took his pen name from a village in Prussia. Why would a French author choose a German pen name? What has changed?

CHAPTER

22

Industrialization, Urbanization, and Revolution, 1832–1851

Chapter Outline

123

Chapter Summary

The revolutions of 1848 were preceded by two decades of industrial expansion and urban growth. The adaptation of steam engines to a variety of machines revolutionized production, from mining to mills and foundries. Literally thousands of miles of railroads created a revolution in transportation. Great Britain led the way in industrialization, but continental states were eager to imitate the British example. Urban populations increased dramatically as rural workers tried to escape from taxes, fluctuating prices, and competition from large landowners. This migration had a dramatic impact on the cities, but the majority of the European population continued to be rural. And in spite of the impact of the factory system, the majority of manufacture was still accomplished by the "putting out" system.

Rapid urban growth was accompanied by social problems of catastrophic proportions. Unpredictable economic cycles resulted in chronic unemployment and food shortages. The teeming cities, with their inadequate water supplies and sanitation, were ideal breeding grounds for disease. Overcrowded streets and shoddy tenements spawned crime, vice, and political unrest. The propertied classes were horrified by the plight of the poor; their attention was increasingly drawn to it by novelists, poets, artists, and reformers. The latter, often women, used charitable organizations, asylums, hospitals, and schools to address the problems of poverty, disease, and prostitution. Governments occasionally produced legislation that provided poor relief or restricted child labor, but they were generally reluctant to interfere. Liberals (in the nineteenth-century sense of the word) equated economic liberty with freedom from government regulation, and believed both were best guaranteed by constitutions, bills of rights, and limited franchises. Others were convinced that solutions to industrial ills could only be provided by socialism's restructuring of society. There were many varieties of socialism, ranging from the utopian to the revolutionary. Some varieties questioned the institution of private property, whereas others demanded that the government assume a more active role in providing for the general welfare.

The French revolution of 1848 was the culmination of many of these factors. Parisian workers—hungry, unemployed, and frustrated by the government's unwillingness to address their problems—brought down the monarchy of Louis Philippe. The new provisional government enacted some important reforms, including universal manhood suffrage, but its support for socialist reforms, such as the national workshops, was only half-hearted. The National Assembly, elected by universal manhood suffrage, instead reflected the rural and conservative French majority. The disappointed Parisian workers returned to their barricades, but this time they were crushed by the military. Property rights were thus protected under the new republic, in spite of the broadened suffrage.

Another popular ideology of the period was nationalism. Italian and German nationalists dreamed of unified states, whereas ethnic minorities in multinational states such as the Austrian Empire, dreamed of independence and self-government. Some multinational states, such as Russia, promoted an official version of nationalism to impose religious and linguistic conformity. In 1848 the Austrian Empire, the defender of the status quo in central Europe, suddenly reeled from a succession of revolts. Italian and German nationalists saw this as a rare opportunity, and the rebellions spread. In the end they all failed—some because the alarmed propertied classes, often rural, turned against the rural rebels; some because the ethnic groups turned against each other; and some because of foreign intervention.

Vocabulary

cottage industry Production by workers who process goods in their own homes to supplement their incomes. Typically the workers are agricultural laborers, the raw materials are supplied by a merchant entrepreneur, and the entire family is involved in the processing.

leprosaria Homes or hospitals for lepers.

secularists People with no religious affiliation; nonbelievers.

suffrage The right to vote; "universal manhood suffrage" means that all adult males can vote.

tariffs Taxes, especially on imported goods. High tariffs protected domestic industries from competition, but they raised prices and reduced choices for consumers.

sedition Disloyalty to the state; treasonous ideas.

communists Originally, socialists who believed in the common ownership of property.

Self-Testing and Review Questions

Identification

After reading Chapter 22, identify and explain the historical significance of each of the following:

1. Young Italy

2. June Days

3. *Communist Manifesto*

4. Treaty of Nanking

5. Adam Mickiewicz

6. Flora Tristan

7. Slavophiles

8. Corn Laws

9. Chartists

10. Stephen Széchenyi

11. *Risorgimento*

12. Frédéric Chopin

13. Frankfurt parliament

14. Louis Blanc

15. Charles Lyell

16. George Sand

17. Daniel O'Connell

18. Alexandre Dumas

19. Giuseppe Verdi

20. Alexander Herzen

Chronology

Identify the events or issues associated with the following dates. Some of these dates may be significant for more than one reason. After you finish, answer the questions that follow.

1839

1840

1847

February 1848

March 1848

April 1848

June 1848

March 1849

April 1849

July 1849

August 1849

1851

1. The turning point of the revolutions of 1848 was June 1848. What events of that month made it significant?

2. How was *The Communist Manifesto* chronologically related to the events of 1848?

Matching Exercises

In each set, match the terms on the left with those on the right.

Set A

_____ 1. *Travels in Icaria*   a. Friedrich Engels

_____ 2. *Organization of Labor*   b. Wilhelm Weitling

_____ 3. *The Conditions of the Working Class in England*   c. Louis Blanc

_____ 4. *Guarantees of Harmony and Freedom*   d. Pierre-Joseph Proudhon

_____ 5. *What Is Property?*   e. Étienne Cabet

Set B

_____ 1. Louis Philippe   a. king of Bavaria

_____ 2. Francis Joseph   b. king of Sardinia and Piedmont

_____ 3. Charles Albert   c. leader who rejected the "crown from the gutter"

_____ 4. Frederick William IV   d. ruler who abdicated the French throne in 1848

_____ 5. Ludwig I   e. aristocrat who succeeded to the Austrian throne in 1848

Set C

_____ 1. Alexandre Dumas   a. *Jane Eyre*

_____ 2. George Sand   b. *The Mysteries of Paris*

_____ 3. Eugène Sue   c. *Human Comedy*

_____ 4. Charlotte Brontë   d. *The Count of Monte Cristo*

_____ 5. Charles Dickens   e. *Oliver Twist*

_____ 6. Honoré de Balzac   f. *Indiana*

Set D

_____ 1. David Friedrich Strauss   a. "historian of the people"

_____ 2. Jules Michelet   b. British nationalist historian

_____ 3. Friedrich C. Schlosser   c. controversial historian of early Christianity

_____ 4. Thomas Macauley   d. German nationalist historian

_____ 5. Adolphe Thiers   e. prime minister and historian

Set E

_____ 1. Alphonse de Lamartine   a. sent an army to defeat Lajos Kossuth

_____ 2. Giuseppe Mazzini   b. helped overthrow Louis Philippe

_____ 3. Joseph Radetzky   c. helped overthrow Pius IX

_____ 4. Alfred von Windischgrätz   d. defeated Charles Albert

_____ 5. Alexander Herzen   e. opposed Nicholas I

Multiple-Choice Questions

1. The *Zollverein* promoted
   a. a merging of German socialist movements.
   b. the abolition of slavery and child labor.
   c. a customs union in the German states.
   d. German unification under the Habsburgs.

2. A role model for the conventional, domestic woman was
   a. George Sand.
   b. Flora Tristan.
   c. Emma Martin.
   d. Queen Victoria.

3. Some militant women in the new French Republic of 1848 were called
   a. Chartists.
   b. Vésuviennes.
   c. daguerrotypes.
   d. Icarists.

4. The Crystal Palace was
   a. the site of an industrial exhibit in Victorian London.
   b. the utopia that Étienne Cabet promised workers.
   c. the home of the ruler of a united Germany, planned by the Frankfurt parliament.
   d. a soccer stadium.

5. The Taiping Rebellion was partly the result of British aggression in
   a. Singapore.
   b. India.
   c. China.
   d. New Zealand.

6. One issue of particular political significance in Ireland was
   a. the temperance movement.
   b. the abolition of slavery.
   c. the repeal of the Corn Laws.
   d. the repeal of the Act of Union.

7. Which of these is *not* true of the industrial era?
   a. European populations declined along with agriculture as peasants left the land and moved into the cities.
   b. The growth of railroads and other transportation systems was encouraged and subsidized by Western governments.
   c. Squalid, overcrowded housing, deplorable sanitary conditions, and industrial pollution all contributed to the spread of disease.
   d. Reform movements sprang up to promote education and temperance and to deplore blood sports, child labor, and prostitution.

8. During the revolutions of 1848,
   a. the various national minorities of the Austrian Empire banded together to make their collective demands of the central government.
   b. German socialists joined nationalists in the Frankfurt parliament.
   c. early successes in Paris and Vienna alarmed the middle classes.
   d. Charles Albert gained papal support for his cause.

9. Honoré Daumier and J. W. M. Turner were
   a. socialists.
   b. novelists.
   c. scientists.
   d. painters.

10. The president of the second French Republic was
    a. Alphonse de Lamartine.
    b. Louis-Napoleon Bonaparte.
    c. Pierre-Joseph Proudhon.
    d. Louis Blanc.

Essay Questions

Using material from this and previous chapters, write an essay on each of the following topics. When appropriate, include dates and cite detailed examples to support your arguments.

1. Nationalists in Italy and Germany dreamed of political unification, but nationalists elsewhere promoted the disintegration of certain states. To which states was nationalism the greatest threat? How did these states deal with the events of 1848?

2. Early socialists believed that they were acting on behalf of the people and expected a groundswell of popular support for their programs. Using the French experience of 1848 as an example, explain why this anticipated popular support never materialized.

3. Both Marx and Metternich chose London as their place of refuge. What characteristics of British society encouraged their choice?

4. Many targets of mid-century reform movements—alcohol, blood sports, slavery, vice—had existed for centuries. Why did these reform movements flourish at this particular time?

5. How did the memory of the "great" French Revolution (in 1789) affect the events of 1848? In what ways were revolutionaries trying to repeat those earlier successes? How were counter-revolutionaries trying to prevent any such success?

Skill Building: Maps

Locate the following regions on the map of Europe. Why was each significant in this chapter?

a. Ireland

b. Berlin

c. Vienna

d. Piedmont and Sardinia

e. Venetia

f. Hungary

g. Galicia

h. Birmingham

i. Prague

j. Frankfurt

k. Lyons

l. Palermo

m. Lombardy

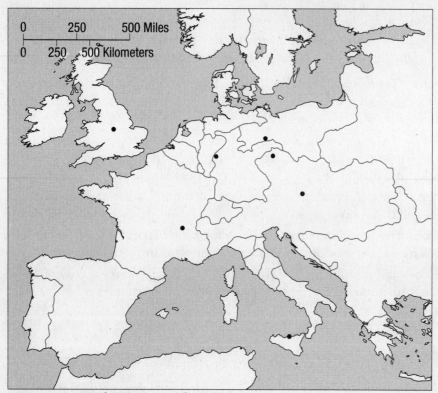

Europe in Mid-Nineteenth Century

1. Lightly shade in the areas where German was spoken. Use contrasting colors to show the distribution of the following languages: Italian, Hungarian, Czech, Polish. What problems would need to be resolved for each of these "nations" to become a political state?

2. Why did Charles Albert need Lombardy to unify Italy? Why did this first step present such formidable problems? Why did the year 1848 seem the perfect time to solve them?

3. You have read that the rebels of the June Days in Paris were "deported." Where would the French deport French citizens? What location did Britain use for its "Siberia"?

Enrichment Exercise

In 1851, Henry Mayhew published the first three volumes of his monumental study, *London Labour and the London Poor,* the most detailed description of an early industrial city and its people in any language. Most libraries contain a copy of Mayhew's work in one of its many modern editions, most of them abridgments. Select one of these, read about a hundred pages, and write a brief essay about life in the nineteenth century. What useful purpose was served by Mayhew's documentation of this squalor? What were his motives?

Document Analysis

DOCUMENT 1

Domestic Ideology and Household Management

Sarah Stickney Ellis, who published under the name Mrs. Ellis, was the most widely read commentator in England on women's domestic role. Here she argues that women must give as much care to household management as their husbands do to business. Women's domestic life is in that sense equivalent to business for men. Note how she uses metaphors that compare domestic life to a kind of castle that must be strongly fortified against the outside world.

The man who voluntarily undertakes a difficult and responsible business, first inquires *how* it is to be conducted so as best to ensure success: so the serious and thoughtful woman, on entering upon the duties of domestic life, ascertains by reflection and observation, in what manner they may be performed so as to render them most conducive to the great end she has in view, the promotion of the happiness of others. . . .

In other countries, where the domestic lamp is voluntarily put out, in order to allow the women to resort to the opera, or the public festival, they are not only careless about their home comforts, but necessarily ignorant of the high degree of excellence to which they might be raised. In England there is a kind of science of good household management. . . . Not only must elegance be called in, to adorn and beautify the whole, but strict integrity must be maintained by the minutest calculation as to lawful means, and self-gratification must be made the yielding point in every disputed case. Not only must an appearance of outward order and comfort be kept up, but around every domestic scene there must be a strong wall of confidence, which no internal suspicion can undermine, no external enemy break through.

Source: *The Select Works of Mrs. Ellis: Comprising "The Women of England," "Wives of England," "Daughters of England," "Poetry of Life," etc. Designed to Promote the Cultivation of the Domestic Virtues* (J. and H. G. Langley, 1844).

Questions

1. What does Mrs. Ellis mean when she writes of "minutest calculation as to lawful means"? What sort of "disputed cases" is she anticipating?

2. If Mrs. Ellis's ideal is to be a manager, what assumption is she making about labor?

3. The advice given here seems to apply only to women living under certain conditions. From your reading of the text, to what class do these women belong?

DOCUMENT 2

Mazzini's Idea of Nationalism

Although Mazzini believed that people's first duty was to humanity, he linked love of humanity with love of nation or nationalism. Nationalism was essential to the "brotherhood of the Peoples" that he advocated. He insisted that social problems could not be solved outside of a nationalist context.

Do not beguile yourselves with the hope of emancipation from unjust social conditions if you do not first conquer a Country for yourselves; where there is no Country there is no common agreement to which you can appeal; the egoism of self-interest rules alone, and he who has the upper hand keeps it, since there is no common safeguard for the interests of all. Do not be led away by the idea of improving your material conditions without first solving the national question. You cannot do it. Your industrial associations and mutual help societies are useful as a means of educating and disciplining yourselves; as an economic fact they will remain barren until you have an Italy.

Source: Joseph Mazzini, *The Duties of Man*, trans. Ella Noyes (J. M. Dent and Sons, 1907), pp. 52–53.

Question

1. Does Mazzini appear to be addressing his arguments to people already convinced of the need for an Italian state or to a group skeptical of the possibility? What historical factors and traditions made his task more difficult?

DOCUMENT 3

The Troubling Sight of Famine

The Irish famine deeply troubled the British view of their country's prosperity and progress. In this passage, one investigator traveling through the Irish countryside at the beginning of the famine describes the most upsetting features.

I did not see a child playing in the streets or on the roads; no children are to be seen outside the doors but a few sick and dying children. . . . In the districts which are now being depopulated by starvation, coffins are only used for the more wealthy. The majority were taken to the grave without any coffin, and buried in their rags: in some instances even the rags are taken from the corpse to cover some still living body.

. . . On arriving at Cappagh, in the first house I saw a dead child lying in a corner of the house, and two children, pale as death, with their heads hanging down upon their breasts sitting by a small fire. The father had died on the road coming home from work. One of the children, a lad seventeen years of age, had been found, in the absence of his mother, who was looking for food, lying dead, with his legs held out of the fire by the little child which I then saw lying dead. Two other children had also died. The mother and the two children still alive had lived on one dish of barley for the last four days. On entering another house the doctor said, "Look there, Sir, you can't tell whether they are boys or girls." Taking up a skeleton child, he said, "Here is the way it is with them all; their legs swing and rock like the legs of a doll, they have the smell of mice."

Source: Adapted from W. Steuart Trench, *Realities of Irish Life* (Longmans, Green, and Co., 1847).

Questions

1. When tragic circumstances such as these occurred, what were the duties of a government, according to the customs and beliefs of the day? What had been the duties of Louis XVI when he was confronted by the hungry women of Paris (see Chapter 20)? What has changed and why?

2. From your reading of the chapter, what might the English government have done to eliminate the causes of the famine? Would such solutions have been politically possible?

DOCUMENT 4

Contrasting Views of the Parisian National Workshops

National workshops were set up by the city government of Paris during the revolution of 1848 to provide work for the unemployed. They aroused great controversy, as can be seen from the two selections that follow. The conservatives emphasized the potential for anarchy in the organization of thousands of unemployed, whereas workers in the workshops stressed the obligation of the new republic to provide work.

The Conservative View (From the Parisian newspaper *Le Constitutionnel*, 22 June 1848)

The national workshops received a growing population. The men were supported during their strikes by the government, which paid them for doing nothing. They were encouraged by speeches that were hostile to the masters. The men's solidarity in their strikes was confirmed, and they became more and more hostile to the employers. As this system developed the alarm increased in industry and commerce. The workers' poverty helped swell what the employers regarded as the army of anarchy.

The Response of the Workers (an undated declaration of workers in one of the national workshops)

We are not people asking for charity. The Republic promised work to provide a livelihood for all its children. . . . So give us work so that we may live like free men. . . . Do not forget, Monarchists, that it was not so that we could remain your slaves that we brought about a third revolution. We fought your social system, the sole cause of the disorder and poverty that devours and swallows contemporary society.

Source: Roger Price, ed., *1848 in France* (Cornell University Press, 1975), pp. 102, 104.

Questions

1. Why were the national workshops so controversial? Why did the middle classes see them as a threat to property rights, whereas the working classes saw them as a basic guarantee of social justice? What did each group consider to be the proper role of government?

2. The presence of the documents in this *Student's Guide* demonstrates the long-term influence of one of the historians discussed in this chapter. Name the historian and discuss his or her influence.

CHAPTER

23

The Politics and Culture of the Nation-State, 1851–1871

Chapter Outline

Chapter Summary

The Crimean War was the first major war to disturb the peace of Europe since the fall of Napoleon. Although the Crimean War was no great turning point in history, it was a bloody affair that shocked the West and forced drastic social reform in Russia. It also witnessed another joint Franco-British military expedition, just as in 1827, when the two former enemies were in agreement over the Balkans and the Ottoman Empire. The Russians also learned that there were limits to Austrian gratitude for the Russian intervention in Hungary in 1849. In fact, for the rest of the century, these two former allies would find little common ground in their policies toward the Balkans and the Ottoman Empire.

The adventurism that brought the French into the Crimean War was characteristic of Napoleon III's foreign policy. This nephew of the great Bonaparte, after his election as president of the Second Republic in 1848, took only a few years to overthrow the constitution and establish a Second Empire. As ruler, he sent French troops deep into Algeria, Indochina, the Crimea, and even Mexico. He also sent French troops to assist the Piedmontese in the unification of Italy. After a few bloody battles in 1859, however, he became alarmed at Piedmontese strength and the threat to the Papal States; he then treacherously and unilaterally negotiated with Austria. Thereafter, he sent French troops to defend Rome from the new Italian kingdom, which wanted to evict the pope and establish the Eternal City as its national capital.

The Italian war of unification was masterminded by Camillo di Cavour, the Piedmontese prime minister, and by Victor Emmanuel II. After Napoleon III withdrew his support, however, a rising of Italian patriots throughout the peninsula and the heroics of Giuseppe Garibaldi were required to create the new Italian state. Garibaldi conquered and Victor Emmanuel annexed part of the Papal States. The Italians annexed Venetia after Prussia crushed Austria in 1866, and they were finally able to take the city of Rome when the French withdrew their troops during the Franco-Prussian War.

Otto von Bismarck was the Prussian chancellor who is credited with German unification. Anticipating the opposition of Austria and France, he helped Prussia to build a formidable army and befriended Russia to gain its neutrality. He used a war with Denmark to draw Austria into brief hostilities, then cleverly provoked the French into a disastrous declaration of war. The Franco-Prussian War resulted in the fall of Napoleon III's French Empire, the creation of a new German Empire, and a bitter legacy that led eventually to two world wars. The Austrian Empire, shaken by its humiliating defeat, was restructured to accommodate powerful Hungarian nationalists. The compromise irritated other minorities, such as the Czechs and Rumanians, but the Germans were now allied with the Hungarians in defense of the status quo.

Alexander II, the tsar who came to power in the midst of the Crimean War, changed his country as profoundly as Bismarck and Cavour changed theirs. It was he who freed tens of thousands of serfs from near-slavery. The freed serfs still faced enormous problems, including a staggering debt as they purchased land from their former masters. Alexander also laid the foundations of local government and reformed the legal system, even as the Russian state expanded steadily into Asia. In many ways, nineteenth-century Russian history parallels that of the United States, which also saw the end of slavery and an aggressive expansion into sparsely settled territories. But the United States also fought a costly Civil War that marked the triumph of northern industrial interests over southern agrarian ones and fixed the course of American history for the rest of the nineteenth century.

The turbulence of the political history of these years was mirrored by intense intellectual and cultural ferment. Men of talent and vision, such as Pasteur, made great strides in many fields, although others, such as Darwin, initiated controversy as well. Marx and others attempted to find scientific explanations for social problems. Socialists, communists, mutualists, anarchists, utilitarians, and liberals disagreed on the urgency of the problems and the nature of the solutions. Social problems were also addressed by novelists, poets, and painters, and even opera.

Vocabulary

autocrat	A ruler with absolute and unlimited authority; for example (in theory at least), the tsar.
literati	The intelligentsia; those who are well educated and well read.
civil service	A government bureaucracy, especially one in which appointments and promotions are based on merit or special examinations.
denominational	Affiliated with a particular religious sect (denomination).
sepoy	In India, a native soldier serving the British Raj.
mutualism	A political philosophy holding that interdependence is necessary for personal and social well-being.
anarchism	A political philosophy that advocates the abolition of government and the state.
antiseptic	Cleansing; purifying; literally, a substance that opposes sepsis, or decay.
Russification	An official policy in the nineteenth-century Russian Empire of promoting the autocratic government, the Russian language, and the Orthodox church, and therefore discouraging, repressing, or discriminating against ethnic and religious minorities and political dissent.

Self-Testing and Review Questions

Identification

After reading Chapter 23, identify and explain the historical significance of each of the following:

1. Ferenc Deák

2. Felix zu Schwarzenberg

3. Hung Hsiu-ch'uan

4. *salon des réfusés*

5. Second Reform Bill

6. positivism

7. *zemstvos*

8. Bernadette Soubirous

9. Ferdinand de Lesseps

10. East India Company

11. Benjamin Disraeli

12. *Ausgleich*

13. the liberal empire

14. Crédit Mobilier

15. *The Origin of Species*

16. Eugénie

17. Red Shirts

18. Bundesrat

19. First Vatican Council

20. *Dejeuner sur l'herbe*

21. Harriet Taylor Mill

22. Louis Pasteur

23. *pétroleuses*

24. Königgrätz

25. International Working Men's Association

26. Leopold of Hohenzollern-Sigmaringen

Chronology

Identify the events or issues associated with each of the following dates. Most of these dates are significant for more than one reason. After you finish, answer the questions that follow.

1852

1856

1857

1859

1860

1861

1862

1863

1864

1867

1869

1871

1. When were the serfs freed in Russia? When was slavery abolished in the United States? Speculate on the similarity of the two dates. Could one have provoked or hurried the other?

2. How were the unification movements in Italy and Germany related chronologically? Why?

Matching Exercises

In each set, match the terms on the left with those on the right.

Set A

_____ 1. *The Mill on the Floss*   a. Ivan Turgenev

_____ 2. *War and Peace*   b. Charles Dickens

_____ 3. *Crime and Punishment*   c. Fyodor Dostoevsky

_____ 4. *Great Expectations*   d. Leo Tolstoy

_____ 5. *Fathers and Sons*   e. George Eliot

_____ 6. *The Possessed*   (Use these more than once)

_____ 7. *A Hunter's Sketches*

Set B

_____ 1. Plombières   a. where the French and Piedmontese defeated the Austrians

_____ 2. Villafranca   b. a battle in the Crimean War

_____ 3. Sedan   c. where Cavour held a secret meeting with Napoleon III

_____ 4. Ems   d. a telegram that Bismarck used to start a war

_____ 5. Solferino   e. the battle in which the Prussians defeated the French and captured the emperor

_____ 6. Sevastopol   f. the place where Napoleon III unilaterally withdrew from the War of the Risorgimento

Set C

_____ 1. "Property is theft."
_____ 2. *The Civil War in France*
_____ 3. *On Liberty*
_____ 4. *Social Statics*
_____ 5. *The Subjection of Women*
_____ 6. *The System of Positive Politics . . .*

a. John Stuart Mill
b. Herbert Spencer
c. Pierre-Joseph Proudhon
d. Karl Marx
e. Auguste Comte
(Use one of these twice)

Set D

_____ 1. Wallachia and Moldavia
_____ 2. Nice and Savoy
_____ 3. Schleswig and Holstein
_____ 4. Alsace and Lorraine

a. taken by France from Piedmont-Sardinia
b. taken by Prussia from France
c. invaded by Russia
d. taken from Denmark by Prussia and Austria

Set E

_____ 1. Auguste Comte
_____ 2. Charles Baudelaire
_____ 3. Edouard Manet
_____ 4. Gustave Courbet
_____ 5. Jacques Offenbach

a. French poet, author of *Les fleurs du mal*
b. French philosopher, a pioneer of sociology
c. popular composer of the Second Empire
d. French painter: *The Wrestlers, The Bather*
e. French painter: *Olympia, Universal Exhibition*

Multiple-Choice Questions

1. The *Syllabus of Errors* was
   a. an attack on modern ideas issued by Pope Pius IX.
   b. a critique of mutualism and anarchism by Karl Marx.
   c. a report on the causes of the Sepoy mutiny in India.
   d. a report on medical conditions in the Crimean War by Florence Nightingale.

2. Verdi's opera about ancient Egypt, written for the opening of the Suez Canal, was
   a. *La Traviata.*
   b. *Aïda.*
   c. *Semiramide.*
   d. *Der Meistersinger.*

3. Which one of these made important discoveries about heredity that went largely unnoticed in his lifetime?
   a. Gregor Mendel
   b. Louis Pasteur
   c. Joseph Lister
   d. Felice Orsini

4. Georges-Eugène Haussmann is best remembered for
   a. his clumsy diplomacy, which ignited the Franco-Prussian War.
   b. founding the *salon des réfusés.*
   c. planning the boulevards of Paris.
   d. building the Suez Canal.

5. The masterpiece *Der Ring des Nibelungen* was written by
   a. Friedrich Froebel.
   b. Alexander Bach.
   c. Felix zu Schwarzenberg.
   d. Richard Wagner.

6. The expression "Dual Monarchy" refers to
   a. the Habsburg state after a cooperative agreement between Austria and Hungary.
   b. Austria and Prussia's joint rule over the German states.
   c. the Russian Empire of the tsar, symbolized by a two-headed Phoenix.
   d. the rule of Victor Emmanuel II in northern Italy and Garibaldi in the south.

7. When Bismarck spoke of "blood and iron," he was calling for
   a. *Ausgleich.*　　　　　　　　c. *zemstvos.*
   b. *Realpolitik.*　　　　　　　d. *Realschulen.*

8. Nihilists were
   a. followers of Bakunin who wished to abolish all government.
   b. reformers who demanded the end of slavery.
   c. disillusioned Russian youth, depicted by Turgenev.
   d. antiestablishment artists of the Second Empire.

9. One important result of the Sepoy rebellion was
   a. the Taiping movement.　　　　c. the Jhansi revolt.
   b. the Meiji restoration.　　　　d. the Government of India Act.

10. The establishment of Maximilian as ruler over Mexico was a failed project of
    a. Alexander II.　　　　　　　c. Napoleon III.
    b. William I.　　　　　　　　d. Lord Palmerston.

Essay Questions

Using material from this and earlier chapters, write an essay on each of the following topics. When appropriate, include dates and cite detailed examples to support your arguments.

1. The French leftist parties often claimed to be more patriotic than their right-wing counterparts, and point to a number of historical events to support their argument. Does the Commune of 1871 support this viewpoint?

2. Compare the roles of Cavour and Bismarck in the unification of Italy and Germany, respectively. Who had the more difficult task, and why?

3. Describe the social, political, and cultural factors behind the emancipation of the serfs in Russia and analyze the ways in which autocratic and aristocratic power shaped the outcome.

4. To what extent do the various theories of Karl Marx related in the text reflect the principal preconceptions of his age about history? science? romanticism? anarchism? Was Marx essentially an original thinker, or did he take many of his ideas from other sources?

5. What events of the pontificate of Pius IX, detailed in this and the previous chapter, might explain his reactionary pronouncements?

Skill Building: Maps

A. *Locate the following regions on the map of Europe. Why was each significant in the present chapter?*

   a. Oder River

   b. Vistula River

   c. Schleswig

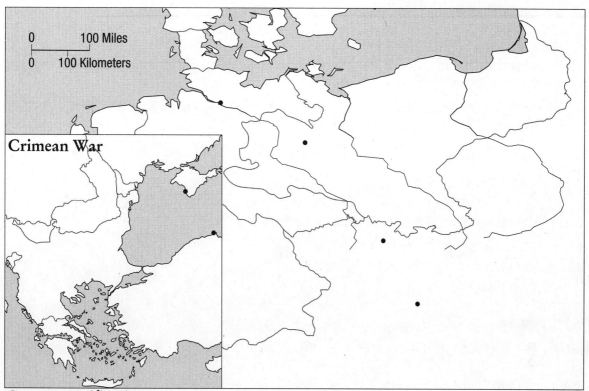

Crimean War

German Unification

    d. Prussia

    e. Elbe River

    f. Mecklenburg

    g. Sinope

    h. Vienna

    i. Berlin

    j. Holstein

    k. the Crimea

    l. Hamburg

    m. Alsace-Lorraine

    n. Bavaria

    o. Könniggrätz (Sadowa)

    p. Sevastopol

q. Austrian Empire

1. What were the boundaries of Prussia before German unification? Mark them on your map. What were the boundaries of the new German state? Why did Austria and France oppose German unification?

2. Why did Austria oppose Italian unification? Explain France's policy considering the behavior of these other states.

B. *Locate the following regions on the map of Italy.*

a. Piedmont

b. Venetia

c. (Duchy of) Modena

d. Papal States

e. Sardinia

f. Savoy

g. Solferino

h. Lombardy

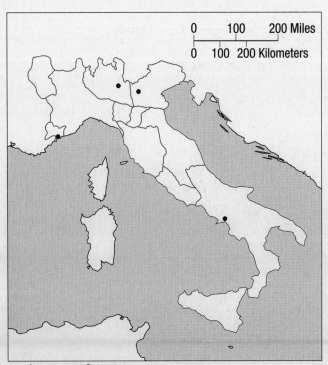

Italian Unification

i. (Duchy of) Parma

j. Tuscany

k. Two Sicilies

l. Sicily

m. Nice (city)

n. Magenta

o. Naples (city)

1. Why was French militancy assistance necessary before Piedmont could successfully annex other Italian states?
2. Why did the pope oppose the unification of Italy under Piedmont?

Enrichment Exercise

Opera is best experienced live, because the music is only one aspect of the art form; there are also poetry, drama, set and costume design, and often choreography. If you are fortunate enough to have a local opera company, try to attend a live performance of a nineteenth-century work. (Many of the most popular operas were written in that century!) If you cannot attend a live performance, many operas by Verdi and Wagner are now available on videocassettes, with English subtitles; select one that particularly interests you (the text describes several). For maximum enjoyment, visit the reference section of a library and read a plot summary in one of the many encyclopedias of opera before attending or viewing the tape. Afterwards, write a one-page summary of your experience. Why did opera become the most important form of entertainment in the eighteenth and nineteenth centuries? How did the setting, the plot, and other factors reflect the life and times of the composer?

Document Analysis

Document 1

The Crimean War and the Revolution in Nursing

Amidst catastrophic casualties from disease and horrid sanitation, Florence Nightingale led a group of volunteer nurses to the Crimea. Her action shocked polite society, because nursing was a job that attracted lower-class women. In those days, nursing often led to prostitution and bad behavior, but in Nightingale's case, it made her a heroine and started nursing on the road to respectability. This excerpt is taken from one of her major reform brochures, "Introducing Female Nurses Into Military Hospitals" (1858).

There is no doubt that the admission of women to ward service is beset with difficulties. Nurses are careful, efficient, often decorous, and always kind, sometimes drunken, sometimes unchaste.

The nurses should be strong, active women, of unblemished character, and should be irreversibly dismissed for the first offence of unchastity, drunkenness, or dishonesty, or proved impropriety of any kind.

Their rules should be simple, very definite, should leave them at the absolute disposal of the surgeon. Their dress should be uniform.

Give them plenty to do, and great responsibility—two effectual means of steadying women.

"In quietness and in confidence shall by your strength." Quietness has been from the beginning of its publicity the one thing wanted in this work. I know the fuss, which from its beginning surrounded it, was abhorrent to us: but the work, which is all we care for, has throughout suffered from it. One hospital, naval, military, or civil, nursed well, and gradually training a few nurses, would do more good to the cause than an endless amount of meetings, testimonials, pounds, and speeches. This never will, never can be a popular work. Few good ones are, without the stern fructifying element of moral restraint and influence; and though the streams of this are many, its source is one. Hearts are not touched without Religion. Religion was not given us from above in impressions and generalities, but in habits of thought and action, in love of God and of mankind, carried into action.

Source: Excerpted from Lucy Ridgely Seymer, ed., *Selected Writings of Florence Nightingale* (Macmillan, 1954), pp. 17–19.

Questions

1. What do you suppose were the principal duties of a nurse in the mid-nineteenth century? Considering the horrors of war and the exclusion of women from many jobs, why was nursing considered appropriate for women of any class?

2. Florence Nightingale combined the highest ideals of religion and military service in developing nursing as a career for respectable women. Discuss those ideals in terms of the movements and philosophies of the nineteenth century.

DOCUMENT 2

Bismarck by Letters

Historians helped develop a portrait of Otto von Bismarck as a clear-sighted master statesman who patriotically plotted the unification of Germany. Statements in Bismarck's letters to his wife, however, suggest that the public version of the man may contain gaps and discrepancies. Trying to resolve image, myth, and truth creates historical problems.

Half an hour ago a cabinet courier woke me with war and peace. Our policy drifts more and more into the Austrian wake; and when we have once fired a shot on the Rhine, it is over with the Italian-Austrian war, and in its place a Prussian-French comes on the scene, in which Austria, after we have taken the burden from her shoulders, stands by us, or fails to stand by us just so far as her own interests require. She will certainly not allow us to play a very brilliant victor's part.

As God wills! After all, everything here is only a question of time, nations and individuals, folly and wisdom, war and peace; they come and go like the waves, but the sea remains. There is nothing on this earth but hypocrisy and jugglery; and whether fever or grapeshot tear off this fleshly mask, a likeness will, after all, turn up between a Prussian and an Austrian, which will make it difficult to distinguish them. The stupid, and the clever too, look pretty much alike when their bones are well picked. With such views, a man certainly gets rid of his specific patriotism.

Source: Adapted from Otto von Bismarck, *Prince Bismarck's Letters to His Wife, His Sister, and Others,* trans. Fitzhugh Maxse (Scribner's, 1878), pp. 131–132.

Questions

1. When do you suspect this letter was written? What clues are provided?
2. Does Bismarck's fatalism seem to incline him toward war or peace?

DOCUMENT 3

A New Lifestyle in Russia

Nikolai Gavrilovich Chernyshevsky (1828–1889) inspired a generation and more of young Russians with his novel What Is To Be Done? *(1864). In it he created characters who tried to live better lives than those dictated by the norms of autocratic Russian society. Here one of the heroes, Dmitry Sergeich, opens by telling Vera, his partner in a "phony marriage," about his plans to support her.*

"I will find employment in my profession, though it will not pay me much; but there will be time left to attend to patients, and, taking all things together, we shall be able to live."

"Yes, dear friend, we shall need so little; only I do not wish to live by your labor. I too will live by my labor; isn't that fair? I should not live at your expense."

"Who told you that, dear Verochka?"

"Oh! he asks who told me! Your books are full of such thoughts."

"In my books? At any rate I never said such a thing to you. When, then, did I say so?"

"When? Haven't you always told me that everything rests on money?"

"Well?"

"And do you really consider me so stupid that I cannot understand books and draw conclusions from premises? Everything rests on money, you say, Dmitry Sergeich; consequently, whoever has money has power and freedom, say your books; then, as long as woman lives at man's expense, she will be dependent on him, will she not? You thought that I could not understand that, and would be your slave? I know that you intend to be a good and benevolent despot, but I do not intend that you should be a despot at all. And now this is what we will do. You shall cut off arms and legs and administer drugs; I, on the other hand, will give lessons on the piano."

Source: Adapted from N. G. Chernyshevsky, *What Is To Be Done? Tales about New People,* trans. Benjamin R. Tucker and Ludmilla B. Turkevich (Random House, 1960), pp. 108–109.

Questions

1. Are the young people presented here idealistic? nihilistic? optimistic? Do you suppose their attitudes were acceptable to their parents and elders?
2. Many years later, Lenin also wrote an essay entitled, "What Is To Be Done?". To what extent might he have been thinking of Chernyshevsky's nonconforming youth?

DOCUMENT 4

Positivism and Politics

Auguste Comte's theory of positivism was not merely theoretical. It had concrete political application. Subjecting everything to scrutiny, positivists challenged both those who held to the reins of government by tradition alone and those who would change society through revolution. Rather, they believed that government should function under the leadership of those qualified to understand social laws or, more precisely, bureaucrats.

>Positivism will lay down a definite basis for the reorganization of society. It will offer a general system of education for the adoption of all civilized nations, and by this means will supply in every department of public and private life fixed principles of judgment and of conduct.

>The primary object, then, of positivism is twofold: to generalize our scientific conceptions, and to systematize the art of social life.

>This will lead us to another question. The regenerating doctrine cannot do its work without adherents; in what quarter should we hope to find them? Now, with individual exceptions of great value, we cannot expect the adhesion of any of the upper classes in society. They are all more or less under the influence of baseless metaphysical theories and of aristocratic self-seeking. They are absorbed in blind political agitation and in disputes for the possession of the useless remnants of the old theological and military system. Their action only tends to prolong the revolutionary state indefinitely, and can never result in true social renovation.

Source: Adapted from *Auguste Comte and Positivism: The Essential Writings,* Gertrude Lenzer, ed. (University of Chicago Press, 1975), p. 318.

Questions

1. How did the ideas and principles of the Enlightenment and the French Revolution affect Comte's thought? Does he generally agree with them or react against them?

2. How do you suppose positivists viewed romanticism? socialism?

CHAPTER
24

Empire, Industry, and Everyday Life, 1871–1894

Chapter Outline

THE ADVANCE OF INDUSTRIAL SOCIETY

Innovation Takes Command
Facing Economic Crisis
The Birth of Management, the Service Sector, and Department Stores
Changes for Traditional Laborers

THE POLITICAL FOUNDATIONS OF MASS SOCIETY

Workers, Politics, and Protest
Expanding Political Participation in Western Europe
Power Politics in Central and Eastern Europe

THE RACE FOR EMPIRE

Taming the Mediterranean, Conquering Africa
Acquiring Territory in Asia
The Rise of Japan
The Paradoxes of Imperialism

THE COMPLEXITIES OF IMPERIAL SOCIETY
  The European Exodus
  The "Best Circles"
  Approaches to Reforming Society
  Professional Sports and Organized Leisure
  Social Consciousness and Imperial Culture

Chapter Summary

Late nineteenth-century industry produced an amazing variety of products. Besides basic commodities like raw textiles and cast iron, the factories in the West also churned out consumer goods for a new mass market and steel for railroads and ships. Although Great Britain remained the world leader, industrialization continued to spread across the continent of Europe and to North America, with its abundance of natural resources. Germany emerged as the leader in Europe, enriched by the territories and war reparations it took from France as a result of the Franco-Prussian War. Most governments, eager to emulate the British path to wealth and power, encouraged investment and industrial development. Some protected domestic industries with tariffs.

The new consumer products, available from department stores and mail-order catalogs, found a ready market in the growing middle classes, which were eager to add luxury to their lives. A certain amount of extra income was now available among the growing numbers of government bureaucrats, industrial managers, service personnel, and skilled laborers. Industrial workers, often the victims of economic cycles and technological change, increasingly joined unions or formed workers' organizations to take collective action. The expansion of suffrage in several countries also provided the opportunity for political action. Socialism continued to spread, with Marxism, anarchism, and nonviolent doctrines competing for support. Nevertheless, for many workers, peasants, and persecuted national minorities, emigration from Europe was the only solution.

New technology and the spread of at least minimal literacy affected the nature of literature and created a new popular press with profits from advertising revenues based on circulation. The press spread the new consumer culture and affected political campaigns; public opinion would become an important factor in determining government policy; and the manipulation of public opinion became a critical aspect of governing. Alarmed by Catholic solidarity in the western and southern German states annexed in 1871, Bismarck launched an anti-Catholic campaign in Germany; his motives were political, not religious, because he later courted the Catholics to help him oppose the growing workers' movement. In Britain, Gladstone also courted public opinion in his campaigns, using it to push Disraeli into action over the Balkans in 1878.

The Balkans once again disturbed European peace. Bismarck, whose newly unified Germany dominated the continent after the Franco-Prussian War, tried to preserve peace by forming alliances with both Austria-Hungary and Russia. But the latter two countries had sharply conflicting interests in the Balkans, and at the Congress of Berlin Bismarck was forced to side with Austria-Hungary. Eventually he was able to placate the Russians and lure them back into his alliance system, but significant damage had been done. Bismarck also convinced Italy to become an ally, although that country also had longstanding differences with Austria-Hungary. After Bismarck's forced retirement, German foreign policy was managed by much less able men, and the folly of two decades of baiting the French would poison European relations for years to come.

The tensions in Europe were also aggravated by the new imperialism; European states established colonial rule throughout Africa, Asia, and the Pacific. The motives for imperialism were complex, including missionary zeal, military strategy, trade routes, a sense of responsibility based on racist assumptions, and simple greed. Imperialist enterprises also were popular with the press and its readers, and eased some of the population pressures that were causing unprecedented emigration. European culture and technology would profoundly change the non-Western societies with which they came in contact, but the experience of imperialism would also result in many changes in Europe, some of them as subtle as the influence of Japanese prints on impressionist painters.

Vocabulary

tortuous	Twisting, winding; not to be confused with "torturous."
hydroelectric	Relating to electricity created by water-driven turbines. Notice that this method, the most common in the first decades of electric power, requires the active cooperation of government, because rivers are not traditionally privately owned.
muckrakers	Journalists of the late nineteenth and early twentieth centuries who exposed public corruption and private vice.
aegis	Zeus' shield, which he gave to Athena; metaphorically the word refers to guidance, protection, patronage, as in "under the aegis of . . . "
jingoism	Any warlike, bullying behavior by a nation; the term was derived from the poem quoted in the text.
pogrom	An organized assault against a group of people, carried out with the cooperation of public officials, such as the persecutions of Jews in tsarist Russia.
ghetto	Originally, the section of a city in which Jews were forced to live; later, any neighborhood containing only a single ethnic group.
décolletage	A low-cut neckline.
prophylaxis	Any practice that prevents illness or disease.
rugby	A type of football in which the players are permitted to touch the ball with their hands; the name derives from Rugby School in England. Many elements of rugby are found in American and Canadian football.
soccer	A type of football in which only the goalkeeper is allowed to use his hands. During the 1880s and 1890s the game was spread around the world by the British navy, and it was the first major sport to pay working-class athletes salaries to play for professional clubs.
Malthusian	Referring to the ideas of Thomas Malthus (1766–1834), who predicted that human populations would outstrip food production, resulting in overcrowding, famine, and chaos.

Self-Testing and Review Questions

Identification

After reading Chapter 24, identify and explain the historical significance of each of the following:

1. Leopold II

2. Labour party

3. Bon Marché

4. *Rerum Novarum*

5. Henry Stanley

6. Xhosa

7. Annie Besant

8. impressionists

9. Isasaki Yataro

10. Indochina

11. Taaffe ring

12. Comte de Chambord

13. *Kulturkampf*

14. Boers

15. Bayreuth

16. Cecil Rhodes

17. Emilia Pardo Besant

18. *The Story of an African Farm*

19. Indian National Congress

20. quinine

Chronology

Identify the events or issues associated with the following dates. Some of these dates may be significant for more than one reason. After you finish, answer the questions that follow.

1871

1873

1876

1877

1878

1881

1884

1888

1891

1892

1894

1. Which events of 1881 discussed in the book are interrelated? How?
2. What is the chronological connection between the expansion of literacy, the rise of the popular press, and the popular novel?

Matching Exercises

In each set, match the terms on the left with those on the right.

Set A

_____ 1. Emile Zola   a. a French painter

_____ 2. Armand Peugeot   b. a Dutch painter

_____ 3. Georges Boulanger   c. a pioneer of the automobile

_____ 4. Edgar Degas   d. a French writer, author of *Au bonheur des dames*

_____ 5. Vincent Van Gogh   e. political leader who almost overthrew the Third Republic

Set B

_____ 1. *Peer Gynt*   a. Leo Tolstoy

_____ 2. *The Mayor of Casterbridge*   b. Henrik Ibsen

_____ 3. *Anna Karenina*   c. Thomas Hardy

_____ 4. *A Doll's House*   d. Fyodor Dostoevsky

_____ 5. *The Brothers Karamazov*   (Use one of these twice)

Set C

_____ 1. Karl Benz   a. Austro-Hungarian prime minister

_____ 2. Edouard von Taaffe   b. Austro-Hungarian foreign minister

_____ 3. Gyula Andrássy   c. Norwegian composer

_____ 4. Antonín Dvořák   d. Czech composer

_____ 5. Edvard Grieg   e. German inventor

Set D

____ 1. Cochin China   a. Great Britain

____ 2. Malay peninsula   b. France

____ 3. Turkestan   c. Germany

____ 4. Cameroun   d. Belgium

____ 5. Burma   e. Russia

____ 6. Cape Colony   (Use these more than once)

____ 7. Tunisia

____ 8. Congo

Set E

____ 1. Three Emperors League   a. Germany, Austria-Hungary, Italy

____ 2. Dual Alliance   b. Russia, Austria-Hungary, Germany

____ 3. Triple Alliance   c. Germany and Russia

____ 4. Reinsurance Treaty   d. Austria-Hungary and Germany

Multiple-Choice Questions

1. The Second International was
   a. Bismarck's international congress, the greatest since the Congress of Vienna.
   b. a federation of socialist and labor organizations.
   c. the British bank, its vaults swollen with wealth derived from imperialism.
   d. a sort of world's fair, at which the Eiffel Tower was unveiled.

2. After his father was assassinated, this tsar made political repression and religious persecution into national policy.
   a. Alexander II
   b. Alexander III
   c. William II
   d. Nicholas II

3. The Congress of Berlin
   a. overturned the Treaty of San Stefano.
   b. created a large Bulgaria friendly to Russia.
   c. ended the *Kulturkampf.*
   d. unified Germany.

4. Under the Third Republic, the French electorate
   a. remained hostile to monarchy and loyal to democracy.
   b. used universal manhood suffrage to deliver the government into the hands of radicals.
   c. lost the desire for imperialist conquests overseas.
   d. became increasingly antisemitic.

5. Charles Parnell was a proponent of
   a. Home Rule.
   b. the People's Will.
   c. Land and Liberty.
   d. the Fabian society.

6. Which of these is *not* true of industrialization in the late nineteenth century?
   a. The concept of limited-liability corporations encouraged investments.
   b. Newspapers remained expensive and their readership was limited to the wealthier classes.
   c. Cartels and trusts promoted monopoly.
   d. Department stores marketed a variety of new consumer products.

7. Bismarck's foreign policy after 1871 was designed to
   a. increase German power and influence, even at the risk of war.
   b. befriend France through concessions and alliances.
   c. isolate France while soothing the differences between Russia and Austria-Hungary.
   d. drive the Ottoman Empire out of Europe.

8. The Fabian society advocated
   a. a new kind of painting, independent of photography's influence.
   b. the violent overthrow of the tsarist regime, because even peaceful dissent was illegal.
   c. socialist reform, brought about through peaceful, constitutional change.
   d. the spread of Christianity through imperialist expansion.

9. A birth control clinic was opened in Amsterdam by
   a. Vera Zasulich.   c. May Morris.
   b. Mary Cassat.   d. Aletta Jacobs.

10. The Midlothian campaign was a great success for
    a. William Gladstone.   c. Cecil Rhodes.
    b. William Morris.   d. Benjamin Disraeli.

Essay Questions

Using material from this and earlier chapters, write an essay on each of the following topics. When appropriate, include dates and cite detailed examples to support your arguments.

1. Write a defense of imperialism on moral grounds using arguments typical of mainstream nineteenth-century European thought. How might a twentieth-century person refute those arguments? On what different premises do the arguments rest?

2. How did the policies of Bismarck the German chancellor (after 1871) differ from those of Bismarck the Prussian chancellor (described in Chapter 23)? How were they the same?

3. In the nineteenth century, Russia expanded eastward, establishing colonial outposts, absorbing native peoples, and building a railroad across the wilderness. What other country does this resemble? Why are these parallels important? How are the two countries different?

4. In the age of imperialism, Europeans exported their culture to the rest of the world. How were European thought, art, and culture affected by new contacts with the non-Western world?

5. How did the "second industrial revolution" differ from the first one? Were these differences fundamental? Were Marx's ideas more applicable to one or the other?

Skill-Building: Maps

A. *Locate the following on the map of eastern Europe. Why was each significant in the present chapter?*

   a. Bessarabia

   b. Ukraine

   c. Kiev

   d. Lithuania

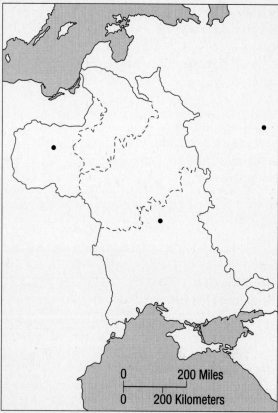

Eastern Europe

  e. Romania

  f. Warsaw

  g. Moscow

1. Shade in the Pale of Settlement on the map. Discuss the history and significance of the Pale.

B. *Locate the following on the map of the world. Why was each significant in the present chapter?*
   a. Egypt

   b. Jamaica

   c. India

   d. Hong Kong

   e. Annam

   f. Canada

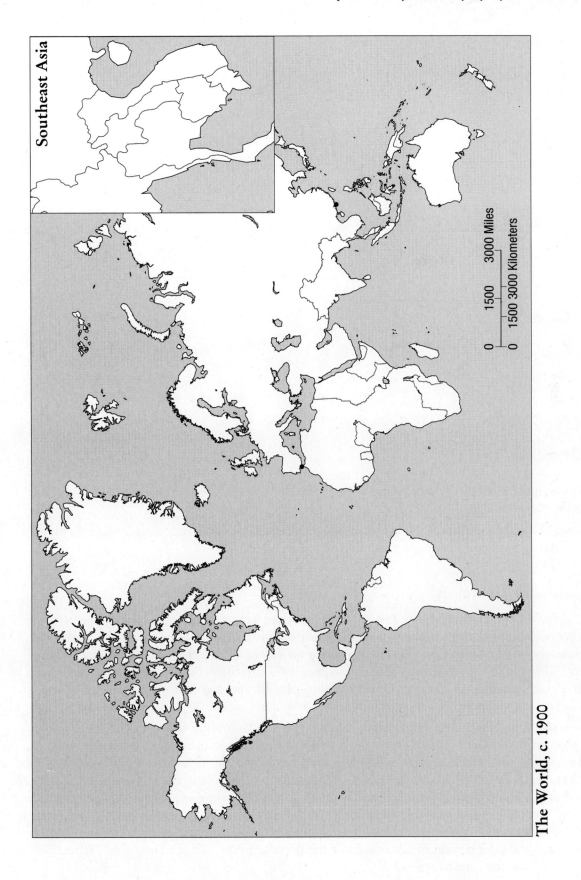

Southeast Asia

The World, c. 1900

3000 Miles

1500   3000 Kilometers

g. Australia

h. Transvaal

i. Nigeria

j. Province

k. China

l. Gibraltar

m. Siam

n. Burma

o. Cambodia

p. Laos

q. Tonkin

r. New Zealand

s. Rhodesia

1. Shade in the parts of the world that belonged to the British Empire. Discuss the factors that led to the great size of this empire.
2. Siam (Thailand), located in southeast Asia between Burma and Indochina, was one of the few Asian countries that managed to remain independent. Why?

Enrichment Exercises

1. Henrik Ibsen's drama *A Doll's House* (1879) shocked his contemporaries by its portrayal of a Norwegian housewife striving to establish her individual identity. Read the play and try to view one of the several productions available on video: the 1959 version with Julie Harris and Christopher Plummer; the much-discussed 1973 interpretation of Nora by Jane Fonda; or a fine Canadian production of 1989 with Claire Bloom and Anthony Hopkins. Write a brief paper explaining Nora's reaction to her life and her world. Was Ibsen a feminist?
2. For an immersion in the imperialist milieu, view the following films, in the order listed. First, see *Zulu Dawn* (1979), which deals with the breakdown of relations between the Zulu nation and the British regime in South Africa, leading to the hostilities at Ulandi in 1878. Next, see *Zulu* (1964), about the efforts of a small British force against overwhelming odds at Rorke's Drift, during the same war. Both films were acclaimed for their "historical accuracy," especially in portraying the warfare of the time. The two together give a vivid portrayal of overbearing imperial government, military arrogance, and the sort of heroics that captured the imagination of Europeans in the popular press. Write a front-line "report" on the war from the Zulu perspective.

3. Many late nineteenth-century novels have captured the imagination of modern filmmakers. There are several excellent versions of *Anna Karenina,* and Roman Polanski's 1980 film *Tess,* based on Thomas Hardy's novel *Tess of the D'Urbervilles,* is a classic in its own genre. A recent French film, *Germinal,* based on a novel by Emile Zola, has received much praise and should be available on video by 1995. Read any of these novels and then write an essay on (1) how well the novel reflects nineteenth-century conditions and values, and (2) why the novel might appeal to modern filmmakers.

Document Analysis

DOCUMENT 1

The Department Store

The department store fascinated people, not only for the way it operated as a gigantic commercial institution but also for its effect on that new species, the shopper. Emile Zola, a major French writer, published an entire novel about the department store and its transformation of Parisian society. This excerpt describes the owner's relationship to his female customers. Note the religious metaphors and the casual antisemitism.

> It was for woman that the stores competed against each other, for woman whom they continually laid a trap with their sales, after having stunned her with their displays of goods. They had awakened in her flesh new desires, they were an immense temptation to which she succumbed fatally, first yielding to the purchases of a good housekeeper, then won over by coquettishness and finally devoured. In setting up things for sale, in democratizing luxury, the stores became a terrible agent of spending, ravaging households, exploiting the passion for ever more expensive fashions. And if, in the department store a woman was queen, adulated and flattered where she was weak, surrounded by kind attentions, she reigned there as a queen drunk with love, . . . who paid for every one of her follies with a drop of blood. Beneath his gallantry, Mouret [the owner] allowed himself the brutality of a Jew selling something by the ounce; he raised a temple to her, he had her flattered by a legion of sales people, and created the rituals of a new cult; he thought of nothing but her, tried without rest to find even bigger seductions; and when he had emptied her pockets and wrecked her nerves, he was as full of a secret contempt as a man whose mistress had made the mistake of surrendering to him.

Source: Emile Zola, *Au Bonheur des dames* (François Bernouard, 1928), pp. 83–84.

Questions

1. Is Zola more upset about the shallow materialistic values or about the role and responsibility of women that are implicit in "shopping"?

2. Compare this document with that about Mrs. Ellis' household manager in the Document Analysis section of Chapter 22. How do the authors differ on the subject of consumerism?

DOCUMENT 2

Imperial Behavior

Imperialists exercised power over native peoples and over imperialist agents of lower rank, such as soldiers. The English explorer of Africa, Henry M. Stanley, gave this advice on how to control both Africans and military men.

Some explorers say: "One must not run through a country, but give the people time to become acquainted with you, and let their worst fears subside."

Now on the expedition across Africa I had no time to give, either to myself or to them. The river bore my heavy canoes downward; my goods would never have endured the dawdling requirement by the system of teaching every tribe I met who I was. To save myself and my men from certain starvation, I had to rush on and on, right through. But on this expedition, the very necessity of making roads to haul my enormous six-ton wagons gave time for my reputation to travel ahead of me. My name, purpose, and liberal rewards for native help, naturally exaggerated, prepared a welcome for me, and transformed my enemies of the old time into workmen, friendly allies, strong porters, and firm friends. I was greatly forbearing also; but, when a fight was inevitable, through open violence, it was sharp and decisive. Consequently, the natives rapidly learned that though everything was to be gained by friendship with me, wars brought nothing but ruin.

When a young white officer quits England for the first time, to lead blacks, he has got to learn and unlearn a great deal. We *must* have white men in Africa; but the raw white is a great nuisance there during the first year. In the second year, he begins to mend; during the third year, if his nature permits it, he has developed into a superior man, whose intelligence may be of transcendent utility for directing masses of inferior men.

My officers were possessed with the notion that my manner was "hard," because I had not many compliments for them. That is the kind of pap which we may offer women and boys. Besides, I thought they were superior natures, and required none of that encouragement, which the more childish blacks almost daily received.

Source: Adapted from Henry Morton Stanley, *Autobiography*, ed. Dorothy Stanley (Houghton Mifflin Co., 1909), pp. 342–343, 384–385.

Question

1. Stanley was hardly typical of upper-class British explorers or British imperialism. He was a Welsh orphan who worked his way to New Orleans as a cabin boy, was adopted by an American merchant, served in the Confederate army for several years, and was later employed by the New York *Herald* (not the British government) to find Livingstone, although he had little African experience. Later, he helped the power-hungry king of Belgium organize his control of the Congo. What insights do each of these facts provide in understanding the document?

DOCUMENT 3

New Customs, New Countries

Rose Schneiderman (1882–1972), future labor leader, emigrated with her family from Russian Poland to the United States in 1890. She soon noticed the different ways in which men and women adapted to the new culture.

Mother had been here only a short time when I noticed that she looked older and more old-fashioned than father. It was so with most of our women, especially those who wore wigs or kerchiefs on their heads. So I thought that if I could persuade her to leave off her kerchief she would look younger and more up to date. So, one day, when we two were alone in the house, I asked her playfully to take off her kerchief and let me do her hair, just to see how it would look.

She consented reluctantly. She had never before in her married life had her hair uncovered before anyone. I was surprised how different she looked. I handed her our little mirror. She glanced at herself, admitted frankly that it looked well and began hastily to put on her kerchief.

"Mamma," I coaxed, "please don't put the kerchief on again—ever!"

At first she would not even listen to me. I began to coax and reason. I pointed out that wives often looked so much older because they were so old-fashioned, that the husbands were often ashamed to go out with them.

Mother put her finger on my lips.

"But father trims his beard," I still argued. Her face looked sad. "Is that why," she said, "I too must sin?"

Source: Adapted from Doris Weatherford, *Foreign and Female Immigrant Women in America 1840–1930* (Schocken Books, 1986), pp. 235–236.

Questions

1. Why were immigrant men and children more likely than women were to adopt the customs of a new country?
2. Do you think that the author's mother might have berated her daughter for not wearing a kerchief, or thought of her as a "sinner"?

DOCUMENT 4

Stanley, Again

The explorer Stanley, like other public figures, had many different faces, including the one he displayed in his autobiographical writings. The makers of popular culture took the stories of the rich and famous and turned them into rollicking rhymes, ballads, and stories. In the early 1890s, this song about Stanley would regularly bring down the house at the London Gaiety, a combination of burlesque and musical-comedy theater for urban folk. With many verses and full of puns, this popularization showed how far imperial culture had spread.

Oh, I went to find Emin Pasha, and started away for fun,
With a box of weeds and a bag of beads, some tracts and a Maxim gun. . . .
I went to find Emin, I did, I looked for him far and wide;
I found him right, I found him tight, and a lot of folks beside,

Away through Darkest Africa, though it cost me lots of tin,
For without a doubt I'd find him out, when I went to find Emin!

Source: Ernest Short, *Fifty Years of Vaudeville* (Eyre and Spotteswoode, 1946), p. 43.

Questions

1. Stanley's final expedition into Africa (1887–1889) was to rescue Emin Pasha, a German who had adopted a Turkish lifestyle and was governor (*pasha*) of the eastern Sudan. Emin had been isolated by a serious native uprising against Anglo-Egyptian rule. What does the ballad suggest about the power of the press to influence popular culture?

2. Does the songwriter's view of imperialism—"a box of weeds and a bag of beads, some tracts and a Maxim gun"—differ significantly from our own?

Practice Questions for Examinations for Part III (Chapters 16–24)

1. How did the discovery and colonization of the New World affect the economies and cultures of the principal colonial powers in western Europe?

2. Trace the history of Russia from the first tsars to the close of the nineteenth century. What were the principal themes in Russian history?

3. Discuss the role of nationalism in European affairs from the French Revolution to the unification of Germany. Was nationalism mostly beneficial, or was it harmful?

4. To what extent did the bitter experience of the religious wars affect the new philosophical directions in European thought—especially political and scientific—in the seventeenth and eighteenth centuries?

5. Compare and contrast European colonialism in the seventeenth and eighteenth centuries with imperialism in the nineteenth century. How are the two movements similar? How are they different?

6. Trace the evolution of the British parliamentary system from the reign of Elizabeth I to the age of Victoria. What factors of British culture and society contributed to this unique political institution?

7. Describe the effects of industrialization on European economy, society, and politics in the eighteenth and nineteenth centuries.

PART

IV

The Crisis of the West:
1894–Present

CHAPTER

25

Modernity and the Road to War, 1894–1914

Chapter Outline

EUROPEAN IMPERIALISM CHALLENGED
  The Trials of Empire
  Empire Threatened: The Russian Revolution of 1905
  Colonial Resistance Expands

ROADS TO WAR
  Competing Alliances and Clashing Ambitions
  The Race to Arms
  War Finally Arrives

Chapter Summary

As the last century ended, Europeans began to define a new society that was self-consciously described as "modern." Private life was subject to unusual scrutiny, as governments became concerned about the falling birthrate and moralists expressed alarm at the changing nature of marriage, the new attitudes of women, the increased use of birth control, and the increasingly public discussion of sexual issues. Sigmund Freud's theories of human sexuality were part of a growing scientific interest in the mind, which included studies of conditioned behavior and attempts to measure intelligence and even to identify criminal tendencies. Freud also spoke and wrote about the existence of an unconscious mind that revealed itself only through dreams and fantasies; mental illnesses could be treated through a process called psychoanalysis.

Just as Freud challenged many traditional assumptions, so too did philosophers such as Friedrich Nietzsche, who rejected scientific certainty and even the logical systems that had been the hallmark of most Western thought since the Enlightenment. His work, and that of contemporaries such as Henri Bergson, stressed irrational forces such as intuition and will. Theories about these forces were sometimes twisted to support irrational and emotional ideologies such as ethnocentrism, racism, antisemitism, and militarism, which were multiplying throughout Europe. At the same time, scientists continued to break new ground, especially in physics, where Albert Einstein and others developed theories that literally changed the way the new century would envision the universe.

The fine arts were also transformed, as new schools of painting self-consciously competed for attention. Fauvists rejected the natural colors of the impressionists, cubists split physical reality into geometric planes, the expressionists explored the bizarre and primitive, and the art nouveau movement rejected all of these, clinging to graceful lines and decoration. Art collectors who had defied the critics and invested in the impressionists were now wealthy, and the art market expanded to include speculation in the new schools as well as more secure investment in the "old masters." Many of the forces that shaped modern art also affected modern music—the influence of primitive and non-Western cultures, the study of the inner mind, and the new relativism in physics and philosophy, to say nothing of the fame and money that notoriety could bring. Composers embraced dissonant harmonies and melodies based on mathematically random sequences of notes. The public was assured that, in time, they would come to appreciate the new music, because such matters were subjective and relative.

The political debates at the turn of the century centered around such issues as socialism, electoral reform, and, increasingly, extreme nationalism and antisemitism. Western socialists argued about what degree of cooperation with capitalism (if any) was appropriate. The Russian marxists in exile split into two factions, Mensheviks and Bolsheviks. Increasingly aggressive anarchists assassinated several heads of state and other famous people. Liberals argued that radicalism could only be tamed by extension of the franchise, and suffragists pointed out the injustice of denying the vote to women. In many countries, social problems were increasingly blamed on national minorities, with Jews singled out for special persecution in Russia.

Antisemitism was also common in the Habsburg states, in Germany, and in France, where the government was badly shaken by the Dreyfus affair.

Meanwhile, the European states were drifting toward war. The diplomatic isolation of France had ended by 1894, but the kaiser clumsily managed to antagonize the British and drive them into the French camp when he encouraged the Boers in southern Africa and confronted the British in both overseas incidents and an expensive arms race. The French wooed the British, backed down to them in the Fashoda incident, and cooperated with them in the Boxer Rebellion, but the British were reluctant to enter into entangling alliances. The Russo-Japanese War strained Anglo-French relations and caused a revolution in Russia, but German bullying in the Moroccan crisis pushed the British and French together once again. In 1908, Austria-Hungary caused another crisis by annexing Bosnia and Herzegovina; the Russian government, weakened by parliamentary disputes, was unable to act.

During the Balkan wars, Austria-Hungary once again showed that it was determined to prevent the creation of a significant southern Slav state. The result was that Bosnian terrorists assassinated the emperor's brother in 1914. The Serbian government was involved in the murder, and Austria soon gave the Serbs a tough ultimatum. Russia, unwilling to be humiliated again by doing nothing, decided to support the Serbs, whereas Germany promised to support Austria-Hungary. Uncertain of French neutrality, the Germans decided to attack France, but did so by violating Belgian neutrality, which Britain was treaty-bound to uphold. Thus most of the major European states drifted into a war that none of them really wanted, many thought was inevitable, and none tried very hard to prevent.

Vocabulary

charisma — A personality and leadership quality that inspires loyalty and popular support.

gramophone — An early trademark for the phonograph; now a generic term for it.

hysteria — An emotional illness characterized by irrational fear and excitability; the condition was thought to be exclusive to women until Freud observed otherwise.

libido — Primitive sexual urges.

neurotic — Emotionally unstable, obsessive.

paradigm — A working model or pattern that demonstrates an intellectual concept; this is a new meaning for an old word and will not be found in older dictionaries.

pathology — The study of disease, abnormality, or deviation.

pragmatism — A philosophy featuring the practical application of ideas and experience; the belief that the value of an idea is proved by its practical consequences.

pseudoscience — Ideas falsely represented as based on objective proof or scientific research.

psyche — The mind; from the Greek word for spirit or soul.

psychoanalysis — A method of studying the unconscious mind and treating mental illness, pioneered by Freud.

psychotherapy — The treatment of emotional or mental illness—for example, by psychoanalysis.

relativism — The theory that truth and knowledge are not absolute but depend on physical circumstances or individual perspective.

Sorbonne	Formerly the prestigious college of letters and seat of the University of Paris, named for the medieval benefactor who endowed it. In recent decades, the site of University of Paris III and IV.
suffragist	An advocate of women's suffrage.
typology	A classification system based on physical types.
Zionist	An advocate of the creation of a Jewish state in Palestine.

Self-Testing and Review Questions

Identification

After reading Chapter 25, identify and explain the historical significance of each of the following:

1. Leo XIII

2. Entente Cordiale

3. Schlieffen plan

4. Pyotr Stolypin

5. Duma

6. Boxer Rebellion

7. Young Turks

8. *H. M. S. Dreadnought*

9. Dreyfus affair

10. V. I. Lenin

11. soviets

12. Bloody Sunday

13. Sun Yat-Sen

14. Boer War

15. Francesco Crispi

16. Millicent Garrett Fawcett

17. Alfred Nobel

18. secessions

19. expressionism

20. $E = mc^2$

21. Apollonian and Dionysian

22. William Butler Yeats

23. cubism

24. Alfred Binet

25. Marie Curie

26. *Degeneration*

27. ego, id, and superego

28. Bernard Berenson

29. Karl Kautsky

30. quantum theory

Chronology

Identify the events or issues associated with the following dates. Most of the dates are significant for more than one reason. After you finish, answer the questions that follow.

1894

1895

1898

1900

1902

1904

1905

1908

1911

1912

1913

1914

1. Construct a chronology of international crises from the 1890s until 1914. Which countries seem to be trying to avoid war? Which seem inclined to disregard the danger?

2. Do the avant-garde works of art and music created a century ago seem old-fashioned? up-to-date? still bizarre? Why?

Matching Exercises

In each set, match the terms on the left with those on the right.

Set A

____ 1. *The Protestant Ethic and the Spirit of Capitalism*

____ 2. *Reflections on Violence*

____ 3. *Sexual Inversion*

____ 4. *The Interpretation of Dreams*

____ 5. *The Jewish State*

____ 6. *Lay Down Your Arms*

a. Havelock Ellis
b. Bertha von Suttner
c. Theodor Herzl
d. Sigmund Freud
e. Max Weber
f. Georges Sorel

Set B

____ 1. Isadora Duncan

____ 2. Susan B. Anthony

____ 3. Henriette Caillaux

____ 4. Sigrid Unset

____ 5. Emmeline Pankhurst

____ 6. Maria Montessori

____ 7. Maud Gonne

a. author of *Jenny*
b. militant British suffragist
c. famous educator
d. Irish nationalist
e. pioneer of modern dance
f. American suffragist
g. defendant in a lurid murder trial

Set C

____ 1. Sarajevo

____ 2. Adowa

____ 3. Algeciras

____ 4. Jameson raid

____ 5. Agadir

____ 6. Fashoda

a. an incident that led to the Boer War
b. a confrontation between France and Britain on the Nile
c. a confrontation between France and Germany in Morocco
d. site of an assassination that led to the First World War
e. an Italian military defeat in Ethiopia
f. an international conference that disappointed Germany

Set D

____ 1. Henri Matisse

____ 2. Paul Cézanne

____ 3. Pablo Picasso

____ 4. Gustav Klimt

____ 5. Edvard Munch

____ 6. Wassily Kandinsky

a. *Boy in a Red Vest*
b. *Les Demoiselles d'Avignon*
c. *The Scream*
d. the Blue Rider exhibit in Munich
e. Viennese painter
f. a founder of fauvism

Set E

____ 1. Bildung

____ 2. Sinn Fein

____ 3. Jugendstil

____ 4. élan vital

____ 5. *trasformismo*

a. the art nouveau in German lands

b. the political strategy of Giovanni Giolitti

c. a philosophical concept of Henri Bergson

d. an Irish political movement

e. character through education

Set F

____ 1. Richard Strauss

____ 2. Igor Stravinsky

____ 3. Arnold Schoenberg

____ 4. Béla Bartók

____ 5. Vaslav Nijinsky

____ 6. Oskar Kokoschka

a. composer of *The Rite of Spring*

b. composer of *Salome* and *Elektra*

c. famous dancer, choreographer of *The Rite of Spring*

d. Viennese expressionist painter of *Bride of the Wind*

e. author of *The Theory of Music*

f. studied Hungarian folk music and dissonant harmonies

Multiple-Choice Questions

1. Which of the following is the correct chronological order of these events?
   a. Sino-Japanese War, Balkan Wars, Boer War, Russo-Japanese War, Spanish-American War
   b. Sino-Japanese War, Boer War, Russo-Japanese War, Spanish-American War, Balkan Wars
   c. Sino-Japanese War, Spanish-American War, Boer War, Russo-Japanese War, Balkan Wars
   d. Sino-Japanese War, Spanish-American War, Russo-Japanese War, Boer War, Balkan Wars

2. "God is dead," according to
   a. William Butler Yeats.
   b. Albert Einstein.
   c. Friedrich Nietzsche.
   d. Gabriele D'Annunzio.

3. Nicholas II found it easiest to deal with
   a. Octobrists.
   b. Kadets.
   c. Bolsheviks.
   d. Social Democrats.

4. Zola's famous article "J'Accuse!" was written in defense of
   a. Alfred von Tirpitz.
   b. Alfred Dreyfus.
   c. Alfred Nobel.
   d. Alfred Binet.

5. The famous French leader who helped organize a unified socialist party was
   a. Georges Braque.
   b. Georges Sorel.
   c. Raymond Poincaré.
   d. Jean Jaurès.

6. The mayor of Vienna whose rabid antisemitism poisoned Austrian politics was
   a. Karl Lueger.
   b. Gabriele Münter.
   c. Franz Kafka.
   d. Gustav Mahler.

7. Kaiser William II was remembered for all of these except:
   a. rebuilding the city of Berlin into a modern metropolis.
   b. engaging in an expensive and provocative arms race with Great Britain.
   c. implementing a foreign policy that closely followed the strategies of Otto von Bismarck.
   d. encouraging Austria-Hungary to deal firmly with Serbia in 1914.

8. The scientist famous for his experiments on conditioned behavior was
   a. Antoine Becquerel.   c. William James.
   b. Ivan Pavlov.   d. Alfred Binet.

9. The Slavs of the Habsburg Empire were especially outraged by
   a. reformism.   c. secessions.
   b. eugenics.   d. Magyarizing.

10. The famous writer Oscar Wilde was imprisoned for
    a. homosexual acts.   c. anarchist plots.
    b. Irish activism.   d. antisemitism.

Essay Questions

Using material from this and previous chapters, write an essay on each of the following topics. When appropriate, cite dates and present detailed examples to support your arguments.

1. The impressionists had struggled against the art establishment to obtain recognition; by the turn of the century, they had *become* the art establishment. How did this development encourage avant-garde movements in art and music in the new century? How does an artist (or composer) obtain recognition in modern mass culture? Give numerous examples from the text.

2. The "starving artist"—that is, the artist whose ideas are unappreciated and unrewarded—is a very different sort from the skilled medieval craftsman whose guild controlled supply and fixed prices or the baroque musician who received patronage from an aristocratic court. How do artists and composers of the modern age earn money? How has this change affected the art they create?

3. To what extent was each of the principal participants in the First World War responsible for its outbreak?

4. Max Weber gave Protestant values the credit for the development of capitalism in Europe. What economic and geographic facts can you present to refute his argument?

5. Argue for or against the following statement: The rise of irrational and antiscientific philosophical schools in the modern world was a reaction to the triumph of science in much the same way that nonrealistic art flourished after the rise of photography.

6. How did nationalism and racist theories contribute to the spread of antisemitism? What other factors might have been involved?

Skill Building: Maps

A. *Locate the following regions on the map of North Africa. Why was each significant in the present chapter?*

   a. Egypt

   b. Tripoli

   c. Algeria

   d. French West Africa

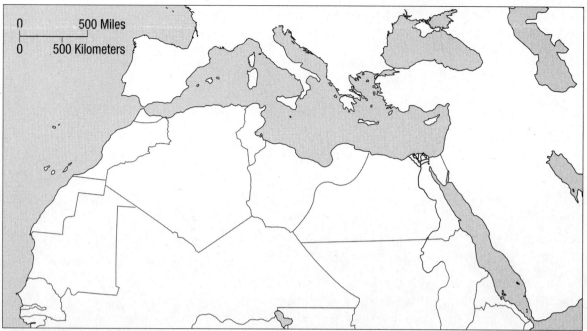

North Africa in 1914

    e. Anglo-Egyptian Sudan

    f. Morocco

1. By the outbreak of the First World War, the entire Mediterranean coast of Africa was controlled by European states. Which state(s) controlled Morocco? Algeria? Tunisia? Tripoli? Egypt? Color the map to show the various colonial powers. Why did European nations compete to control Africa?

B. *Locate the following regions on the map of the Balkans. Why was each significant in the present chapter?*

    a. Bosnia-Herzegovina

    b. Montenegro

    c. Serbia

    d. Greece

    e. Romania

    f. Bulgaria

    g. Ottoman Empire

    h. Albania

    i. Macedonia

The Balkans in the Early Twentieth Century

    j. Novi Bazar

    k. Sarajevo

1. Which Balkan states were clients of Russia? of the Ottoman Empire? of Austria-Hungary?
2. Why did these allegiances make a difference in the years leading up to World War I?

C. *Locate the following regions on the map of east Asia. Why was each significant in the present chapter?*

    a. Vladivostok

    b. Korea

    c. Port Arthur

    d. Philippines

    e. Japan

    f. Manchuria

    g. Chinese Empire

    h. Russian Empire

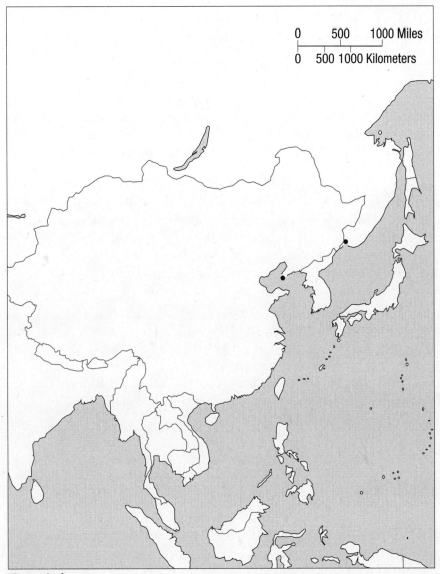

East Asia

1. Why was control of Port Arthur contested by China, Japan, and Russia?
2. Mark the route of the Trans-Siberian Railway. What geographical handicaps did Russia suffer in the Russo-Japanese War? What role did the railway play?

Enrichment Exercise

The film *Potemkin*, sometimes called *The Battleship Potemkin* (1925), was the masterpiece of Russian director Sergei Eisenstein and a landmark in the history of cinema. It dramatizes the Revolution of 1905, the brutality of the tsarist troops at Odessa, and the naval mutiny. Although the film was obviously intended as propaganda, the sets, costumes, and emotions are undeniably authentic. Prior to this work, most directors had used a fixed camera aimed at a stage; Eisenstein's use of closeups, montages, and other devices was revolutionary and even controversial, and helped to liberate cinematography as a new art form. After viewing *Potemkin*, write an essay about the experience. Was the propaganda effective, and why?

Document Analysis

DOCUMENT 1

Art and Anarchy

Some modern artists explicitly rejected middle-class values and the stiff manners of high society. Instead they turned to peasants, the working class, and poor people for inspiration. Several artists found working-class politics attractive, and as the playwright and artist Wassily Kandinsky explained, a concept such as anarchism could be translated into artistic terms.

> "Anarchy" is what many call the current state of painting. The same word is also used here and there to characterize the present state of music. People falsely use the term to denote planless disruption and disorder. Anarchy is really methodicalness and order, which is not established through external and ulti- mately futile force, but through a *sensation of the good.* In other words, limits are also established here, but these limits must be called *internal* and they will replace the external ones.

Source: Wassily Kandinsky, quoted in Peter Jelavich, *Munich and Theatrical Modernism: Politics, Playwriting, and Performance, 1890–1914* (Harvard University Press, 1985), pp. 231–232.

Questions

1. Does Kandinsky's definition of anarchy agree with any that you have learned from this text or elsewhere? Does Kandinsky believe explanations of art must be rational?
2. To whom are his words ultimately addressed?

DOCUMENT 2

Suffragists Turn Militant

When founded in 1903, the Women's Social and Political Union differentiated itself from other women's groups by its militant tactics. Emmeline Pankhurst explains why this organization used such extreme methods to get attention.

> The contention of the old-fashioned suffragists, and of the politicians as well, has always been that an educated public opinion will ultimately give votes to women without any great force being exerted in behalf of the reform. . . . In the year 1906 there was an immensely large public opinion in favor of woman suf- frage. But what good did that do the cause?
>
> From the very first . . . we made the public aware of the woman suffrage movement as it had never been before. . . . We threw away all our conventional notions of what was "ladylike" and "good form," and we applied to our meth- ods the one test question, Will it help? Just as the [Salvation Army] took religion to the street crowds in such fashion that the church people were horrified, so we took suffrage to the general public in a manner that amazed and scandalised the other suffragists. . . .
>
> Women have concealed themselves for thirty-six hours in dangerous posi- tions, under the platforms, in the organs, wherever they could get a vantage point. They waited starving in the cold, sometimes on the roof exposed to a win- ter's night, just to get a chance of saying in the course of a Cabinet Minister's

speech, "When is the Liberal Government going to put its promises into practice?"

Source: Emmeline Pankhurst, *Mrs. Pankhurst's Own Story* (Hearst's International Library, 1914), pp. 61, 62, 235.

Question

1. How are Pankhurst's tactics related to those of Kandinsky? How are their rationales similar?

DOCUMENT 3

The Student Response to Bloody Sunday

Tsarist Russia was considered immune to revolution, so Bloody Sunday was a shock to people such as W. S. Woytinsky, a young student. Returning from a trip to Italy with his father, he rushed to observe university reaction to the massacre in St. Petersburg.

> I had an uneasy feeling of having deserted my real world while I wandered in a strange land in bygone centuries. I left Florence on the first morning train.
>
> A general meeting of students had been called to take a stand on the massacre of January 9. . . . All the speakers . . . called for strikes in all Russian universities, institutes, and colleges. Their arguments were moral and political: We cannot study when the soil under our feet is soaked with blood. . . . We must show the workers and peasants that the students are on their side.
>
> Behind the speaker's desk hung a full-length portrait of the Tsar. . . . A pole rose to the top of the painting and tore the canvas in two. "Away with the Tsar!" roared the crowd. Bystanders rushed to the portrait and tore off pieces of the canvas. I did my part and emerged with a piece [of] at least two square feet.
>
> The crowd, in high spirits, was moving toward the door when a young man addressed me in broken Russian. "Pardon, but could I see your piece? Oh, it looks fine. Must be from a sleeve or the trousers. I have two pieces but they are not worth much—just drapery. . . . Would you kindly give me yours? This is for a New York paper."

Source: W. S. Woytinsky, *Stormy Passage: A Personal History Through Two Russian Revolutions to Democracy and Freedom, 1905–1960* (Vanguard, 1961), pp. 11–12.

Questions

1. Woytinsky, repulsed by the violent repression of Bloody Sunday, comes to sympathize with the revolutionaries and oppose the tsar. What tactics does this meeting suggest for future revolutionary groups? Has Emmeline Pankhurst thought of this?
2. Why are students, usually members of the privileged classes, often drawn to such causes?

DOCUMENT 4

The Austrian Ultimatum

The Austrian government waited until July 23 to send Serbia an ultimatum after the June 28 assassination. This abridged version of the ultimatum shows how harshly the Dual Monarchy could treat small nations and its own minorities. Austrian officials deliberately framed the ultimatum to start a war, because they hardly expected to Serbs to agree. In fact, Serbia accepted most of the conditions and only balked at the intervention of Austrian officials (no. 5), which would have meant a dilution of Serbian sovereignty.

> The Royal Serbian Government shall undertake:
> 1. To suppress any publication which incites hatred and contempt of the Austro-Hungarian Monarchy.
> 2. To dissolve immediately the society styled "Narodna Odbrana."
> 3. To eliminate without delay from public instruction in Serbia everything that serves to foment propaganda against Austria-Hungary.
> 4. To remove from the military service, and from the administration in general, all officers and functionaries guilty of propaganda against the Austro-Hungarian Monarchy.
> 5. To accept the collaboration in Serbia of representatives of the Austro-Hungarian Government for the suppression of the subversive movement directed against the territorial integrity of the Monarchy.
> 6. To take judicial proceedings against accessories to the plot of the 28th of June; delegates of the Austro-Hungarian Government will take part in the investigation relating thereto.
> 7. To proceed without delay to the arrest of Major Voija Tankositch.
> 8. To prevent by effective measures the cooperation of the Serbian authorities in the illicit traffic in arms across the frontier.
> 9. To furnish the Imperial and Royal Government with explanations regarding the unjustifiable utterances of high Serbian officials.
> 10. To notify the Imperial and Royal Government without delay of the execution of the measures comprised under the preceding heads.
>
> The Austro-Hungarian Government expects the reply at the latest by 5 o'clock on Saturday evening the 25th of July.

Source: Abridged from Charles F. Horne, ed., *Source Records of the Great War* (National Alumni, 1923), 1:288–289.

Questions

1. Consider that the elderly Archduke Franz Ferdinand and his wife were brutally murdered, that he was the brother of the emperor and sole heir of the Habsburg dynasty, and that the weapon used in the assassination had been supplied to the Bosnian terrorists by the Serbian government. Did the Austrian government have a casus belli—that is, justification for a declaration of war? If you had been an Austrian and a patriot, would you have considered the ultimatum an unwarranted provocation?

2. If Lee Harvey Oswald had been proven to be an agent of the Cuban government in the assassination of Kennedy, what would the average American have considered an appropriate response to Cuba?

CHAPTER
26

War, Revolution, and Reconstruction, 1914–1929

Chapter Outline

NIGHTMARES FROM THE PAST, BOLD VISIONS OF THE FUTURE
Disillusionment and Dreams in the Arts
The Bolsheviks in Power
Fascism on the March

Chapter Summary

The initial German offensive of the war bypassed French defensive systems along the Franco-German border, and swept instead through Belgium and then into France. But the Germans failed to capture Paris because of stubborn Belgian and French resistance. Both sides, unwilling to relinquish territory, settled into fortified fronts that would move little during the next four years. The Russian offensive similarly stalled in the east. German battleships, constructed during the bitter arms race of the previous decade, proved unsuccessful against the British navy, and the Germans were forced to rely on submarines to harass the Allied and neutral shipping on which Britain depended. The war expanded when Japan and Italy joined the Allies and the Ottoman Empire and Bulgaria joined Germany and the other Central Powers. The costs of the war mounted as literally millions of casualties were incurred by both sides, and the entire economies of the belligerents were organized to contribute to the cause. Citizens were called upon to put aside social and political differences, such as labor disputes, and to contribute selflessly to the struggle for national survival. Propaganda demonized the enemy and declared the war a sacred cause.

Civilian suffering, mounting casualties, and incompetent leadership on both sides led to revolts. The French army and German navy experienced mutinies, and the Irish took advantage of the British involvement in the war to stage an ill-fated rebellion against British rule. More significantly, in 1917 the March Revolution in Russia swept away the tsar and his centuries-old dynasty. A Provisional Government was established to deal with the war as well as the competing political and economic factions in Russia that had been frustrated by decades of neglect. At that point, the Bolshevik leader Lenin was shipped into Russia by the Germans, who correctly guessed that he was capable of causing trouble in the enemy camp. After Lenin gained widespread support by promising to end the war, transfer power to the soviets, and redistribute land, his Bolsheviks overthrew the Provisional Government and made him dictator in November 1917. He promptly pulled Russia out of the war, ceding a third of European Russia to Germany in return for peace.

By 1918 the military situation had changed drastically. The Russians had abandoned the Eastern Front, the Austro-Hungarian Empire had virtually collapsed, German industry was exhausted, American troops were arriving on the Western Front, and new weapons, especially tanks, were breaking the stalemate of trench warfare. The failure of a last desperate German offensive in the summer turned the momentum against the Central Powers. The kaiser, with whom the Allies refused to negotiate, was forced to abdicate so that an armistice could be arranged. The fighting ended on November 11, 1918.

In 1919, while diplomats met in various Paris suburbs to conclude the terms of peace, civil war raged in Russia, and Lenin called for world revolution. Convinced that the European war had broken the back of capitalism, workers in the many lands shocked by defeat raised red flags and proclaimed communist regimes. In Germany a parliamentary republic was proclaimed at Weimar; the left-wing radicals were defeated in Berlin and Munich, and a right-wing military coup was foiled by a general strike.

In Paris, diplomats adopted many of Wilson's idealistic Fourteen Points, but only after heated debate. They created a League of Nations, but left a number of important decisions to be decided by the new organization itself. They generally agreed to the nationalist demands of central and southern Europeans, creating new states from the former Austrian, Ottoman, and

Russian empires. At Versailles, where the peace with Germany was signed, it was agreed that Germany would pay reparations to France, Belgium, and Britain. (Germans were told by demagogic leaders that they had not lost the war and had been betrayed into accepting this humiliation—a lie, widely believed, that helped the rise of Nazism.) The former colonies and possessions of the German and Ottoman empires were to be governed as mandates of Britain, France, and Japan. Deprived of these colonies and saddled with enormous debts, the Weimar Republic would suffer economic problems throughout the 1920s.

Lenin, whose untimely exit from the war made him unwelcome at Versailles, used the military secret police to crush his enemies in Russia. He was also able to win back a number of the territories he had ceded to Germany. The Bolsheviks controlled an increasingly centralized government. The peasants, who had been driven to desperation by wartime confiscations, supported the new regime because it restored free trade in produce and consumer goods. The new communist state made a number of reforms, notably in education, medical care, and pensions; it legalized birth control and abortion; and it encouraged the arts. Intellectuals debated the extent to which the arts should serve the state and the audiences to whom they were directed. This era came to an end with Lenin's death in 1924. The power struggle that followed was won after a few years by Stalin, under whom Russia became increasingly totalitarian. Dictatorships also sprang up in Poland, Hungary, and Italy, but these were generally anticommunist and nationalistic, fed by postwar frustration, economic hardship, and fear of socialism.

During the 1920s, new consumer products and new industrial concepts, such as scientific management, stimulated all western economies. The roles and behavior expected of women changed, and the relationships between the sexes were the subject of both scholarly and popular studies. New media, film and radio, helped spread a universal culture of automobiles, electric appliances, off-the-rack fashions, and American jazz. Many intellectuals and artists, disillusioned by the costly war that had failed to fulfill its promises, remained skeptical or darkly described a totalitarian future that would engulf the whole world. Others celebrated the promise of technology or tried to create new art and literature that reflected the new age.

Vocabulary

belle époque	Literally "the beautiful era," the nostalgic term for the period of European history immediately preceding the First World War.
draconian	Severe; the word refers to the harsh law code of the ancient Athenian statesman Draco.
dystopian	The opposite of utopian. If a utopia is an ideal society, a dystopia is the worst possible society.
en masse	In a group.
Great War	The 1914–1918 war that involved all of Europe and some other nations. From 1914 to 1939, what we today call World War I was called the Great War.
jazz	Popular music of African-American origin that became the rage in Europe after the First World War.
mandate	In this context, a commission by the League of Nations to a member nation authorizing it to govern one of the former territories or colonies of the states defeated in the world war; a territory or colony so governed.
normalcy	Normality; the word *normalcy* was coined by Warren Harding in his presidential campaign of 1920 to indicate his intention to return the country to prewar conditions.

propaganda	Allegations made to further one's cause or to undermine someone else's.
putsch	The German word for coup, an attempt to seize control of the government.
reparations	Payments made to repair damage one has caused.

Self-Testing and Review Questions

Identification

After reading Chapter 26, identify and explain the historical significance of each of the following:

1. Battle of Jutland

2. Battle of Verdun

3. *union sacrée*

4. National Service Act

5. Zimmerwald movement

6. Grigori Rasputin

7. April Theses

8. Georges Clémenceau

9. Freikorps

10. Weimar Republic

11. Black and Tans

12. War Communism

13. Theodor van de Velde

14. David Lloyd George

15. war-guilt clause

16. League of Nations

17. Little Entente

18. *Sturmabteilung*

19. Beer Hall Putsch

20. Dail Eireann

21. *Metropolis*

22. dada

23. Green Armies

24. Zhenotdel

25. Comintern

26. March on Rome

27. Worker Opposition

28. Treaty of Rapallo

29. Lateran Agreement

30. Cheka

Chronology

Identify the events or issues associated with each of the following dates. Several of these dates may be significant for more than one reason. After you finish, answer the questions that follow.

1914

1916

1917

1918

1919

1922

1924

1926

1929

1. When was the *Lusitania* sunk? When did the United States enter the war? What does the chronology indicate about the common belief that the former caused the latter?

2. How might the March Revolution in Russia have contributed to the American declaration of war? How did the November Revolution and the Treaty of Brest-Litovsk affect the Allies?

Matching Exercises

In each set, match the terms on the left with those on the right.

Set A

____ 1. Sergei Eisenstein
____ 2. Vladimir Mayakovsky
____ 3. Felix Dzerzhinsky
____ 4. Alexander Kerensky
____ 5. Leon Trotsky

a. leader overthrown by Lenin
b. leader of the secret police
c. leader of the Red Army
d. Soviet filmmaker
e. Soviet poet

Set B

____ 1. Jozef Pilsudski
____ 2. Béla Kun
____ 3. Miklós Horthy
____ 4. Eduard Beneš
____ 5. Georg Grosz

a. angry expressionist artist
b. Polish dictator
c. Czech nationalist
d. Hungarian communist dictator
e. Hungarian nationalist dictator

Set C

____ 1. *All Quiet on the Western Front*
____ 2. *The Trail, The Castle*
____ 3. *Ulysses*
____ 4. *Remembrance of Things Past*
____ 5. *Orlando, Mrs. Dalloway*
____ 6. *The Wasteland,* "The Hollow Men"

a. T. S. Eliot
b. Virginia Woolf
c. Erich Maria Remarque
d. Franz Kafka
e. Marcel Proust
f. James Joyce

Set D

____ 1. Karl Liebknecht
____ 2. Paul von Hindenburg
____ 3. Walter Rathenau
____ 4. Friedrich Ebert
____ 5. T. von Bethmann-Hollweg

a. wartime foreign minister of Germany
b. wartime chancellor of Germany
c. German commander on the Western Front
d. Spartacist leader
e. leader of the Weimar Republic

Set E

____ 1. Rosa Luxemburg
____ 2. Kaethe Kollwitz
____ 3. Alexandra Kollontai
____ 4. Nadezhda Krupskaya

a. anarchist and revolutionary
b. pacifist artist
c. Soviet novelist and commissar
d. Spartacist leader

Multiple-Choice Questions

1. The Second International
   a. vigorously opposed the war as a capitalist plot against the workers.
   b. wavered in its opposition to the war, to the disgust of Lenin.
   c. supported the war, which it believed created new opportunities for revolution.
   d. was called on by Lenin in 1919 to be an agent of world revolution.

2. The New Economic Policy in Russia was to
    a. revive agriculture by permitting local free markets.
    b. supply the Red Army by brutal confiscations and requisitions in the countryside.
    c. build a new heavy industry infrastructure in five years.
    d. crush the last vestiges of petty-bourgeois capitalism and profiteering.

3. Which is the correct chronological order of these events?
    a. Verdun, Marne, *Lusitania,* Caporetto
    b. Marne, *Lusitania,* Verdun, Caporetto
    c. Caporetto, Marne, Verdun, *Lusitania*
    d. Marne, Verdun, Caporetto, *Lusitania*

4. The Bloomsbury Group consisted of
    a. an antiwar movement.
    b. unconventional writers.
    c. avant-garde painters.
    d. museum curators.

5. The Bauhaus movement consisted of
    a. unconventional writers, led by Ludwig Hilbersheimer.
    b. avant-garde painters, led by Hugo Stinnes.
    c. functionalist architects, led by Walter Gropius.
    d. right-wing antisemites, led by Adolf Hitler.

6. Erich Ludendorff was
    a. a supporter of the Kapp Putsch and other antirepublican causes in postwar Germany.
    b. vilified by antisemites for his handling of the German economy.
    c. a Spartacist leader, murdered while in government custody.
    d. the creator of lurid pacifist paintings in the expressionist style.

7. The Easter Rebellion
    a. overthrew the tsar and briefly brought representative government to Russia.
    b. overthrew the Provisional Government as a result of Lenin's promises to the workers.
    c. almost overthrew the Weimar Republic but failed to gain popular support.
    d. tried to overthrow British rule in Ireland but was crushed by the military.

8. Germany was granted a seat in the League of Nations by the
    a. Treaty of Rapallo.
    b. Lateran Agreement.
    c. Treaty of Locarno.
    d. Treaty of the Trianon.

9. During the Great War, combat typically involved
    a. artillery bombardment, poison-gas attacks, life in trenches.
    b. hand-to-hand combat, cavalry charges, airplane dogfights.
    c. mechanized armies penetrating hundreds of miles into enemy territory.
    d. all of the above.

10. Mussolini
    a. negotiated a reconciliation between the Italian state and the pope.
    b. overthrew Victor Emmanuel III and created a fascist dictatorship.
    c. integrated women into combat units of the army.
    d. reached a compromise with the socialist opposition.

Essay Questions

Using material from this and previous chapters, write an essay on each of the following topics. When appropriate, include dates and cite detailed examples to support your arguments.

1. How did the new Soviet state compare to the societies projected by socialist leaders of the nineteenth century? In what ways was the new Soviet state similar to the tsarist regimes of the past?

2. Given Germany's unprovoked attacks on Belgium and France, the destruction in those countries during four years of war, and Germany's prolonging of the war in the hope of territorial gain, was Article 231 unreasonable? What arguments could be made that it was?

3. What historical experiences made it so difficult for central and eastern European states to embrace democracy and parliamentary rule?

4. The Great War wasn't really the first "world war," because previous wars, especially those of the late eighteenth and early nineteenth century, had been global in scope. What factors distinguished this war from other wars and made it one of the great turning points in world history?

5. What had each of the victors hoped to gain from the war? What happened in the negotiations? How successful were they?

Skill Building: Maps

A. *On the map of the Western Front, locate the following:*

  a. Belgium

  b. Liège

  c. Marne River

  d. Artois

  e. Germany

  f. Luxembourg

  g. Ypres

  h. Paris

  i. Verdun

  j. France

  k. French/German border

1. One of the reasons the French suffered heavy casualties at places such as Verdun was the stubborn determination of the high command to yield not even one yard of French soil to the enemy. What historical experiences probably caused this inflexible and disastrous policy?

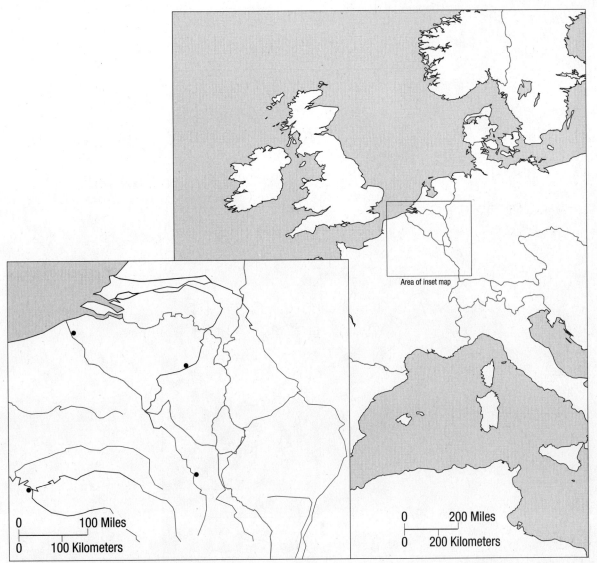

Area of inset map

0   100 Miles

0   100 Kilometers

0   200 Miles

0   200 Kilometers

World War I: The Western Front

2. How much of the war was fought on French soil? on German soil? Why would some German demagogues later proclaim that Germany had never lost the war but had been betrayed by her leaders?

B. On the map of Europe in the 1920s, locate the following:

   a. France

   b. Italy

   c. Czechoslovakia

   d. Romania

   e. Lithuania

   f. Estonia

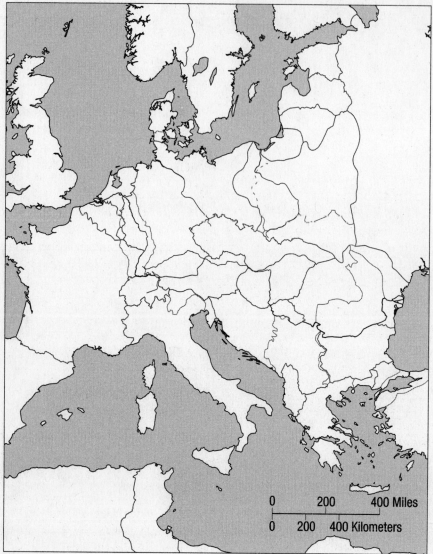

Europe in the 1920s

g. Germany

h. Austria

i. Hungary

j. Yugoslavia

k. Latvia

l. Poland

m. Turkey

1. On the map, shade in the territories that had belonged to Germany in the prewar period. German anger over the loss of so many territories would lead to another world war. The Austrian empire suffered even greater losses but accepted them. Why?

2. Notice the strip of land that extended from Poland to the Baltic Sea, separating the extreme eastern portion of Germany from the rest of the state. Why was this done? How do you suppose the Germans felt about this?

Enrichment Exercises

1. The idealism of the prewar Marxists, the exhilaration they felt during the November Revolution in Russia, and their subsequent disillusionment are all brilliantly captured in Warren Beatty's three-hour, award-winning film *Reds* (1981). The film tells the story of the left-wing American journalist John Reed, whose eyewitness account of the Revolution, *Ten Days That Shook the World,* became the basis for Eisenstein's 1927 film of the same name. After reading Reed's book or viewing *Reds,* write an essay explaining the attraction that communism held for Reed and his friends. (Both films are available on videotape.)

2. Remarque's antiwar novel *All Quiet on the Western Front* became the basis of American director Lewis Milestone's controversial film of 1930. This film, made during the first years of talking pictures, was over two hours long, cost over a million dollars, and employed literally thousands of extras; it was also one of the early recipients of academy awards. The film helped turn American public opinion toward isolationism and was a sensation in Germany, where Remarque was forced to leave the country (the film having reached a different audience than the book!). After reading the novel and viewing the film in its uncut version, write an essay relating the experiences of Paul Baumer and his friends. Why did the Nazis consider this film dangerous?

3. The young Ernest Hemingway drew on personal experience in his 1929 novel *A Farewell to Arms,* which told of an American ambulance driver on the Italian front and his ill-fated affair with a British nurse. In 1932, Gary Cooper and Helen Hayes starred in a Hollywood movie of the novel that audiences loved and Hemingway hated. Read the book, see the film, and write an essay about both. How do they differ? Why did American movies become notorious for cashing in on the popularity of a literary work, and then tinkering with the plot? Hemingway is often characterized as glorifying masculinity and macho adventure; from the evidence in this novel, how did he feel about the war?

Document Analysis

DOCUMENT 1

A View from the Front

World War I was laden with experiences—tragic, comic, heroic, resistant—and produced conflicting accounts. Czech author Jaroslav Hasek (1883–1923) took the comic, sarcastic approach in describing his experiences on the Eastern Front under the Habsburgs and then as a Russian prisoner of war. In this selection, a Habsburg general reviews the troops.

> Apparently by way of encouraging the rank and file as a whole, he asked where the young recruit came from, how old he was, and whether he had a watch. The young recruit had a watch, but as he thought that he was going to get another one from the old gentleman, he said he hadn't got one, whereupon the aged general gave a fatuous smile, such as Franz Josef used to put on . . . and

said, "That's fine, that's fine," whereupon he honored a corporal, who was standing near by, asking him whether his wife was well.

"Beg to report, sir," bawled the corporal, "I'm not married."

Whereupon the general, with a patronizing smile, repeated, "That's fine, that's fine."

Then the general, lapsing still further into senile infantility, asked Captain Sagner to show him how the troops number off in twos from the right, and after a while, he heard them yelling, "One—two, one—two, one—two."

The aged general was very fond of this. At home he had two orderlies, and he used to line them up in front of him and make them number off: "One—two, one—two."

Austria had lots of generals like this.

Source: Jaroslav Hasek, *The Good Soldier Schweik*, trans. Paul Selver (Doubleday, 1963), pp. 363–364.

Questions

1. To what extent is Hasek's view of the general colored by his Czech nationalism?

2. How did the bumbling Habsburg rule described here compare to what was to come—decades of Nazi and then Communist oppression?

DOCUMENT 2

The "Fourteen Points"

Woodrow Wilson's plan for peace had global impact because it offered terms on which the Central Powers might be willing to negotiate an end to the war. It also addressed issues that were seen to have caused war in the first place.

1. Open covenants of peace, openly arrived at. Diplomacy shall proceed always frankly and in the public view.

2. Absolute freedom of navigation upon the seas, outside territorial waters.

3. The removal, so far as possible, of all economic barriers and the establishment of an equality of trade conditions.

4. Adequate guarantees given and taken that national armaments will be reduced.

5. A free, open-minded, and absolutely impartial adjustment of all colonial claims. In determining all such questions of sovereignty the interests of the populations concerned must have equal weight with the equitable claims of the Government whose title is to be determined.

6. The evacuation of all Russian territory.

7. Belgium must be evacuated and restored. Without this healing act the whole structure and validity of international law is forever impaired.

8. All French territory should be freed and the invaded portions restored; and the wrong done to France by Prussia in 1871 in the matter of Alsace-Lorraine should be righted.

9. A readjustment of the frontiers of Italy should be effected along clearly recognizable lines of nationality.

10. The peoples of Austria-Hungary, whose place among the nations we wish to see safeguarded and assured, should be accorded the freest opportunity of autonomous development.

11. Rumania, Serbia, and Montenegro should be evacuated; occupied territories restored; Serbia accorded free and secure access to the sea; and international guarantees of the political and economic independence and territorial integrity of the several Balkan states should be entered into.

12. Nationalities which are now under Turkish rule should be assured an unmolested opportunity of autonomous development, and the Dardanelles should be permanently opened as a free passage to the ships and commerce of all nations.

13. An independent Polish state should be erected which should be assured a free and secure access to the sea.

14. A general association of nations must be formed, for the purpose of affording mutual guaranties of political independence and territorial integrity to great and small states alike.

Source: Abridged from Charles F. Horne, ed., *The Great Events of the Great War* (National Alumni, 1920), 6:3–6.

Questions

1. How did Wilson's idealistic goals undermine some of the advantages that would normally belong to the victors?
2. Why does Wilson, in his concern for self-determination for small nations, have nothing to say about Ireland?
3. How might the Treaty of Brest-Litovsk have influenced this document?

DOCUMENT 3

Champion of the New Russian Woman

Socialist doctrine preached that women would gain rights from the mere fact of revolution. Alexandra Kollontai, in contrast, believed that changing women's status would take a special effort, cultural as well as political. Objecting to tighter social control by Bolshevik leaders, she moved out of the mainstream into the revolutionary backwater. She explains herself as follows:

There were differences of opinion in the Party. I resigned from my post as People's Commissar on the ground of total disagreement with the current policy. Little by little I was also relieved of all my other tasks. I again gave lectures and espoused my ideas on "the new woman" and "the new morality." The revolution was in full swing. The struggle was becoming increasingly irreconcilable and bloodier; much of what was happening did not fit in with my outlook. But after all there was still the unfinished task, women's liberation. Women, of course, had received all rights but in practice, of course, they still lived under the old yoke: without authority in family life, enslaved by a thousand menial household chores, bearing the whole burden of maternity, even the material cares, because many women now found life alone as a result of the war and other circumstances.

Source: Alexandra Kollontai, *The Autobiography of a Sexually Emancipated Communist Woman*, trans. Salvator Attanasio (Herder and Herder, 1971), p. 40.

Questions

1. Although many women were involved in the Russian revolution, Kollontai was the only woman on the Bolshevik central committee, the only woman to hold a policy-making position. Does one usually serve a cause better by resigning in protest from such a position or by staying in it?

2. How might the special circumstances of revolutionary Russia have affected Kollontai's decision?

Document 4

A Way of Life

It was difficult for soldiers to leave the front after the experience of war. Here are two extracts from German soldiers' writing that show why the volunteer armies had such appeal.

> I simply can't live without my people. . . . I can't live without my corps. . . . I have no other training, no wife or children, only my men. . . . What place would I have in the world without my soldier's greatcoat; what good would I be in this world without you?

> When blood whirled through the brain and pulsed through the veins as before a longed-for night of love, but far hotter and crazier. . . . The baptism of fire! The air was so charged then with an overwhelming presence of men that every breath was intoxicating, that they could have cried without knowing why. Oh, hearts-of-men, that are capable of this!

Source: Quoted in Klaus Theweleit, *Male Fantasies* (University of Minnesota Press, 1987), 1:60.

Questions

1. The idea that group violence can be exhilarating and even addictive to some people is suggested by recent reports on subjects ranging from urban gangs to soccer hooligans. To most people, however, the same activities are repulsive. What is it that these former soldiers seem to miss? comradeship? responsibility? self-importance? being shot at and shelled? killing? What features of civilian life compared unfavorably with their wartime experiences?

2. Did all countries experience problems with groups of returning veterans? Which countries did? What conditions seem to have led to the creation of groups like the Freikorps?

CHAPTER
27

An Age of Castastrophes, 1929–1945

Chapter Outline

WORLD WAR II

The German Onslaught
War in the Pacific
The Holocaust
Society at War
From Resistance to Allied Victory
Uncertain Victories

Chapter Summary

The economic misery that descended on the West in the Great Depression upset the fragile economic equilibrium of the 1920s. The United States had become a creditor to many European states after the First World War and a major industrial power partly at the expense of European industry. Unemployment drastically affected the industrial classes but left some other classes relatively unhurt, creating political tensions. The depression upset international trade, already complicated by war debts, reparations payments, and tariff barriers. In addition to these problems, imperial powers also had to cope with growing unrest in their colonies.

The Soviet Union, lacking stock markets and the like, was economically isolated from the West, and seemed to outsiders to be immune from business cycles and collapses. In fact, the USSR was undergoing tremendous economic change as its new leader, Stalin, broke with Lenin's version of Marxism. Stalin was determined to transform Russia into a modern industrial state, even though it meant transferring workers from place to place and from job to job. He also wanted to impose central planning on the agricultural system, but this meant putting down opposition from peasants who had prospered under Lenin's New Economic Policy (NEP). Vilifying resisters as "kulaks" or profiteers, Stalin murdered, imprisoned, or relocated millions of peasants. As famine engulfed the country, scarce food was allotted only to those who supported Stalin, and millions died. Political opponents were arrested and potential rivals subjected to show trials. Soviet citizens were encouraged to be patriotic, and women were encouraged to bear children for the state. Even the arts were forced to conform to Stalin's taste or be suppressed.

In Germany, Hitler and his stormtroopers, aided by Nazi sympathizers in government and the courts, provoked public disorder, blamed it on the socialists, and then offered themselves as the only party capable of restoring order and the only alternative to communism. Supported by right-wing businessmen such as Alfred Hugenberg, Hitler's Nazi Party made dramatic electoral gains in 1930 and 1932, winning support in all classes that feared socialism. The record of the Weimar Republic did little to engender grass-roots loyalty. In 1933, Hitler became chancellor of the Republic; a fire in the Reichstag provided the excuse he needed to censor the press and curtail political opposition. He rigged the March elections and then suspended the constitution; thereafter, he was free to implement his programs. Germans were indoctrinated through government propaganda and agencies such as the Hitler Youth. Jews were driven from government jobs and key professions, and Nazis were given preference. The *Sturmabteilung* (SA) and its leaders, now embarrassing and potentially dangerous, were purged.

Hitler used central planning and trade deficits to prime the German economy. He encouraged industry by rebuilding the German military, developing new transportation systems, and carefully regulating labor. His laws against Jews became progressively harsher, denying them citizenship and other civil rights. Many Jews emigrated, forfeiting their possessions; those who remained behind were subjected to escalating mistreatment and even physical attack. Fascism and antisemitism permeated policies throughout eastern Europe; Hitler found admirers in Romania, Hungary, Austria, Bulgaria, and elsewhere.

Other countries did not go to such extremes. In the United States and Great Britain, radical solutions to the depression were generally rejected, and moderate reforms and programs to alleviate suffering were implemented. In France, right-wing organizations plotted against the Third Republic but were foiled by an unusual coalition of moderates and leftists. In the West, the arts, free of state control, were vigorous, irreverent, and often commercialized. The spread of totalitarianism, militarism, and censorship were issues of deep concern in most of the West.

The relative peace of the 1920s was shattered in 1931 when Japan, its government now dominated by its military, invaded China. Events quickly grew worse as the world slid toward another world war. The League of Nations proved unable to restore the peace, because Western members feared another crippling war. Hitler withdrew from the League and began to rebuild the German military in defiance of the Versailles Treaty. In 1935, the Italians, under Mussolini, invaded Ethiopia. In 1936, Hitler occupied the Rhineland. The opportunity to push back a weak German army was fading quickly. The Spanish Civil War (1936–1939) provided both Germany and Italy, now allies, with an opportunity to test their troops in the cause of fascism. In 1938, Hitler annexed Austria and bullied Czechoslovakia; the West tried appeasement. In 1939, Hitler and Stalin signed a peace pact, but both began to shore up their borders. Hitler's invasion of Poland provoked declarations of war by Britain and France.

With shocking ease the German army quickly crushed Poland, Norway, and France in 1939–1940; the British, alone in the West, fought on. In 1941, Hitler invaded Russia, and in December the Japanese attacked the United States naval base at Pearl Harbor, bringing that reluctant country into the war. As Nazi armies rolled through eastern Europe, millions of Jews and others were rounded up and shipped to death camps. In 1942, the U.S. Navy, after some initial defeats, won some important victories in the Pacific and turned the war inexorably against Japan. In 1943, stubborn Soviet resistance turned back the Nazi army in the east, while the Americans and British drove the Germans from North Africa and invaded Italy. In 1944, with the Germans in retreat in the east and the south, the Allies landed in Normandy and liberated France. In 1945, Germany was overrun from three fronts, and Japan's unwillingness to admit defeat was ended by two atomic bombs. The bloodiest war in history was over, but the security of the world was far from settled.

Vocabulary

Aryan — Any member of a nation that speaks an Indo-European language. The Nazis made this word disreputable by using it to describe a pure Germanic race, a concept that was neither biologically nor linguistically sound.

Axis — Originally a nickname for the alliance between Hitler and Mussolini (the "Rome-Berlin Axis"), later used to refer to the entire German-led coalition, including Japan, during World War II.

authoritarian — Demanding automatic obedience and submission.

demagogue — A politician who uses oratorical skill to arouse base emotions and manipulate public opinion. Hitler and Mussolini were demagogues.

fait accompli — An accomplished fact.

fascism — A political ideology stressing extreme nationalism, national unity through obedience to central authority, and the central coordination of industry, labor, and the economy. Fascism is antidemocratic, repressive, and generally militaristic.

Federal Reserve Bank — An agency of the American government set up in 1913 to control the availability of credit and currency.

Führer	Leader; the title Hitler used as head of the Nazi party and later as head of state. He preferred it to titles such as Chancellor, probably because they implied constitutional limitations.
genocide	The extermination of an entire ethnic group; for example, what Hitler tried to accomplish in the Holocaust.
guinea	In Britain, a monetary value equal to 21 shillings (old style), or £1.05 (metric). The prices of British luxury items are often quoted in guineas rather than pounds sterling.
gypsies	An itinerant ethnic group, originally from India, found throughout Europe since the Middle Ages.
kulak	A word for a clenched fist, used by Stalin to describe well-to-do Russian peasants, implying that they were usurers.
Lebensraum	Room to live, or "elbow room," a German expression justifying expansion into eastern Europe.
mesmerized	Hypnotized; derived from Franz Mesmer (1734–1815), a physician who is often (probably incorrectly) thought to have been a pioneer of hypnotism.
NASDAP	The abbreviation of Nationalsozialistische Deutsche Arbeiterpartei (National Socialist German Labor Party), commonly called "Nazis."
Pacific Rim	A 1990s expression for countries of the Far East that border the Pacific.
purge	To clear or rid a body of impurities; therefore, to eliminate disloyal or useless members of a party or government.
swastika	An ancient design adopted by the Nazis as a symbol of the party and of Aryan supremacy.
technocrat	A technician or specialist with managerial authority.
Wehrmacht	The German army.

Self-Testing and Review Questions

Identification

After reading Chapter 27, identify and explain the historical significance of each of the following:

1. phony war

2. Winston Churchill

3. Nuremberg Laws

4. Mohandas K. Gandhi

5. Atatürk

6. kolkhoz

7. Reichstag fire

8. Dachau

9. autobahn

10. Schützstaffel

11. Edward VIII

12. Werner Heisenberg

13. *Quadragesimo Anno*

14. Stalingrad

15. Vidkung Quisling

16. Hideki Tojo

17. Final Solution

18. Five-Year Plan

19. the Hundred Days*

20. Engelbert Dollfuss

21. *Kristallnacht*

22. Atlantic Charter

23. Manhattan Project

24. Condor Legion

25. Munich Conference

Chronology

Identify the events or issues associated with each of the following dates. Several of these dates may be significant for more than one reason. After you finish, answer the questions that follow.

1929

1932

1933

1934

1935

---

* Not to be confused with Napoleon's Hundred Days in 1815.

1937

1938

1939

1941

1943

1944

1945

1. What events mark the increasing campaign of terror against Jews in Germany? When did the Holocaust begin? Was war a cause or a cover for the Holocaust? Discuss.
2. To what extent were American politicians during the Great Depression probably influenced by the radical political and economic solutions being tried in Europe?

Matching Exercises

In each set, match the terms on the left with those on the right.

Set A

____ 1. *Darkness at Noon*   a. Charlie Chaplin
____ 2. *Guernica*   b. Marlene Dietrich
____ 3. *The Magic Mountain*   c. Virginia Woolf
____ 4. *The Three Guineas*   d. Arthur Koestler
____ 5. *The Blue Angel*   e. Thomas Mann
____ 6. *Modern Times*   f. Pablo Picasso

Set B

____ 1. Ernst Roehm   a. Austrian chancellor
____ 2. Heinrich Himmler   b. Swedish hero
____ 3. Kurt Schuschnigg   c. German filmmaker
____ 4. Joseph Goebbels   d. leader of the SA
____ 5. Raoul Wallenberg   e. leader of the SS
____ 6. Fritz Lang   f. Hitler's propaganda chief

Set C

____ 1. *Gleichschaltung*   a. a book by Adolf Hitler
____ 2. *Blitzkrieg*   b. vacations for workers
____ 3. *Anschluss*   c. lightning warfare
____ 4. *Volksgemeinschaft*   d. political conformity for civil servants
____ 5. *Mein Kampf*   e. the people's community
____ 6. *Kraft durch Freude*   f. the annexation of Austria

Set D

___ 1. Mikhail Sholokhov   a. Russian poet whose works were suppressed

___ 2. Sergei Prokofiev   b. Russian novelist, author of *And Quiet Flows the Don*

___ 3. Grigori Zinoviev   c. Russian composer of *Peter and the Wolf*

___ 4. S. A. Stavisky   d. Russian politician and rival of Stalin

___ 5. Anna Akhmatova   e. caused a scandal in France

Set E

___ 1. Neville Chamberlain   a. the Vichy government

___ 2. Léon Blum   b. the Falange

___ 3. Henri-Philippe Pétain   c. the Popular Front

___ 4. Benito Mussolini   d. the Free French

___ 5. Francisco Franco   e. the Pact of Steel

___ 6. Charles de Gaulle   f. "peace in our time"

Multiple-Choice Questions

1. The causes of the global depression of the 1930s did not include
   a. poor harvests and food shortages.
   b. a decline in consumer purchases resulting from poor industrial wages.
   c. the American stock market crash of 1929.
   d. international trade problems, worsened by tariff barriers and reparation payments.

2. The Camelots du Roi and Croix de feu were
   a. parties of the Popular Front.
   b. right-wing political factions.
   c. elite corps of the Free French.
   d. agencies of the resistance.

3. On the Night of the Long Knives,
   a. a group of army officers tried to assassinate Hitler.
   b. Stalin had Kirov, Zinoviev, and Kamenev arrested and Trotsky killed.
   c. Hitler ordered the assassination of Roehm and other Nazi rivals.
   d. Franco and the army rebelled against the republic.

4. Babi Yar was the site of
   a. a labor camp.
   b. a massacre.
   c. a critical battle.
   d. a colonial revolt.

5. The artistic style favored by Stalin was called
   a. communist expressionism.
   b. socialist realism.
   c. bourgeois revisionism.
   d. naturalism.

6. Which is the correct chronological order for the following events?
   a. fall of France, Pearl Harbor, Stalingrad, Normandy, Hiroshima
   b. Pearl Harbor, fall of France, Stalingrad, Normandy, Hiroshima
   c. Pearl Harbor, Stalingrad, fall of France, Hiroshima, Normandy
   d. Stalingrad, Pearl Harbor, fall of France, Normandy, Hiroshima

7. Hitler's political strategy included
   a. taking care to avoid trouble with the law before he took power.
   b. manipulating the public's fear of socialism and public disorder.
   c. expressing respect for human rights and democracy.
   d. presenting himself as well educated, cultured, and a patron of the fine arts.

8. Which of the following was true of the 1930s?
   a. Mussolini, inspired by Hitler's innovations, created a fascist state in Italy and was ostracized.
   b. The United States avoided any sort of government intervention in the economy and attracted many imitators.
   c. Antisemitism, limited to Nazi Germany, prompted strong sanctions from the major Western powers.
   d. The ideological issues of the Spanish Civil War attracted foreign intervention.

9. The Blitz was
   a. Germany's war strategy.
   b. Hitler's public-relations offensive.
   c. the bombing of London.
   d. Operation Barbarossa.

10. The Sudetenland, coveted by Hitler, was located in
    a. Finland.
    b. Yugoslavia.
    c. Czechoslovakia.
    d. Poland.

Essay Questions

Using material from this and previous chapters, write an essay on each of the following topics. When appropriate, include dates and cite examples to support your arguments.

1. Did the Versailles Treaty help cause the Second World War? Why or why not?

2. The apologists for Joseph Stalin argued that his Five-Year Plans and other programs created an industrialized Russia instrumental to the defeat of Hitler's Germany. Discuss his reforms and argue for or against this theory. How important was Russia's role in the defeat of Hitler?

3. Some historians have argued that Hitler was a monster created by western European appeasement in the years preceding the war. Argue for or against this position.

4. How could the Holocaust have been permitted to happen? Trace the rise of totalitarianism and the spread of antisemitism in the years after World War I. Could such a nightmare happen again?

5. Explain the appeal of fascism in Europe between the wars. Why did fascism have special appeal in certain countries and less in others?

Skill Building: Maps

A. Locate the following regions on the map of east Asia and the Pacific. Why was each significant in the present chapter?

   a. Japan

   b. Pearl Harbor

   c. Coral Sea

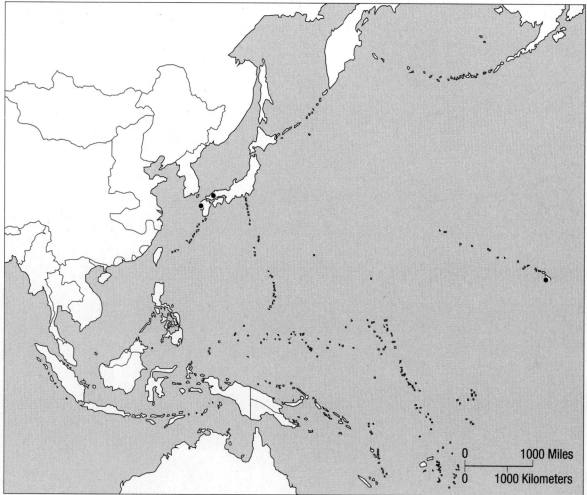

East Asia and the Pacific

d. Philippines

e. Netherlands East Indies

f. Hiroshima

g. Soviet Union

h. Manchuria

i. Midway Island

j. Korea

k. Burma

l. French Indochina

m. Nagasaki

n. China

1. Which countries were occupied by the Japanese? Did the Japanese really believe they could defeat the United States? How and why?

B. *Locate the following on the map of Europe. Why was each significant in the present chapter?*
   a. Weimar

   b. Munich

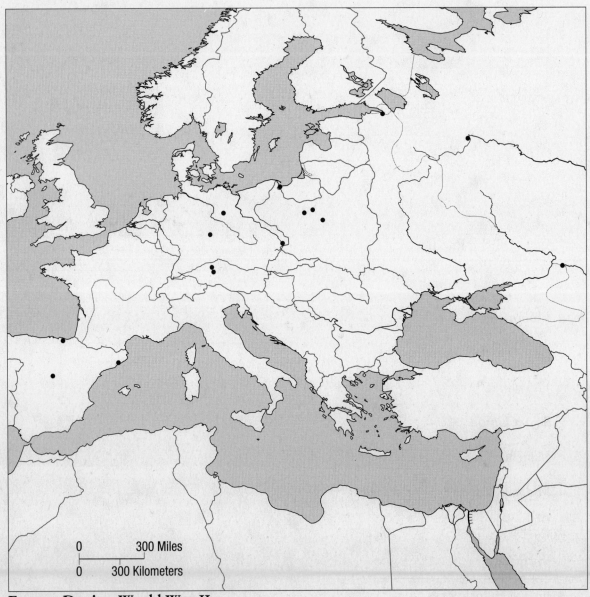

Europe During World War II

c. Barcelona

d. Danzig

e. Rhineland

f. Leningrad

g. Stalingrad

h. Dachau

i. Berlin

j. Madrid

k. Guernica

l. Warsaw

m. Sudenteland

n. Moscow

o. Auschwitz-Birkena

p. Treblinka

q. Suez Canal

r. Transjordan

s. Vichy France

t. Sobibor

u. Palestine

v. Yugoslavia

w. Ukraine

1. Which countries were allied with Hitler during the war? Which remained neutral? Why was Switzerland allowed to remain neutral?

2. How much of Europe was under Nazi occupation at one time or another? Who controlled the greatest amount of territory—Hitler, Napoleon, or Charlemagne?

3. Why were Hitler's extermination camps located where they were?

Enrichment Exercises

1. In *Alexander Nevsky* (1938), Eisenstein made his first film in ten years, this time for Stalin, who was trying to instill a new patriotism into the Russians to replace Lenin's internationalism. The film depicts a thirteenth-century invasion of Russia by Teutonic Knights. The Russians are handsome and peace loving, the Germans monstrous caricatures. Prokofiev's brilliant sound track parodies heavy German romantic music and light Slavic melodies, contributing subtly to the propaganda. The cast was enormous and the battle scenes particularly impressive. View the film, preferably the new version with the sound track re-recorded, and write an essay about the experience. Judging from this film, does war seem to have been inevitable in 1938?

2. The Nazis also produced a superb example of cinema as propaganda in *The Triumph of the Will*, a film about the sixth Nazi Party Congress in Nuremberg in 1934, directed by Leni Reifenstahl, one of the first important women in cinematography. Hitler's ability to captivate a crowd is evident even to those who do not understand German. View this film and write an essay describing Hitler's appeal in 1934 Germany.

3. In the last days of World War II, British author George Orwell published *Animal Farm: A Fairy Story*. This clever tale tells how the animals overthrow an incompetent farmer and take over the farm; they then try to create a utopia of animal solidarity and equality, but instead drift toward totalitarianism. The book is brief and entertaining; there is also an animated film version from 1955, but it is not recommended. Read *Animal Farm* and write a review. Does the plot closely parallel the history of one country? How effective is Orwell's little satire?

Document Analysis

DOCUMENT 1

Republican Relationships

The Spanish Civil War brought not only fighting on the battlefield but also a reexamination of entrenched attitudes in daily life. Among republicans in Madrid or Barcelona the end of monarchy brought a search for egalitarian relationships between men and women. That search intensified when the civil war broke out, although Franco's side promised a return to "traditions." Before he won, however, two different women reported what the civil war was like during sieges and blackouts.

ROSA VEGA, A SCHOOLTEACHER IN MADRID: It was so dark that I often bumped into people in the streets. But never once was I molested or in any way made aware that I was a woman. Before the war there would have been remarks of one sort or another—now that was entirely gone. Women were no longer objects, they were human beings, persons on the same level as men. There were many bad things, no doubt, in the Popular Front zone, but the fact that both sexes were humanly equal was one of the most remarkable social advances of the time.

MARIA SOLANA, A SOCIALIST YOUTH MEMBER: The war bred a new spirit in people, it was amazing. I was often sent round villages on propaganda missions with other party youth and there wouldn't be enough beds. I, the only woman, would sleep in the same bed with two or three youths and nothing would happen—absolutely nothing. There was a new sense of human relationships.

Source: Adapted from Ronald Fraser, *The Blood of Spain. An Oral History of the Spanish Civil War* (Pantheon, 1979), p. 286.

Questions

1. Did Vega really believe that most Spanish men indiscriminately molested women if given the opportunity? Did the absence of molestation prove that sexual equality had been achieved? Was Vega's optimism justified?

2. If Solana were forced into such sleeping arrangements by some natural disaster in royalist Spain, such as an earthquake, would the youths have behaved like animals? Is the male behavior described by these women really remarkable? Could it have been caused by something other than republican virtue?

DOCUMENT 2

Resistance!

After the "Final Solution" went into effect in 1941, Nazis pretended to be deporting Jews for resettlement when in fact they were rounding them up for death camps. Many Jews, however, knowing that the worst awaited them, determined to resist. Here is an excerpt from a Resistance Manifesto published in the Vilnius ghetto in January 1942:

Let us not be led like sheep to the slaughter!

I. *Let us defend ourselves during a deportation!*

For several months now, day and night, thousands and tens of thousands have been torn away from our midst. . . . The illusion still lives within us that they are still alive somewhere, in an undisclosed concentration camp, in a ghetto.

In the face of the next day which arrives with the horror of deportation and murder, the hour has struck to dispel the illusion: There is no way out of the ghetto, except the way of death!

No illusion greater than that our dear ones are alive.

II. *On guard over national honor and dignity*

We work for Germans and Lithuanians. Everyday we come face to face with our employers, the murderers of our brothers. Great the shame and pain, observing the conduct of Jews, stripped of the awareness of human dignity.

Comrades!

Don't give the foe the chance to ridicule you!

When a German ridicules a Jew—don't help him laugh!

Don't play up to your murderers!

Denounce the bootlickers at work!

Denounce the girls who flirt with Gestapo men!

Work slowly, don't speed!

Show solidarity! If misfortune befalls one of you—don't be vile egotists—all of you help him.

Jewish agents of the Gestapo and informers of all sorts walk the streets. If you get hold of one such, sentence him—to be beaten until death!

Source: Excerpted from Lucy S. Dawidowicz, *A Holocaust Reader* (Behrman House, 1976), pp. 334-336.

Question

1. Why is the author of this document experiencing difficulty convincing the Jews of eastern Europe that the Holocaust is taking place?

DOCUMENT 3

Uniforms and Order

Young fascist toughs, from the Blackshirts of Mussolini to the various Nazi groups named in this selection, seemed to love to march about in uniforms. The Great War may partly explain this phenomenon: some of them were veterans, and many of them belonged to the generation that had just missed the war. A love of shiny boots was so characteristic of fascism that the British Parliament passed a law restricting paramilitary uniforms to certain government employees, a law that some believe retarded the growth of fascist movements in Britain. In 1936, one of the contributors to Fodor's popular guidebooks, L. Ráskay, "was struck by the enormous number of different uniforms" he saw when his train entered Nazi Germany. He was hesitant to mention the subject for fear that it might be construed as politically sensitive, but he finally asked a fellow passenger, who was a jeweler.

I learnt that most of the uniforms in Germany have nothing to do with militarism. He himself [the jeweler] . . . was now in the National Socialist Vanguard organisation and often wore uniform once a week. The youths in our compartment who wore brown shirts and jackets were members of the S.A. . . . The members are all in civil callings and only use their free time to work for the Party, which . . . is now synonymous with the State. He pointed out a particularly fine-looking fair man, wearing a . . . black uniform over his brown shirt, indicating that he was a high officer in the S.S. . . . I was not surprised to hear that many other Party organisations wear uniform, as well as the hundred thousand German youths who are now roped in for service. . . . Children are very uniformed as well, the smallest belonging to the so-called "Young People," the bigger ones to the Hitler Youth. The girls also have their uniformed organisation, the B.D.M. (Bund Deutscher Mädel).

[A young English boy, commenting on the difference between the British and the Germans, observed:] "When an English soldier has finished his day's work he takes off his uniform as quickly as possible and gets into his beloved flannel trousers. When, however, a German civilian has finished his work he tears home to change his civilians for a uniform." . . .

This, however, has nothing to do with the militarism of old times—it is a leaning towards voluntary organisation and discipline which to us English seems strange . . . though there is no reason why we should grudge others a pleasure we do not covet ourselves. Especially when a love of uniform is combined with a love of peace, as in the case of my neighbor, the friendly jeweler who declared in every second sentence that no one in Germany desires war.

Source: Eugene Fodor, ed., *1936 . . . On the Continent: The Entertaining Travel Annual* (Fodor's Travel Guides, 1985), pp. 452–454.

Questions

1. The English traveler is trying to be tolerant and not to offend the German; the German is trying to reassure the Englishman, and both are denying that uniforms have anything to do with militarism. Is this an example of self-deception and denial? What similar values seem to have pervaded European relations in the 1930s? Why?

2. The love of uniforms was not restricted to fascists; many young American servicemen were convinced that uniforms were attractive to members of the opposite sex. What other reasons, practical or symbolic, innocent or sinister, might explain people's affection for uniforms during this period?

3. The Versailles Treaty placed legal limitations on the size of the German army; to what extent might the Germans' love of uniforms have been in defiance of this hated treaty?

4. Why do people seem to walk differently when wearing a uniform? Do clothes affect behavior? Does being an anonymous member of a group affect behavior? Could the Uniform Act really have deterred the rise of fascism in Britain?

DOCUMENT 4

The Fate of the Kulaks

Aleksandr Solzhenitsyn (b. 1918) was a young Russian captain who, because of indiscreet letters to a friend, spent eleven years (1945–1957) in a labor camp in Siberia. In 1963, in a period of "de-Stalinization," the Soviet government permitted publication of his stunning One Day in the Life of Ivan Denisovitch, *which depicted the brutal life of prisoners under Stalin. He became a literary celebrity abroad and won the Nobel Prize in 1970, but Stalinism was resurrected in the Soviet Union and his works were again suppressed; in 1974, Solzhenitsyn was forced into exile.* The Gulag Archipelago, *his most important work, is a massive study of the Soviet prison system, together with hundreds of tales of Stalin's atrocities that he collected from victims in the camps; many of the horrors he witnessed personally. Solzhenitsyn speculated that Stalin murdered 15 million Soviet citizens via the purges, collectivization, and brutal relocation of peasants. His tales of enforced starvation and his estimate of the death toll were doubted for years, but with the release of Soviet information since the mid-1980s, his figures no longer seem unreasonable.*

> . . . [T]hey began to haul prisoners in barges . . . during the liquidation of the "kulaks." These rivers [the Northern Dvina, Ob, and Yenisei] flowed straight north, and their barges were potbellied and capacious. . . . [I]t was the only way they could cope with the task of carting all this gray mass from living Russia to the dead North. People were thrown into trough-like holds and lay there in piles or crawled around like crabs in a basket. . . . Sometimes they transported this mass out in the open without any cover, and sometimes they covered it with a big tarpaulin—in order not to look at it, or to guard it better, but certainly not to keep off the rain. The journey in such a barge was no longer prisoner transport, but simply death on the installment plan. Anyway, they gave them hardly anything to eat. Then they tossed them out in the tundra—and there they didn't give them anything at all to eat. They just left them there to die, alone with nature. (I, 578)
>
> [F]or the *special settlements* the Cheka . . . chose places on stony hillsides . . . where it was impossible to dig down to water, and nothing would grow in the soil. . . . [M]any such special settlements died off to a man. . . . In 1930, [in

Vasyugan,] 10,000 families (60,000–70,000 people as families then went) passed through Tomsk and from there were driven farther, at first on foot . . . although it was winter. . . . (The inhabitants of villages on the route were ordered out afterward to pick up the bodies of adults and children.). . . . [T]hey were marooned on patches of firm ground in the marshes. *No food or tools were left for them.* The roads were impassable, and there was no way to the world outside, except for two brushwood paths. . . . Machine-gunners manned barriers on both paths and let no one through from the death camp. They started dying like flies. Desperate people came out to the barriers begging to be let through, and were shot on the spot. . . . They died off—every one of them. (III, 362–363)

Source: Aleksandr Solzhenitsyn, *The Gulag Archipelago, 1918–1956,* trans. Thomas P. Whitney and Harry Willetts, 6 vols. in three (Harper and Row, 1973–1978).

Questions

1. Stalin reportedly said that "a single death is a tragedy, a million deaths is a statistic." What insight does this statement provide about the totalitarian dictator's fear of articulate and independent thinkers such as Solzhenitsyn?

2. Hitler and Stalin, between them, may have been responsible for the death of 20 million people or more, *not counting war casualties*! How could this have happened? Were they worse than the psychopathic rulers of previous ages, or did they simply have better managerial, bureaucratic, and industrial systems with which to commit mass murder? Did their crimes require an unprecedented level of national support and cooperation?

CHAPTER

28

The Atomic Age, 1945–1962

Chapter Outline

THE RETURN OF PROSPERITY ON THE BRINK OF NUCLEAR WAR
The Welfare State and Conditions of Everyday Life
Angry Young Men and "New Look" Women
Kennedy, Khrushchev, and the Atomic Brink

Chapter Summary

By the spring of 1945, the Soviet armies had pushed into Germany from the east while the Americans and British attacked from the west and south. Hitler refused to admit defeat, so the armies kept advancing until they met at Berlin and occupied the city, and the continent, together. Because much of the continent lay in ruins, without agriculture, industry, transportation, and basic necessities, the occupation would be of long duration. In the Soviet zone, the Russian troops looted, drove citizens to the West, and set up puppet governments. Stalin, for defensive purposes, clearly intended to keep a string of satellite states between the USSR and western Europe. Furthermore, communist guerrillas in Greece, Turkey, and elsewhere, seemed to be trying to expand this buffer zone. As early as 1945, Churchill coined the term "iron curtain" to describe the increasingly hostile frontier between the West and the Russian-occupied East. Cooperation between the erstwhile allies, even when pursuing and punishing Nazi war criminals, became strained.

Truman determined to prevent the violent overthrow of such areas as Greece, Turkey, and Iran by sending military aid. Communists had played an important role in the wartime resistance, and consequently they became a significant force in party politics in such war-torn countries as France and Italy. In 1947, to forestall a popular drift toward communism in the West, his secretary of state, Gen. George C. Marshall, announced a major program of economic aid to rebuild the European economy. Countries accepting this aid would naturally be drawn into the American political orbit, so the Soviets opposed the concept. When Czechoslovakia and Poland tried to join the Marshall Plan, they were crudely prevented, and the Soviets even tried to drive their former allies from their occupation zones in the city of Berlin. The West successfully countered this provocation with the Berlin airlift and created NATO (North Atlantic Treaty Organization); the Soviets "tested" an atomic bomb. By 1950, Europe was divided into two hostile, well-armed camps.

The communist threat was not restricted to Europe. In 1949, Mao Zedong defeated Chiang Kai-shek in the Chinese civil war, but the new People's Republic of China was not recognized by the United Nations, of which Chiang's government had been a charter member. In 1950, the Soviet-supported North Korean regime invaded the U.N.-recognized Republic of Korea. The United Nations authorized a "police action" to roll back the invaders. Meanwhile, in Indochina, communist Viet-Minh battled the French. In 1953 the Korean War ended in stalemate, but soon after, the French were pushed from Indochina.

The bankrupt British and French governments, unable to afford the costs of putting down rebellions in their former colonies, were retreating from the responsibilities of empire. In 1947–1948, for example, the British withdrew from Palestine, India, Pakistan, Burma, and Ceylon. In 1955, having lost Indochina, France determined to resist the independence movement in Algeria. The long and bloody war that followed badly divided the French and brought down the Fourth Republic.

The Cold War placed a strain on the resources of the United States, which bore the main responsibility for the defense of Europe and large parts of Asia. The arms race with the Soviet Union brought industrial growth but also inflation; it inspired technological advances but also incurred enormous public debt. The art and literature of the times were affected by memories of the war and the Holocaust, and by the threat of the atomic bomb. There was no respite from the draft, from security precautions, from spy scares. The fear of communist spies stealing military secrets was based partly on reality, but the dangers were exaggerated by demagogic politicians and exploited in films and popular fiction.

In 1956, Russian tanks crushed a freedom movement in Hungary. The Suez crisis embarrassed the United States, which had been courting the Arab states but needed allies such as France and Britain in Europe. The new Soviet premier, Khrushchev, was a contradictory figure who encouraged criticism of Stalin but not of socialism. He was determined to hold his ground in Germany (the Berlin Wall), and he also tried to gain a foothold in the western hemisphere by placing nuclear missiles in Cuba. U.S. President John F. Kennedy demanded their withdrawal in October 1962, and after several tense days, Khrushchev agreed. A possible nuclear disaster was averted.

Vocabulary

Afrikaners People of Dutch descent who have lived in South Africa since the seventeenth century. They speak a dialect of Dutch called Afrikaans; the Boers spoken of in Chapter 25 were Afrikaners.

collaborators Those who cooperated with the Nazi occupation of their homelands.

cooptation Adopting the arguments of one's political opponents.

GNP Gross national product, the total economic output of a nation.

impasse A deadlock or stalemate.

per capita Per person.

pied noir An inhabitant of Algeria of European (usually French) descent.

police action The Korean War was never formally declared because the North Korean state did not legally exist in the eyes of the United Nations. The term *police action* denied the North Koreans any official acknowledgment and assigned them the status of bandits or pirates.

quagmire A bog; a situation one cannot get out of.

rapprochement Agreement; cordial relations.

Self-Testing and Review Questions

Identification

After reading Chapter 28, identify and explain the historical significance of each of the following:

1. Kielce

2. Treaty of Rome

3. Stanislaw Mikołajczyk

4. Tito

5. Voice of America

6. Council of Europe

7. Bay of Pigs

8. Jackson Pollack

9. apartheid

10. SEATO

11. Dien Bien Phu

12. Golda Meir

13. Rosa Parks

14. *Mater et Magistra*

15. John Foster Dulles

16. Truman Doctrine

17. Nelly Sachs

18. Security Council

19. *Algérie française*

20. Bretton Woods

21. Sputnik

22. Lavrenti Beria

23. Third World

24. Warsaw Pact

25. Fourth Republic

Chronology

Identify the events or issues associated with each of the following dates. Several of these dates may be significant for more than one reason. After you finish, answer the questions that follow.

1945

1947

1948

1949

1950

1952

1954

1956

1960

1961

1962

1. Given the simultaneous communist advances in Europe, Asia, and elsewhere, was the West's suspicion of a world communist conspiracy justified? What other forces could account for these events? Which explanation seemed most likely at the time? What response was appropriate?

2. The Suez and Hungarian crises occurred simultaneously. How was the response to each conditioned by the other? What else that happened that year might have influenced the outcomes?

3. When did the French leave Indochina? When did the Algerian war begin? How did the events in Indochina affect the French response in Algeria?

4. What were the dates of the Berlin Crisis (the airlift)? When was the Berlin Wall built? Note that the two events are separated by twelve years.

Matching Exercises

In each set, match the terms on the left with those on the right.

Set A

____ 1. *Fahrenheit 451*   a. Samuel Beckett
____ 2. *Lucky Jim*   b. Albert Camus
____ 3. *The Stranger*   c. Günter Grass
____ 4. *Waiting for Godot*   d. Kingsley Amis
____ 5. *The Tin Drum*   e. Ray Bradbury

Set B

____ 1. Robert Schuman   a. the Fifth Republic
____ 2. Jean Monnet   b. famous filmmaker
____ 3. Charles de Gaulle   c. existentialist philosopher
____ 4. François Truffaut   d. *The Second Sex*
____ 5. Jean-Paul Sartre   e. a founder of the ECSC
____ 6. Simone de Beauvoir   f. ECSC leader, a founder of the EEC

Set C

____ 1. Jomo Kenyatta   a. India

____ 2. Achmed Sukarno   b. Iran

____ 3. Shah Reza Pahlevi   c. Indonesia

____ 4. Gamal Abdel Nasser   d. Ghana

____ 5. Kwame Nkrumah   e. Kenya

____ 6. Mohandas K. Gandhi   f. Egypt

Set D

____ 1. James Bond novels   a. George Orwell

____ 2. *The Double Helix*   b. James Dean

____ 3. *1984*   c. Marlon Brando

____ 4. *Rebel Without a Cause*   d. Ian Fleming

____ 5. *The Wild One*   e. James Watson

Set E

____ 1. Georgi Malenkov   a. hack scientist, a favorite of Stalin

____ 2. T. D. Lysenko   b. censored the arts for Stalin

____ 3. Boris Pasternak   c. Khrushchev's predecessor

____ 4. Andrei Zhdanov   d. Czech foreign minister, murdered in 1948

____ 5. Wladislaw Gomulka   e. Polish leader in 1956

____ 6. Jan Masaryk   f. author of *Dr. Zhivago*

Multiple-Choice Questions

1. At the Nuremberg trials,
   a. Julius and Ethyl Rosenberg were found guilty of treason.
   b. Lavrenti Beria and other friends of Stalin were purged.
   c. Anna Akhmatova and other opponents of Stalin were purged.
   d. twelve Nazis were sentenced to death for war crimes.

2. The Marshall Plan
   a. created a World Bank and an International Monetary Fund.
   b. divided Germany in two in order to prevent a third world war.
   c. offered massive U.S. economic aid to war-torn Europe.
   d. divided Korea at the 38th parallel.

3. Which of these is in the correct chronological order?
   a. Berlin Crisis (airlift), Korean War, Dien Bien Phu, Suez Crisis, Cuban Missile Crisis
   b. Suez Crisis, Berlin Crisis, Korean War, Cuban Missile Crisis, Dien Bien Phu
   c. Berlin Crisis, Suez Crisis, Korean War, Cuban Missile Crisis, Dien Bien Phu
   d. Korean War, Dien Bien Phu, Suez Crisis, Berlin Crisis, Cuban Missile Crisis

4. The Mau Mau uprising took place in
   a. Algeria.   c. South Africa.
   b. East Africa.   d. the Congo.

5. The unfortunate Hungarian leader who tried to liberate his country from Soviet control was
   a. János Kádár.
   b. Josip Broz.
   c. Imre Nagy.
   d. Andrei Zhdanov.

6. The first chancellor of the German Federal Republic (West Germany) was
   a. Walter Ulbricht.
   b. Ludwig Erhard.
   c. Julius Rosenberg.
   d. Konrad Adenauer.

7. The Christian Democrat leader in Italy after World War II was
   a. Vittorio De Sica.
   b. Roberto Rossellini.
   c. Alcide De Gasperi.
   d. Pope John XXIII.

8. Dictatorship in western Europe was not completely wiped out by World War II; it lived on in
   a. Norway and Sweden.
   b. Spain and Portugal.
   c. Ireland and Denmark.
   d. Belgium and Holland.

9. Nikita Khrushchev's policies included
   a. approval of Stalin's "cult of personality" and his version of socialism.
   b. unwillingness to fight a nuclear war over Cuba.
   c. refusal to use Soviet troops in Hungary.
   d. encouraging the North Koreans to invade the south.

10. Great Britain was an important member of
    a. NATO.
    b. COMECON.
    c. the Warsaw Pact.
    d. ECSC.

Essay Questions

Using material from this and previous chapters, write an essay on each of the following topics. When appropriate, include dates and cite examples to support your arguments.

1. Discuss the steps taken toward European unification in the postwar decades. What was the attraction of a common market? What were the problems?

2. Explain the series of events and incidents that caused the former allies—the USSR and the West—to become enemies in the Cold War. Could the Cold War have been avoided?

3. What factors caused the collapse of the British and French empires in the postwar years? Have the regions that the European powers precipitously left been peaceful? prosperous? Why?

4. What assumptions did Gandhi and Martin Luther King make when they adopted the tactics of nonviolent resistance? Would these tactics have worked as well against the Soviet government? Give examples to support your argument.

5. Compare the policies of Stalin and Khrushchev. How were they similar? How were they different?

Skill Building: Maps

A. *Locate the following on the map of Europe. Why was each significant in the present chapter?*

    a. Frankfurt

    b. Iron Curtain

    c. Berlin

    d. West Germany

    e. Yugoslavia

    f. Albania

    g. France

    h. Ireland

    i. Portugal

    j. Netherlands

    k. Norway

    l. Sweden

    m. Denmark

    n. Hungary

    o. Romania

    p. Turkey

    q. Bulgaria

    r. Hanover

    s. Hamburg

    t. East Germany

    u. Greece

    v. Poland

    w. USSR

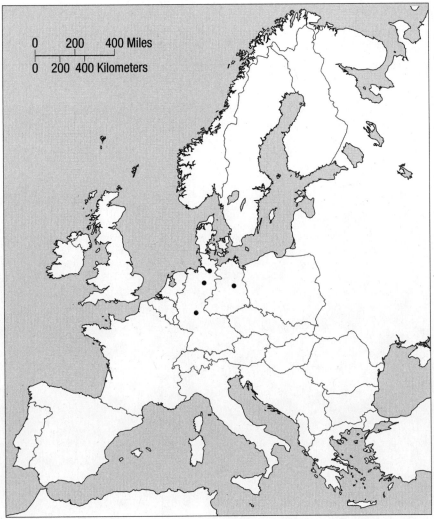

Cold War Europe

   x. United Kingdom

   y. Spain

   z. Luxemburg

  aa. Belgium

  bb. Finland

  cc. Czechoslovakia

  dd. Austria

  ee. Switzerland

   ff. Bulgaria

  gg. Finland

1. Which countries were said to be "behind" the Iron Curtain? Which were members of NATO? Which were neutral? On the map, use different colors to shade in these three groups. What was the significance of NATO? of the Warsaw Pact?

2. Which countries became members of the EEC? What was the significance of the EEC?

B. Locate the following on the map of Africa. Why was each significant in the present chapter?

   a. Tunisia

   b. Libya

   c. Sudan

   d. Ethiopia

   e. Lesotho

   f. South Africa

   g. Morocco

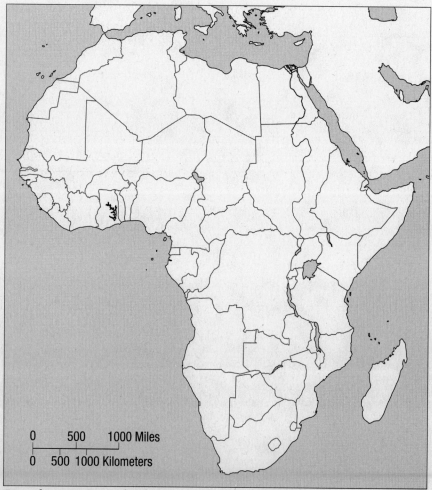

0   500   1000 Miles

0   500   1000 Kilometers

Decolonization of Africa

h. Egypt

i. Algeria

j. Liberia

k. Namibia

l. Swaziland

1. Did the borders of the new African states conform to the old colonial borders or to the traditional tribal territories of precolonial times? Why?
2. Given the ethnic conflicts that have plagued European history, why were similar problems not foreseen in Africa?

Enrichment Exercise

One of the favorite literary devices of the postwar period was to place the story and characters in some imaginary future, often a horrible setting in which certain objectionable elements of the present had become dominant features of life. Aldous Huxley's novel *Brave New World* (1932) and movies such as *Things to Come* (1936) and Charlie Chaplin's *Modern Times* (1936) helped popularize this genre and probably helped shape George Orwell's *1984* (1948). Other grim views of the future included the end of the world via nuclear war in Nevil Shute's *On the Beach* (1957); a devastated postnuclear landscape in the B-movie *Panic in the Year Zero* (1962); and a descent into barbarism, as in Ray Bradbury's *Fahrenheit 451*. Choose one of the following:

• George Orwell's *1984* is a condemnation of totalitarianism like *Animal Farm*, but here Orwell shows the government using technology to control and indoctrinate—note that when Winston Smith's electricity is off, the two-way TV screen still functions. England has become a dreary socialist society, endlessly at war, its history under constant revision, the meanings of words twisted to suit the state. Read the book and view the film starring John Hurt and Richard Burton that was made in 1984 (don't bother with the 1954 version). Write a summary of the story listing all the elements of postwar society that Orwell found ominous. How prophetic was he?

• Anthony Burgess's *A Clockwork Orange* (1962) was also set in a gray socialist future, but one in which government is ineffectual, Russian culture and language dominate England, and disaffected, unemployed youths amuse themselves with casual gang violence. (Youth gangs—Teddy Boys, Mods, Rockers—were a problem in Britain, so much so that the film *The Wild One* was banned there until 1967.) Burgess's antisocial protagonist is "cured" by behavioral conditioning, a reference to B. F. Skinner's *Science and Human Behavior* (1953). Read *A Clockwork Orange* (a glossary in the back helps with the slang words) and view the acclaimed film version (1971) by Stanley Kubrick. (Warning: this is a violent and disturbing film.) Write an essay summarizing the story and listing all the elements of postwar society that Burgess found ominous. How prophetic was he? Incidentally, if you enjoy Burgess's work, check out his *1985* (1978), a satire and commentary on Orwell's book.

Document Analysis
DOCUMENT 1
The New Class

Milovan Djilas, a Yugoslavian communist and longtime radical, was part of the Tito revolution. His analysis of the USSR in The New Class *pointed to the fact that modern communism had not fulfilled its promise of making society "classless." In writing the book, however, Djilas had gone too far even for Tito. He was expelled from the Communist Party in January 1954 and imprisoned at hard labor.*

> The greatest illusion [of communism] was that industrialization and collectivization in the U.S.S.R., and destruction of capitalist ownership, would result in a classless society. In 1936, when the new Constitution was promulgated, Stalin announced that the "exploiting class" had ceased to exist. The capitalist and other classes of ancient origin had in fact been destroyed, but a new class, previously unknown to history, had been formed.
>
> It is understandable that this class, like those before it, should believe that the establishment of its power would result in happiness and freedom for all men. The only difference between this and other classes was that it treated the delay in the realization of its illusions more crudely. It thus affirmed that its power was more complete than the power of any other class before in history, and its class illusions and prejudices were proportionally greater.
>
> This new class, the bureaucracy, or more accurately the political bureaucracy, has all the characteristics of earlier ones as well as some new characteristics of its own.

Source: Milovan Djilas, *The New Class: An Analysis of the Communist System* (Praeger, 1957), pp. 37–38.

Questions
1. Marx had taught that history consisted of Hegelian cycles in which socioeconomic classes struggled against each other, creating still new classes and new struggles. But Marx believed that once the industrial proletariat had triumphed, the dialectical process would end and "history would cease." Is Djilas a Hegelian? a Marxist?
2. Why would Tito probably disapprove of these excerpts from Djilas's book? Do the criticisms of the Soviet Union apply also to Yugoslavia?

DOCUMENT 2
Black Skin, White Masks

Frantz Fanon was born in the French colony of Martinique and became a well-known psychoanalyst after studying in Paris. His influential writing presented decolonization as more than a process of political independence from Europe. Suggesting that a new identity for blacks had to replace the old one, Fanon helped extend the definition of independence from political issues to personal and cultural ones.

> I propose nothing short of the liberation of the man of color from himself....
>
> The black schoolboy in the Antilles, who in his lessons is forever talking

about "our ancestors, the [French]," identifies himself with the explorer, the bringer of civilization, the white man who carries truth to savages—an all-white truth. There is identification—that is, the young Negro subjectively adopts a white man's attitude. . . .

Little by little, one can observe in the young Antillean the formation and crystallization of an attitude and a way of thinking and seeing that are essentially white. When in school he has to read stories of savages told by white men, he always thinks of the [African]. . . . The Negro lives in Africa. Subjectively, intellectually, the Antillean conducts himself like a white man. But he is a Negro. That he will learn once he goes to Europe; and when he hears Negroes mentioned he will recognize that the word includes himself.

Source: Frantz Fanon, *Black Skin, White Masks*, trans. Charles Lam Markmann (Grove, 1967 [1952]), pp. 8, 147–148.

Questions

1. Fanon views himself as a victim of colonialism and discrimination. How common among French citizens in general in 1952 was the sort of education Fanon had received? Do his education and background suggest that the situation was getting better or worse for black citizens of the French Empire?

2. Were the French, in referring to non-European citizens of the French Empire as "French" and assuming their inclusion in the common national culture, behaving hatefully? Would Fanon have preferred an exclusionary policy toward the Antilles schoolboy? Would the schoolboy?

DOCUMENT 3

Childhood and the Welfare State

The welfare state has attracted criticism for making government too impersonal and eroding people's initiative. By providing help for children, the old, the sick, the unemployed, and others in great need, the argument goes, the state does them a psychological disservice. Others debate this criticism. In this selection, Carolyn Stedman remembers what the provisions she received as a British child growing up in the 1950s meant to her development.

The 1950s was a time when state intervention in children's lives was highly visible, and experienced, by me at least, as entirely beneficent. The calculated, dictated fairness of the ration book went on into the new decade, and we spent a lot of time . . . picking up medicine bottles of orange juice and jars of Virol from the baby clinic for my sister. I think I would be a very different person now if orange juice and milk and dinners at school hadn't told me, in a covert way, that I had a right to exist, was worth something. . . . I think that had I grown up with my parents only twenty years before, I would not now believe this. . . . Being a child when the state was practically engaged in making children healthy and literate was a support against my own circumstances. . . .

It was a considerable achievement for a society to pour so much milk and so much orange juice, so many vitamins, down the throats of its children, and for the height and weight of those children to outstrip the measurements of only a decade before. . . . Within that period of time more children were provided with the goods of the earth than had any generation been before. What my mother lacked, I was given; and though vast inequalities remained between me and others of my generation, the sense that a benevolent state bestowed on me, that of my own existence and the worth of that existence . . . demonstrates in some degree what a fully material culture might offer in terms of physical comfort and the structures of care and affection that it symbolizes, to all its children.

Source: Carolyn Kay Stedman, *Landscape for a Good Woman: A Story of Two Lives* (Rutgers University Press, 1987), pp. 121–123.

Questions

1. In addition to food and vitamins, what else did Stedman apparently receive from the government?

2. "From each according to his ability," Marx paraphrased the early socialists, "and to each according to his needs." This statement is now considered naive, and the criticism is made that without economic incentives, people will not work. What other factors affect human behavior, or is all behavior (as Marx himself taught) economically based? Take into account this passage from Stedman.

DOCUMENT 4

At the Berlin Wall

Although the Cold War included real military threats, it was also carried out in newspaper reporting, films, and public rhetoric that emphasized the differences between Soviets and Americans. Early in the 1960s, U.S. President John F. Kennedy received a rapturous greeting in West Berlin when he spoke to hundreds of thousands about the meaning of the Berlin Wall. Thrilled with Kennedy's speech, said one observer, the crowd "shook itself and rose and roared like an animal."

There are some people in the world who really don't understand, or say they don't, what is the great issue between the free world and the Communist world. Let them come to Berlin!

There are some who say that Communism is the wave of the future. Let them come to Berlin!

And there are some who say in Europe and elsewhere we can work with the Communists.

Let them come to Berlin!

And there are even a few who say that it is true that Communism is an evil system, but it permits us to make economic progress.

Lass sie nach Berlin kommen! Let them come to Berlin!

I know of no town, no city, that has been besieged for eighteen years, that still lives with the vitality and the force and the determination of the city of West Berlin.

When all are free the people of West Berlin can take sober satisfaction in the fact that they were in the front lines for almost two decades.

All free men, wherever they may live, are citizens of Berlin. And, therefore, as a free man, I take pride in the words: "Ich bin ein Berliner."

Source: Quoted in Walter Henry Nelson, *The Berliners: Their Saga and Their City* (David McKay, 1969), pp. 181–182.

Questions

1. The Berlin Wall cut across several of the most beautiful streets and squares of the city, cut through neighborhoods, even houses. All of these were intersected by an ugly structure of concrete and barbed wire, with mines and guard towers. Imagine the impact on the subway system and public transportation, on sewers, water, electricity, and gas mains. If cities are the basis of civilization, what did the Berlin Wall symbolize?

2. Presumably the citizens of West Berlin and the United States were already in agreement with Kennedy. To whom else might this speech have been addressed?

CHAPTER

29

Technology, Social Change, and Challenges to Western Dominance, 1962–1979

Chapter Outline

Chapter Summary

By the 1960s, a new technological revolution was sweeping the West. The transistor and later the microchip would permit the miniaturization of most electronic devices, making them cheaper and more portable. An information revolution accompanied the spread of television, and in time communications satellites would enable people around the world not only to learn about events as they happened but to actually see them. The people who determined what the public was shown acquired enormous influence over popular opinion. Special-interest groups soon learned that they could stage events and create "news." Computers were used increasingly in science, manufacturing, and accounting. They performed many of the computations that made space exploration possible; by 1969, slightly more than a decade after the Russians launched the first satellite into orbit, the United States had landed astronauts on the moon. Amazing progress was also made in reproductive technology and in microbiology, as scientists learned more about cell chemistry, heredity, and virology. Surgeons successfully transplanted organs and even replaced them with mechanical devices. Such accomplishments were disturbing to those who had always imagined these processes to be controlled by divine intervention; many of these innovations also posed challenging ethical questions.

As machines took over many tasks from workers, more and more of the labor force found employment in the service sector—bureaucracy, education, medicine—creating what some termed a postindustrial society. Even much agriculture was now run by corporations. Multinational corporations, some of them richer than small nations, marketed their products to global markets and moved their manufacturing operations about in search of the most economical labor force. Workers, too, crossed borders in search of employment. Job security depended more than ever on education.

The social sciences acquired new prestige in the academic world, often using the computer and research procedures similar to those of mathematicians and physicists. B. F. Skinner proposed to make psychology a science by studying only observable and quantifiable behaviors. In France, the anthropologist Claude Lévi-Strauss replaced Jean-Paul Sartre as the most fashionable thinker. The fine arts continued to use the unusual or outrageous to gain attention. In the 1960s and 1970s, one new trend was "pop art," which borrowed images from commercial packaging. In music, the young thronged to hear popular performers such as the Beatles, whereas serious music became increasingly academic and esoteric.

The Cold War continued throughout the 1960s. The United States maintained its leadership of the West, although with increasing difficulty. At the same time that its moral leadership was being challenged by civil rights struggles at home, the United States stubbornly escalated the Vietnam conflict into a major war. The resulting inflation irritated America's European allies. Gaullist France withdrew from NATO, which created hard feelings with its former allies. West Germany pursued trade relationships with the communist bloc. In the Soviet Union, the fall of Khrushchev led to a new, more Stalinist regime under Leonid Brezhnev; the brief period of Soviet liberalization ended, and dissidents were once again persecuted vigorously. As the costs of the war in Vietnam increased and the war itself seemed futile, protest movements spread across the United States. The tactics of protest, many of them borrowed from the civil rights movement, generated much publicity in the mass media and were widely imitated throughout the world. In France, for example, rebellious students fought in the streets against police, and the sympathy they gained from the populace eventually forced the resignation of Charles de Gaulle. In Czechoslovakia, on the other hand, the Soviets ignored public opinion and brutally crushed the dissidents.

The Vietnam War committed American forces so deeply that the Soviets were tempted to try to gain advantage elsewhere. In the Middle East, for example, Soviet-armed Arab states attacked Israel, but they suffered a humiliating defeat that left a legacy of bitterness and terrorism. In 1971, the United States restored relations with the communist government of China. This move created a new equilibrium among the superpowers that enabled the United States to extricate itself from the Vietnam conflict; the worried Soviets also agreed to participate in arms-limitations agreements. As relations between the superpowers stabilized, well short of friendship, dissident groups throughout the world used the new tactic of terrorism to gain publicity for their causes; groups in the Middle East, especially, gained the world's attention with sporadic acts of terrorism. Middle Eastern governments, meanwhile, joined together in OPEC to curtail oil production and put economic pressure on Western economies. The potential for peace was demonstrated when Israel and Egypt, at the urging of American President Jimmy Carter, agreed to end hostilities. But such advances seemed less significant, at least to the West, when in 1979 the fanatical new leader of Iran encouraged his supporters to attack the U.S. embassy in Teheran and take the diplomats in it hostage.

Vocabulary

behaviorist   A psychologist who believes that organisms learn behavior in response to stimuli from the environment, and that these observable behaviors are the only valid and scientific data for psychological study.

cartel   An organization, such as OPEC, in which members agree to cooperate for their common interest in regulating prices, production, and even marketing.

catalyzed   Caused; in chemistry, a catalyst is a substance that causes or modifies a chemical reaction without being itself consumed or changed. This concept carries over into the nonchemical use of the word.

cyborg   A new word combining *cybernetic* and *organism;* thus, an organism partly or completely controlled by mechanical or electronic systems.

detente   A lessening or loosening of tension and hostility between nations.

DNA   The common abbreviation of deoxyribonucleic acid, a chemical found in the nucleus of living cells.

endemic   Native to a particular locality; the opposite of epidemic.

homogeneous   Alike, of the same sort or kind; the opposite of *heterogeneous.*

immolated   Burned; Vietnamese Buddhist monks performed self-immolation to attract media attention in the early 1960s.

in vitro   Latin for "in glass"; in an artificial environment, such as a laboratory, test tube, or Petri dish.

Self-Testing and Review Questions

Identification

After reading Chapter 29, identify and explain the historical significance of each of the following:

1. Camp David Accord

2. OPEC

3. *samizdat*

4. Martin Luther King

5. Prague spring

6. Tet offensive

7. Michnik clubs

8. *The Feminine Mystique*

9. Charter 77

10. Danny the Red

11. Colossus

12. *Viking* and *Voyager*

13. SALT talks

14. Leonid Brezhnev

15. *Humanae Vitae*

16. Bloody Sunday

17. Henry Kissinger

18. Harold Wilson

19. Green Party

20. Six-Day War

21. John Cage

22. Kent State

Chronology

Identify the events or issues associated with each of the following dates. Several of these dates may be significant for more than one reason. When you have finished, answer the questions that follow.

1962

1963

1964

1967

1968

1970

1972

1973

1976

1979

1. What were the dates for the administrations of John F. Kennedy, Lyndon Johnson, Richard Nixon, Gerald Ford, and Jimmy Carter? How were the major events of the 1960s and 1970s influenced by their policies?

2. How did the various protest movements of the period become aware of each other via the electronic and other media? How did they inspire each other? What new tactics emerged?

Matching Exercises

In each set, match the terms on the left with those on the right.

Set A

____ 1. Christiaan Barnard

____ 2. Neil Armstrong

____ 3. Fritz Schumacher

____ 4. Arthur C. Clarke

____ 5. Andy Warhol

a. the first man on the moon

b. pioneer of pop art

c. science fiction writer; author of *2001: A Space Odyssey*

d. the first heart transplant

e. environmentalist; author of *Small Is Beautiful*

Set B

____ 1. Ludwig Erhard

____ 2. Christa Wolf

____ 3. Rudi Dutschke

____ 4. Willy Brandt

____ 5. Robert Rauschenberg

a. radical student

b. modern artist

c. author of *Divided Heaven*

d. promoter of *Ostpolitik*

e. succesor to Adenauer

Set C

____ 1. Valentina Tereshkova

____ 2. Alexei Kosygin

____ 3. Yevgeny Yevtushenko

____ 4. Alexander Solzhenitsyn

____ 5. Vaclav Havel

a. Ukrainian poet; author of *Babi Yar*

b. Brezhnev's colleague

c. dissident Czech playwright

d. astronaut

e. Nobel Prize winner; author of *One Day in the Life of Ivan Denisovitch*

Set D

____ 1. Claude Lévi-Strauss   a. sociologist of postindustrial society
____ 2. B. F. Skinner   b. promoter of creativity through psychedelic drugs
____ 3. Daniel Bell   c. astronaut and politician
____ 4. John Glenn   d. psychologist; advocate of behaviorism
____ 5. Timothy Leary   e. anthropologist; advocate of structuralism

Set E

____ 1. Antonin Novotny   a. Polish author of *Solaris*
____ 2. Alexander Dubcek   b. Slovak populist
____ 3. Wladyslaw Gomulka   c. Czech communist; critic of the preceding
____ 4. János Kádár   d. Hungarian leader
____ 5. Stanislaw Lem   e. unpopular Polish leader

Multiple-Choice Questions

1. Which of these are in correct chronological order?
   a. Prague spring, Kent State, Tet offensive, Yom Kippur War, Six-Day War
   b. Six-Day War, Tet offensive, Prague spring, Kent State, Yom Kippur War
   c. Tet offensive, Kent State, Six-Day War, Yom Kippur War, Prague spring
   d. Kent State, Six-Day War, Tet offensive, Prague spring, Yom Kippur War

2. The discoverers of DNA were
   a. Baader and Meinhof.   c. Crick and Watson.
   b. Brezhnev and Kosygin.   d. Lon Nol and Pol Pot.

3. At Helsinki in 1975, the Soviets promised
   a. to limit production of intercontinental ballistic missiles.
   b. not to pollute the Arctic Sea.
   c. to liberate the Baltic states of Estonia, Latvia, and Lithuania.
   d. not to violate the human rights of its citizens.

4. The pope who called the church council known as Vatican II, which modernized the Roman Catholic church in significant and controversial ways, was
   a. John XXIII.   c. Pius XII.
   b. Paul VI.   d. John Paul I.

5. The Great Society was planned and promoted by
   a. John F. Kennedy.   c. Lyndon B. Johnson.
   b. Richard M. Nixon.   d. Martin Luther King.

6. The Cambodian government was taken over and at least a million people killed by
   a. the Khmer Rouge.   c. Henry Kissinger.
   b. Ngo Dinh Diem.   d. the North Vietnamese.

7. The Cultural Revolution, an attempt to revive revolutionary spirit, was sanctioned by
   a. Ho Chi Minh.   c. the P. L. O.
   b. Daniel Cohn-Bendit.   d. Mao Zedong.

8. The scientific advances of the 1960s and 1970s did *not* include
   a. the invention of the first effective birth-control devices.
   b. the first space exploration and a moon landing.
   c. the growing importance of electronic media.
   d. medical advances such as heart transplants and in vitro fertilization.

9. An attempt to return Spain to dictatorship was averted by the intervention of
   a. Richard Nixon.   c. Francisco Franco.
   b. King Juan Carlos.   d. Charles de Gaulle.

10. The Red Brigades
    a. set off bloody fighting in Northern Ireland.
    b. killed Olympic athletes in Munich.
    c. kidnapped and murdered Aldo Moro.
    d. raided Israel from the West Bank and the Golan Heights.

Essay Questions

Using material from this and previous chapters, write an essay on each of the following topics. When appropriate, include dates and cite examples to support your arguments.

1. How were science and technology changing everyday life in the 1960s and 1970s? What historical precedents were there for such changes? How did the new media affect unrest in both the West and behind the Iron Curtain?

2. The teenagers and young adults of both the West and the Iron Curtain countries gained unprecedented political importance in the 1960s and 1970s. How? Why?

3. How were the world crises in southeast Asia and the Middle East in the 1960s and 1970s equivalent to the nationalist ferment in Europe during the previous century? How were they different?

4. How did Nixon's visit to China change the relationships among the superpowers? How did it contribute to the end of the Vietnam War?

5. It has been noted that the spread of literacy and of electronic media made it easier for demagogues and dictators to control public opinion. Do you think the new technologies of the 1960s and 1970s, such as the computer, would make it easier or more difficult to control people?

Skill Building: Maps

A. *Locate the following regions on the map of the Middle East. Why was each significant in the present chapter?*

   a. Israel

   b. Sinai peninsula

   c. Golan Heights

   d. West Bank

   e. Jerusalem

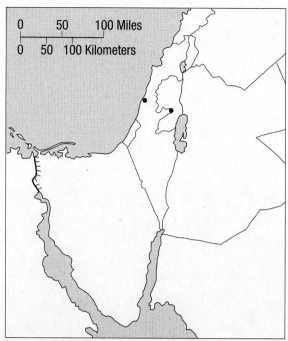

Israel After the Six-Day War

   f. Tel Aviv

   g. Gaza Strip

   h. Syria

   i. Jordan

   j. Egypt

   k. Saudi Arabia

1. To which states was the existence of Israel a direct military threat? Why could Egypt finally agree to terms?
2. Why is the location of Jerusalem politically significant?

B. *Locate the following regions on the map of the Vietnam War. Why was each significant in the present chapter?*

   a. North Vietnam

   b. Laos

   c. Gulf of Tonkin

   d. Hanoi

   e. Cambodia

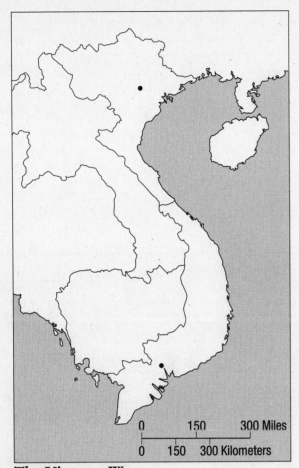

The Vietnam War

   f. Thailand

   g. Saigon

   h. South Vietnam

1. Considering that the People's Republic of China and the Soviet Union were at odds, which was the powerful patron supporting the North Vietnamese in the war against the United States? Given that the North Vietnamese and the Khmer Rouge were enemies, who backed the latter? Why?

Enrichment Exercise

There were many reasons for the enormous expansion of U.S. colleges and universities in the 1960s and 1970s: the G. I. Bill after the Korean War; the fear (caused by Sputnik) that Russian technology was overtaking that of the West; the rising wealth and aspirations of the working and middle classes who wanted their children to have the opportunities formerly reserved for the higher classes. The fact that both faculty and students were drawn from an increasingly diverse population upset the traditional hierarchies, created many new tensions, and significantly contributed to student involvement in the various protest movements, such as the Paris riots of 1968. In Great Britain, the growth of "red brick" universities across the country (in contrast to the stone buildings at Oxford and Cambridge) was a parallel phenomenon. Britain produced a wealth of novelists who saw the red-brick universities as a perfect setting for their sardonic and often hilarious commentary about postwar British society. Some of the best include Kingsley Amis, David Lodge, Tom Sharpe, and Malcolm Bradbury. Choose one of the following:

1. Bradbury's *The History Man* (1975) is a witty, nasty portrayal of snobbish dons, radical professors, bewildered exchange students, and academic ambition. Read the book and write a brief report. How does the British university described here compare to higher education in America? Is the author's view of the social sciences fair? Henry Kissinger once commented that academic intrigues were so vicious because the issues were so small. Would Bradbury agree?

2. Bradbury's *Stepping Westward* (1965) tells of an English professor's experiences as a visiting lecturer in a midwestern American university in the 1960s. David Lodge's *Changing Places: A Tale of Two Campuses* (1975) tells of an English exchange professor at "Euphoria State" in the early 1970s (Lodge taught for a time at the University of California at Berkeley). Read one or both of these books and write a brief report. What do these British authors consider to be the biggest differences between British and American culture in the 1960s or 1970s? Do you agree?

Document Analysis

DOCUMENT 1

At the Barricades

On May 3, 1968, the rector of the Sorbonne, Jean Roche, committed an unthinkable act—he called in the local police to suppress a small but noisy gathering in the university courtyard, thus violating the tradition of sanctuary that had been honored for centuries. The students in question had been demonstrating in support of their colleagues at Nanterre, where the issue since March had been the right to have visitors of the opposite sex in dormitory rooms. The court met on Saturday night (!) and sentenced the arrested students to two-year prison terms, without appeal. Expecting trouble, the government called in special anti-riot forces from the Belgian and Rhineland frontier garrisons, the much-feared C.R.S. (Compagnies républicaines de sécurité) who had earned a reputation for brutality in the recent Algerian troubles. The C.R.S. were often recruited from the rural and working-class populations whose children rarely attended the University of Paris. Janet Flanner, whose elegant letters from Paris (written under the pen name Genêt) appeared regularly in the New Yorker *magazine, described what followed.*

With the Sorbonne locked against them, students began roaming the streets, insulting the C.R.S. guards, who were armed, wore steel helmets, and carried long nightsticks. . . . Violence became the pattern. Street fighting animated the Rue Soufflot, broke out around the Panthéon and the Place Edmund-Rostand, at the corner of the Luxembourg Gardens, and in all the smaller medieval alleyways leading off the lower Boulevard Saint-Michel. Everywhere the students at first advanced with insults as their only weapon, before fleeing to save their scalps from the attacking police clubs. Wednesday night, as if their energy were uncontrollable, the students embarked by the thousand on a long parading march up and down Paris, mounting the Champs-Élysées to the Arc de Triomphe, where they extinguished the flames over the Unknown Soldier's Tomb, had a sit-in around it, and sang the "Internationale."

By Thursday . . . evening . . . the students had started building barricades throughout the Latin Quarter, because barricades are a historic instinctive accompaniment of French rebellions. They dug up the cube-shaped paving blocks from the streets, piled them as ammunition and protection to a height of five or six feet, and in the Rue Gay-Lussac, just off the Luxembourg Gardens, added all the cars that had been parked there. . . . *"Nous sommes chez nous"* ["We are at home"] the students kept saying, as if that medieval section of old academic Paris were their property to despoil or defend. . . . Whether from the students' amateur Molotov cocktails or from the C.R.S. variety of chemical gas bombs . . . all the captive automobiles in the Rue Gay-Lussac . . . were set aflame. As the police closed in, the students began running up apartment-house staircases to continue fighting from the roofs, tipping parapet stones onto the enemy below, and finally knocking on apartment doors to beg shelter. . . . Red Cross stations had been set up in the Boul' Mich', and after midnight women taxi-drivers banded together to take out the wounded students, mostly with bashed heads. The fire department was . . . putting down fires, and there were screams and shouts that could be heard as far off as the Boulevard Saint-Germain. The students fought with unflagging courage until they were knocked down and out by the police.

Source: Janet Flanner (Genêt), *Paris Journal, Vol. II (1965–1971)*, ed. William Shawn (Harcourt Brace Jovanovich, 1977), pp. 250–252.

Questions

1. Many of the residents of the Left Bank and Latin Quarter gave the students shelter. In the following weeks, the communist-dominated C.G.T., a labor union, called a massive general strike in sympathy for the students. Were the students' sleeping arrangements at Nanterre the big issue here? Did the unions really care about sanctuary rights at the Sorbonne?

2. Most of the students in question came from upper middle-class families, and their presence in a university in the 1960s indicates their privileged status. How and why did they become radical?

3. In several days of violent rioting as described above, no one was killed. Two years later, unarmed American students were shot down at Kent State. How were the situations similar? How were they different?

DOCUMENT 2

The Middle East in Conflict

As colonial control over the Middle East waned, intellectuals from the region disagreed about the kind of future the new states should forge. Nasser had suggested Arab unity, but that proved difficult to achieve. Opposition to the new state of Israel provided only the temporary and artificial unity of a common enemy. Some intellectuals, such as the Tunisian Hisham Djaït (b. 1935) proposed a secular government that would protect religious tradition but not enforce it, that would permit people to practice religion as (and if) they chose. Others, such as the Shi ite imam Khomeini, advocated a rejection of virtually everything Western, except weapons technology and the tape cassettes he used to spread his message.

DJAÏT: We are for laicism, but a laicism which will not be hostile to Islam, and does not draw its motivation from anti-Islamic feeling. In our anguished journey we have preserved the very essential of faith, a profound and ineradicable tenderness for this religion which has lighted our childhood and been our first guide towards the Good and the discovery of the Absolute. . . . Our laicism finds its limits in the recognition of the essential relation between the state, certain elements of moral and social behaviour, the structure of the collective personality and the Islamic faith. . . . Reform should not be made in opposition to religion, it should be made at one and the same time by religion, in religion and independently of it.

Source: Quoted in Albert Hourani, *A History of the Arab Peoples* (Harvard University Press, 1991), pp. 444–445.

KHOMEINI: It is often proclaimed that religion must be separated from politics, and that the ecclesiastical world should keep out of the affairs of state. It is proclaimed that high Moslem clerical authorities have no business mixing into the social and political decisions of the government. Such proclamations can come only from the atheists; they are dictated and spread by imperialists. Was politics separate from religion in the time of the Prophet (God salute him, him and his faithful!)? Was there a distinction at that time between the religious and the high functionaries of the state? Were religious and temporal powers separate in the times of the Caliphs? Those are aberrations invented by the imperialists with a view to turning the clergy away from the material and social life of Moslem peoples, and thus to getting a free hand to pillage their wealth. . . .

We need a head of government who is not at the mercy of his lust and other temptations. We need someone to govern us for whom all are equal, for whom all enjoy the same rights and obligations; someone who doesn't indulge in favoritism, who regards his family in the same light as others, who will cut off his son's hands if he steals, and execute his brothers and sisters if they sell heroin.

Source: Ayatollah Ruhollah Khomeini, *Principes de l'Ayatollah Khomeiny: Philosophiques, sociaux, et réligieux*, ed. Jean-Marie Xavière (Libres-Hallier, 1979); English edition: *Sayings of the Ayatollah Khomeini: Political, Philosophical, Social, and Religious*, trans. Harold J. Salemson, ed. Tony Hendra (Bantam Books, 1980), pp. 16–17, 25.

Questions

1. What is the essence of religion to Djaït? to Khomeini? Can these differences be explained by the differences between Sunni and Shi ite Islam?

2. Both of these statements profoundly reflect European influences. How many can you list?

3. What other historical figures have you encountered in the text who shared Khomeini's view of a fusion of church and state? Over the centuries, how successful were the institutions they founded? Do you think Khomeini would have been interested in an argument based on historical pragmatism?

DOCUMENT 3

The Communist Party in Bologna

For several decades after World War II, the Italian Communist Party (PCI) controlled local governments in many regions, in spite of the sometimes fragile but continued domination of the Christian Democrats (DC) at the national level. The DC maintained the old bans on birth control, abortion, and even divorce, in return for the support of the Roman Catholic Church; they were often accused of incompetence and corruption. The PCI claimed to be the friends of labor, the enemies of corruption, and to have fought the Nazis during the war. The citizens of Bologna so consistently voted communist that the ancient city became known as la città rossa *(the red city), a play on its other nickname,* la città grassa *(fat city, because of the legendary quality of its cuisine). Why did the* bolognesi *support the PCI. so consistently? And why did others support the DC in opposition? A poll of the citizens, taken in the early 1960s, was part of a study by Robert H. Evans.*

Opinions of the PCI in Bologna (in percentages, by sex)
M = male, F = female

	True M F	False M F	Don't Know M F	Total M F
The PCI is the only well-organized party in Bologna.	46 34	23 21	31 45	100 100
In Bologna, the communists are too strong; the other parties should reorganize.	38 31	12 10	50 59	100 100
In this part of the country, the Resistance was fought almost exclusively by communists.	25 18	33 26	42 56	100 100
Only the PCI has men really capable of administering Bologna.	20 16	38 36	42 48	100 100
The PCI is declining in Bologna.	8 12	33 26	59 62	100 100
The clergy of Bologna participates too much in politics.	39 31	18 19	43 50	100 100

Opinions of the PCI in Bologna (in percentages, by voters)
C = communist voters, N = noncommunist voters

	True C N	False C N	Don't Know C N	Total C N
The PCI is the only well-organized party in Bologna.	69 29	4 42	27 29	100 100
In Bologna, the communists are too strong; the other parties should reorganize.	10 62	20 8	70 30	100 100
In this part of the country, the Resistance was fought almost exclusively by communists.	47 10	7 55	46 35	100 100
Only the PCI has men really capable of administering Bologna.	46 3	10 68	44 29	100 100
The PCI is declining in Bologna.	2 20	55 20	43 60	100 100
The clergy of Bologna participates too much in politics.	57 29	2 36	41 35	100 100

Why People Vote for the DC (in percentages)
(Totals exceed 100% because of multiple answers)

	Total	Male	Female
They [share] their ideas, believe in their ideology . . .	10	10	10
Are afraid of communism, want to fight it	11	11	11
Are Christians, for religion, for the Church . . .	8	7	9
Want well-being, liberty, a little democracy . . . (and other DC positive answers)	8	12	5
Because they . . . are ignorant, do not understand . . . (and other DC negative answers)	4	5	3
To create a majority to change the present administration . . .	4	5	3
Do not know, no answer	50	43	56
Other answers	6	8	5

Source: Robert H. Evans, *Coexistence: Communism and Its Practice in Bologna, 1945–1965* (University of Notre Dame Press, 1967), pp. 207–209.

Questions

1. How did its relationship with the Roman Catholic Church affect support for the DC? Do women and men differ significantly on this issue? Was this a good strategy for the future?

2. Do the supporters of the PCI seem to be Stalinists? Are they looking forward to a proletarian revolution? Are the supporters of the DC afraid of a communist victory? How is the perception of the communist party in Italy different from that in the United States, and why?

3. Why do you suppose so many voters register no opinion?

DOCUMENT 4

An Antiwar Song of the 1960s

Pete Seeger was a popular American folksinger who achieved some notoriety in the 1950s by refusing to cooperate with a ludicrous House Un-American Activities Committee investigation of folksinging as a possible communist activity. He was blacklisted from television for years, and other popular performers such as Joan Baez refused to appear on TV in protest of this injustice. This antiwar anthem, which was translated into dozens of languages around the world, was inspired by an old Russian song quoted in Mikhail Sholokov's And Quiet Flows the Don: *"Where are the geese? They've gone to the reeds. And where are the reeds? They've been gathered by the girls. And where are the girls? They've taken husbands. And where are the Cossacks? They've gone to war."*

> Where have all the flowers gone, Long time passing,
> Where have all the flowers gone, Long time ago,
> Where have all the flowers gone, Young girls picked them every one,
> When will they ever learn? When will they ever learn?
>
> Where have all the young girls gone, Long time passing,
> Where have all the young girls gone, Long time ago,

Where have all the young girls gone, Gone to young men every one,
When will they ever learn? When will they ever learn?

Where have all the young men gone, Long time passing,
Where have all the young men gone, Long time ago,
Where have all the young men gone, They are all in uniform,
When will they ever learn? When will they ever learn?

Where have all the soldiers gone, Long time passing,
Where have all the soldiers gone, Long time ago,
Where have all the soldiers gone, Gone to graveyards every one,
When will they ever learn? When will they ever learn?

Where have all the graveyards gone, Long time passing,
Where have all the graveyards gone, Long time ago,
Where have all the graveyards gone, Covered with flowers every one,
When will they ever learn? When will they ever learn?

Source: Words and music by Pete Seeger, © copyright 1961 (renewed) by Sanga Music, Inc. All rights reserved. Used by permission.

Questions

1. Would you categorize the aesthetic values of this song as realistic or romantic? How could such an apparently innocent and philosophical sentiment be politically controversial? Does the person expressing these sentiments sound like a communist ideologue or a dangerous radical? Why would anticommunists automatically dislike this song? Are the opinions expressed naive?

2. To what or whom would the person expressing these sentiments probably give his or her highest allegiance? How were these values related to other movements of the decade, such as environmentalism?

3. Why, in an age of high-volume electronic music conceived by committees and created in studios, were simple folksongs such as these popular? With what groups did they gain popularity?

CHAPTER
30

The West and the New Globalism, 1979–Present

Chapter Outline

THE WEST ON THE EVE OF A NEW MILLENNIUM
   A New World Order?
   The West in a Global Age
   Global Culture or Western Civilization?

Chapter Summary

The hostage crisis between the United States and Iran (1979–1981) and the Russian invasion of Afghanistan (1979) were both results of renewed conflicts between the Muslim world and the superpowers. Khomeini, who had suffered under the shah and lived in exile in France, had come to hate the West and all that it represented. He envisaged a state dominated by the Shi ite clergy, of which he was the leader, and claimed that no other form of government was acceptable under Muslim law. The Soviet Union, with a large Muslim population, was nervous about the spread of this sort of fundamentalism across its borders and overreacted. Its invasion of Afghanistan shattered the detente with the United States. President Carter behaved with unexpected and unpopular restraint toward Iran, a policy that probably saved the hostages but certainly cost him any hope of reelection. Saddam Hussein, the Sunni dictator of Iraq, was also concerned about the influence of the unstable ayatollah on his own large Shi ite population; in 1980 he attacked Iran in what proved to be a long, bloody, and indecisive war.

The decade of the 1980s was one of confrontation between the United States and the Soviet Union, which President Reagan described as an "evil empire." The U.S. economy boomed as the government ran up an enormous debt purchasing expensive weapons systems. The debt was increased by America's worsening balance of trade with the nations of the Pacific Rim, which had come to dominate world trade in electronic consumer goods such as television sets and in cameras and automobiles.

An additional problem facing the advanced economies was a heightened awareness of the environmental damage the planet was sustaining. As the West began to take expensive steps to halt pollution, less advanced nations refused to cooperate, suspecting a plot to prevent them from developing. The Iron Curtain countries, where production quotas were important politically, and the press was not free to expose such matters, ignored environmental damage until it reached crisis proportions. In 1986, in perhaps the most dramatic example, a chronically unsafe nuclear reactor in the Ukraine suffered a meltdown and released a radioactive cloud that blew across Europe, to the acute embarrassment of the Soviet government.

In the 1980s, the governments of several Western nations turned away from the welfare state and adopted conservative reforms. Ronald Reagan cut U.S. taxes to encourage investments, and Margaret Thatcher slashed government spending and sold off ("privatised") government-owned enterprises in Great Britain. Germany also reduced welfare expenditures and cut corporate taxes. The French seemed to buck the trends once again; angry at the corruption and arrogance of their conservative government, they finally voted long-time socialist leader François Mitterand into office. His attempts to nationalize key industries and financial institutions so frightened investors that he was forced to revise his policies until they resembled those of his neighbors. Most European economies grew in the 1980s, buoyed by the Common Market.

The people living behind the Iron Curtain were increasingly aware of the prosperity in the West. They resented the poor quality and shortages of even basic necessities. They compared their situation with that of average people in the West, who enjoyed many new consumer goods and technologies that were available only to communist party officials in the East. In the 1980s, strikes broke out across Poland. Suppressing them would have been difficult given the breadth of the movement, the unavoidable global publicity, and the sympathetic pronouncements of the first Polish pope. When martial law failed to crush the Polish labor movement, Solidarity, anti-communists in other communist countries gained hope. In 1985 the new Soviet leader Mikhail

Gorbachev, a pragmatist, proposed a new relationship with the West to slow the economic decline of his nation, which was being worsened by the expensive arms race. But Soviet liberalization, once permitted, became impossible to control. In 1989 communist rule was voted out in Poland, Hungary, and Czechoslovakia. When Chinese students demanded a new openness, however, they were brutally repressed, sending waves of revulsion around the world and hastening the end of the last communist regimes in the West. In November 1989, the Berlin Wall was torn down, and in December the cruel Romanian communist dictatorship was ousted.

The collapse of European communism left chaos in its wake. With factories closing and social services suspended in eastern Europe, waves of emigrants moved westward, joining thousands of "guest" laborers and former colonials and putting enormous strain on the Western economies. The nation-state itself, the basis of government and diplomacy for a millennium, was endangered; European unification in the West had already threatened to make it obsolete. Ethnic groups in Transylvania, Bosnia, and the Caucasus, freed from communist control, revived centuries-old grievances and erupted into tribal warfare. Some would-be powers, such as Saddam Hussein of Iraq, invaded their neighbors, betting that the United States or the United Nations could not summon the will to stop them. In spite of such challenges, the "new world order" that unfolded in the 1990s was filled with promise—an end to apartheid in South Africa, new negotiations in the Middle East, and an emerging global culture—to find new solutions to the continuing challenges of poverty, disease, war, and injustice that had dogged the human race throughout its history.

Vocabulary

bipolarism	Having two poles, such as the earth or a magnet; *multipolar* means having many poles.
dacha	A Russian word for a country house or villa.
ecosystem	An interdependent biological community in a particular physical environment, such as a desert, a tidal pool, or the entire earth.
e-mail	Electronic mail. Messages sent between computers via modems and telephone lines, either directly or indirectly (through networks of computers).
gerontocracy	Government by the elderly.
junta	A Spanish word (pronounced "hoon'ta") for a governing council, often of military officers.
polyglot	Multilingual.

Self-Testing and Review Questions

Identification

After reading Chapter 30, identify and explain the historical significance of each of the following:

1. glasnost

2. Maastricht Treaty

3. Christa Wolf

4. Zentrum party

5. Felipe Gonzalez

6. Sandinistas

7. SDI

8. John Paul II

9. Toni Morrison

10. perestroika

11. Tienanmen Square

12. Rupert Murdoch

13. Reaganomics

14. Margaret Thatcher

15. Helmut Kohl

16. François Mitterand

17. Pompidou Center

18. Solidarity

19. Chernobyl

20. Mikhail Gorbachev

Chronology

Identify the events or issues associated with each of the following dates. Several of the dates may be significant for more than one reason. When you finish, answer the question that follows.

1979

1980

1982

1984

1986

1988

1989

1992

1. The year of the collapse of communism in Europe will almost certainly mark one of the great turning points in history, along with the French Revolution and the two World Wars. Once the political equilibrium has been shattered in this way, how long does it take to restore it? Judging by previous "watersheds," how long might the social and political repercussions continue?

Matching Exercises

In each set, match the terms on the left with those on the right.

Set A

____ 1. *One Hundred Years of Solitude*   a. Naguib Mahfouz

____ 2. *In the Ditch*   b. Salman Rushdie

____ 3. *The Satanic Verses*   c. Buchi Emecheta

____ 4. *Cairo Trilogy*   d. Milan Kundera

____ 5. *The Unbearable Lightness of Being*   e. Gabriel García Marquez

Set B

____ 1. François Mitterand   a. French racist politician of the National Front

____ 2. Jacques Lacan   b. French socialist president

____ 3. Jean-Marie Le Pen   c. French psychoanalyst

____ 4. Valéry Giscard d'Estaing   d. French conservative president

Set C

____ 1. Lech Wałesa   a. leader of the "velvet revolution"

____ 2. Vaclav Havel   b. leader of Solidarity

____ 3. Slobodan Milosevic   c. Polish communist dictator

____ 4. Wojciech Jaruzelski   d. Romanian communist dictator

____ 5. Nicolai Ceausescu   e. Serbian nationalist

Multiple-Choice Questions

1. Which of these lists the events in the correct chronological order?
   a. Falklands War, Maastricht Treaty, unification of Germany, Tienanmen Square
   b. Maastricht Treaty, Falklands War, unification of Germany, Tienanmen Square
   c. Tienanmen Square, Maastricht Treaty, Falklands War, unification of Germany
   d. Falklands War, Tienanmen Square, unification of Germany, Maastricht Treaty

2. The distinguished economist who advocated monetarist or "supply side" theories was
   a. James Watt.   c. Michel Foucault.
   b. Erich Honecker.   d. Milton Friedman.

3. An attempted coup to save hard-line communism was foiled in 1991 by
   a. Mikhail Gorbachev.   c. Ronald Reagan.
   b. Boris Yeltsin.   d. Felix Dzerzhinsky.

4. The Commonwealth of Independent States was
   a. a new arrangement of the states of the former Soviet Union.
   b. the coalition of fundamentalist Muslim states led by Iran.
   c. the new name for unified Germany.
   d. the former Yugoslavia.

5. The war over the Falkland Islands was politically beneficial to
   a. Ronald Reagan.   c. Felipe Gonzalez.
   b. Margaret Thatcher.   d. George Bush.

6. Which of these was the leader of the ANC?
   a. Rupert Murdoch   c. Nelson Mandela
   b. Wole Soyinka   d. F. W. de Klerk

7. Saddam Hussein flouted world opinion in 1990 when he
   a. invaded Iran.   c. invaded Libya.
   b. invaded Kuwait.   d. invaded Israel.

Essay Questions

Using material from this and previous chapters, write an essay on each of the following topics. When appropriate, include dates and cite examples to support your arguments.

1. What important events since 1979 have altered the relationship between the West and the Muslim world? Has it improved or worsened? Why?

2. What would be the advantages of European unification? What historical problems must be overcome? Should the United States encourage the EC (European Community)?

3. Why are states in eastern Europe breaking up into ethnic zones even as western European states are trying to put nationalism behind them and unite for the common good? Are the trends opposite, or are there similarities and parallels?

4. In 1789, France, one of the superpowers of its age, saw its entire political and social system toppled by a revolution. The consequences of the revolution affected European culture and the balance of power for decades. Is the breakup of the Soviet Union a comparable event? How and why?

Skill Building: Maps

Locate the following regions on the map of Europe. Why was each significant in the present chapter?

a. Bosnia-Herzegovina

b. Slovenia

c. Yugoslavia

d. Slovakia

e. Croatia

f. Czech Republic

Eastern and Central Europe

g. Ukraine

h. Poland

i. Lithuania

j. Serbia

k. Belarus

1. After World War I, many of the nations of central and eastern Europe were reorganized into states that conformed approximately to ethnic distribution. Did this create a more stable or a less stable situation? Discuss how the absence of clearly defined natural boundaries might increase international tension.

2. In the seventeenth century, Hobbes declared that tyranny was preferable to anarchy. Would the situation in the former Yugoslavia seem to support or refute this theory?

Enrichment Exercise

In 1983, Malcolm Bradbury, the distinguished British author and social satirist, wrote a book that looked bemusedly at communist society and the Cold War mentality. In *Rates of Exchange*, the mild-mannered academic Dr. Petworth attends a conference in Slaka, an imaginary eastern European state, "land of . . . beetroot and tractor." The book was such a success in Britain that Bradbury later wrote a tongue-in-cheek tourist guide to the same country, *Why Come to Slaka?* (1986). Read *Rates of Exchange* and write a two-page report. Did you learn more about eastern Europe or about the West's perception of it? How many of the stereotypes were based on fact?

Document Analysis

Document 1

A New European

Immigration to Europe accelerated as the colonial empires collapsed. Thousands of Indians and Pakistanis, West Indians, and Africans took advantage of generous immigration laws to move to England. Surinamese and Moluccan faces became common on the streets of Amsterdam. By the early 1990s, one out of every ten residents of France had been born abroad, most of them in Africa but many in southeast Asia. This experience of immigration and multiracial society, sometimes a strain even in the United States where there was plenty of room and a tradition of welcoming immigrants, caused cultural shock in Europe. In the late 1980s, Common Market laws permitted residents of any European country to travel freely to the others, so that no part of Europe became immune. Outbursts of racial bigotry, especially among unemployed whites, and other social problems inevitably followed, but in general the European governments, with popular support, banned discrimination and declared the new Europeans eligible for all state services. Realistically, however, the complete integration of the newcomers into European society would not be quick or simple.

Buchi Emecheta migrated from Nigeria to Great Britain with her husband in the 1960s. Later she separated from him and lived on welfare to maintain her five children. She also began writing novels about the experience of immigrants from the former colonies. Successful as a novelist, Emecheta also earned a degree in sociology and became a social worker at a London center for immigrant youth. In this selection, she describes her ambivalent attitude toward her job.

I was going to teach them to learn to talk in low voices, to show them how to relax with a good book rather than banging draughts, which only stimulated them into a state of high excitement. I was going to introduce them to cultural activities such as listening to music, my own type of music, which in my over-optimistic state I was sure they were going to like. I was going to make them realize that they could achieve things with their lives, lives which were just beginning. I was going to make their visits to [the club] worth their while and make the centre serve as a place of relaxation and civil education, the type of education that would teach them political and social awareness.

How was I to know, then, that all this could be rejected, including me? I was now aware then that I stood for the very type of black image they felt emphasized their failures. They knew that blacks like me who could claim to have made it were a pain to the masses of other blacks who could never make it. They also knew that my type of black suffers from a kind of false consciousness. We think we have been successful in achieving equality with white middle class intellectuals because we say to ourselves, have we not been to the university, have we not gone through the same degree of socialization via the educational system? But we often fail to see that we are middle-class blacks or, to put it more correctly, a black middle class.

Source: Buchi Emecheta, *Head Above Water: An Autobiography* (Fontana Books, 1986), pp. 140–141.

Questions

1. To what extent are Emecheta's frustrations unique to her situation? To what extent are they the universal frustrations of a teacher?
2. Why will some of Emecheta's students "never make it"? Because they are black? Because they are not middle class? Because they are rejecting what she has to offer? What can be done?

DOCUMENT 2

Ending Socialist Economics

By the fall of 1990, living conditions in the Soviet Union had become so bad that its leadership feared for the very existence of the country. The reform president, Mikhail S. Gorbachev, announced the transition to a market economy in October 1990 as a way of saving socialist society and the Soviet Union.

The situation in the people's economy is growing worse. The volume of production is decreasing and economic ties are being disrupted. Separatism is growing. The consumers' market is devastated. The budget deficit and solvency of the state have reached critical levels. Anti-social phenomena and the crime rate are on the rise. . . .

The choice has been made.

There is no alternative to the transition to the market. The whole world experience proved the vitality and efficiency of the market economy. The transition to it in our society is dictated by the interests of the people. Its goal is to create a socially oriented economy, to turn production to the satisfaction of consumers' demands, to overcome the shortages and the shame of the shopping lines—in reality to provide for the economic freedom of citizens, to establish new conditions for encouraging their diligence, creative abilities, initiative and high productivity.

Transition to the market does not contradict the socialist choice of our people.

Through the nationwide market a unified economic space will be created, which will integrate all republics and regions of the country. Transition to the market will allow for creation of an economic basis for voluntary unification of the sovereign republics within the framework of a renewed federation and strengthened union.

Source: *The New York Times,* October 17, 1990.

Questions

1. Does a market economy in fact contradict the "socialist choice" of the people? What did Lenin think? What was the NEP? What did Stalin think?

2. What impact would home computers, fax and copy machines, and other new technology have upon a closed, censored society? Could the Soviet Union have remained a closed dictatorship and still have kept up with the rest of the world's technology?

DOCUMENT 3

A Word About Words

On the eve of his country's "velvet revolution," the Czech dissident writer Vaclav Havel received the German Booksellers Association Peace Prize. He used that occasion to explore the ambiguities of words as tools of power and to affirm the value of clear and informed thinking as a cornerstone of civilization.

I live in a country where the authority and radioactive effect of words are demonstrated by the sanctions which free speech attracts. . . . Could you conceive of something of the kind in the Federal Republic of Germany?

Yes, I do inhabit a system in which words are capable of shaking the entire structure of government, where words can prove mightier than ten military divisions, where Solzhenitsyn's words of truth were regarded as something so dangerous that their author had to be bundled into an airplane and shipped out. Yes, in the part of the world I inhabit the word "Solidarity" was capable of shaking an entire power bloc.

Alongside words that electrify society with their freedom and truthfulness, we have words that mesmerize, deceive, inflame, madden, beguile, words that are harmful—lethal even. The word as arrow.

The words of Lenin—what were they? Liberating or, on the contrary, deceptive, dangerous and ultimately enslaving?

What was the true nature of Christ's words? Were they the beginning of an era of salvation, and among the most powerful cultural impulses in the history of the world—or were they the spiritual source of the crusades, inquisitions, the cultural extermination of the American Indians, and, later, the entire expansion of the white race that was fraught with so many contradictions and had so many tragic consequences. . . .

What a weird fate can befall certain words! . . . The same word can, at one moment, radiate great hope; at another, it can emit lethal rays. The same word can be true at one moment and false the next, at one moment illuminating, at another deceptive.

My intention is to tell you about another lesson that we in this corner of the world have learned about the importance of words . . . that it always pays to be suspicious of words and to be wary of them.

At the beginning of everything is the word.

It is a miracle to which we owe the fact that we are human.

But at the same time it is a pitfall and a test, a snare and a trial.

More so, perhaps, than it appears to you who have enormous freedom of speech, and might therefore assume that words are not so important.

They are.

Source: Vaclav Havel, *Open Letters: Selected Writings 1965–1990*, ed. Paul Wilson (Knopf, 1991), pp. 377–388.

Questions

1. Was the use of language to deceive limited to the communist bloc?

2. In constructing these warnings, does Havel also have in mind a figure from German history? Why is this name unspoken?

DOCUMENT 4

New Words for a New Culture

English journalist Peter Conradi contributed the following article to the lifestyle magazine of The European, *a weekly newspaper published in English but intended to reach the entire European community. Conradi wryly observes that the cultural differences between East and West are rapidly diminishing.*

Russia may have given the world the words "perestroika" and "glasnost," but the language is not above borrowing from abroad. These days the country's *nuvorichi* are snapping up foreign words with as much enthusiasm as they show for foreign cars, holidays and property.

Today's *biznismyen* (and, in the interests of sexual equality, *biznismyenka*) works hard to earn his *baksi* (only US bucks, of course). Sometimes, he will invest them in an *offshornaya campania* or ask his *dealer* to swap them into *voucheri* and *checki*. If he is cautious, he might prefer to put the money into a *trast* or a *kholding*.

The *biznismyen*'s wife, meanwhile, will be down at the sports club, clad in *leggingsi* or *dzhinzi*, doing her daily *shaping*.

The happy couple will spend their evenings at one of Moscow's *naitclubi*, where they can *drinknut* while listening to a *diskjokay*. Then it's home in the Mercedes or Lincoln to a fashionable *cottedge* on the edge of town, to watch *vidiki* on the *televisor*. Holidays might be spent on a *shoptur*—organised by the *sekretersha*, of course.

If things go badly, he may fall foul of *reketeeri*, racketeers from the local branch of the *mafia*. Many of its members are *sportsmyeni*. You will recognise them as they come towards you: they will be wearing *slaksi* and hiding their rippling pectorals beneath a *futbolka*.

Source: Peter Conradi, "Switch on the vidiki in your country cottedge," in *élan: Culture, Life & Style*, p. 31, in *The European*, No. 214 (17–23 June 1994).

Questions

1. The French government has occasionally expressed concern over the influx of foreign words into the language. Why do languages import words? Would you expect a Russian backlash against this trend?

2. Do the changes observed here affect all sectors of Russian society?

Practice Questions for Examinations for
Part IV (Chapters 25–30)

1. Describe the political, social, and cultural changes that occurred in the West as a result of World War I. Measured against the great events of European history (the fall of Rome, the French Revolution), how important was the "Great War"?

2. Trace the evolution and application of communist thought on Russian society from the Bolshevik Revolution of 1917 to the collapse of communism. What pre-revolutionary Russian traditions were preserved in the new system?

3. What conditions—economic, social, psychological—encouraged the rise of European fascism? Could fascism return?

4. How did decolonization and the Cold War affect the relations between the West and the non-European world after World War II?

5. How and why did the world's political, economic, and cultural institutions come to be dominated in the late twentieth century by two super-states, both direct heirs of European culture?

6. How has the explosion of new technology affected history in the twentieth century?

7. Discuss the role of the smaller states of eastern Europe and the Balkans in the great events of the twentieth century—World War I, World War II, the Cold War, and the fall of communism.

Answers to the Self-Testing and Review Questions

Chapter 13

Matching Exercises

Set A:	1. b	2. e	3. f	4. c	5. a	6. d
Set B:	1. e	2. a	3. b	4. c	5. d	
Set C:	1. c	2. a	3. e	4. b	5. d	
Set D:	1. d	2. e	3. b	4. a	5. c	
Set E:	1. b	2. c	3. a	4. e	5. d	

Multiple-Choice Questions

1. a   2. b   3. a   4. b   5. d   6. c   7. b   8. b   9. b   10. a

Chapter 14

Matching Exercises

Set A:	1. d	2. c	3. c	4. a	5. b	
Set B:	1. d	2. a	3. b	4. e	5. c	
Set C:	1. c	2. e	3. a	4. b	5. d	
Set D:	1. f	2. e	3. b	4. a	5. c	6. d
Set E:	1. b	2. a	3. e	4. d	5. c	

Multiple-Choice Questions

1. b   2. b   3. a   4. a   5. d   6. b   7. d   8. c   9. a   10. b

Chapter 15

Matching Exercises

Set A:	1. d	2. c	3. a	4. e	5. b
Set B:	1. e	2. b	3. a	4. c	5. d
Set C:	1. e	2. a	3. c	4. b	5. d
Set D:	1. d	2. c	3. a	4. c	5. b
Set E:	1. d	2. b	3. c	4. e	5. a
Set F:	1. b	2. d	3. a	4. c	5. e

Multiple-Choice Questions

1. d   2. b   3. a   4. c   5. b   6. b   7. d   8. c   9. b   10. c

Chapter 16

Matching Exercises

Set A: 1. d   2. c   3. a   4. b

Set B: 1. c   2. b   3. e   4. a   5. d

Set C: 1. a   2. b   3. c   4. d   5. f   6. e

Set D: 1. e   2. c   3. d   4. b   5. a

Set E: 1. e   2. c   3. f   4. b   5. d   6. a

Multiple-Choice Questions

1. c   2. b   3. c   4. b   5. a   6. d   7. d   8. a   9. b   10. a

Chapter 17

Matching Exercises

Set A: 1. b   2. f   3. c   4. d   5. e   6. a   7. b

Set B: 1. e   2. c   3. b   4. a   5. b   6. d

Set C: 1. c   2. b   3. a   4. e   5. d

Set D: 1. b   2. c   3. a   4. e   5. d

Set E: 1. b   2. d   3. e   4. c   5. a

Multiple-Choice Questions

1. a   2. d   3. c   4. b   5. c   6. d   7. a   8. b   9. c   10. b

Chapter 18

Matching Exercises

Set A: 1. c   2. a   3. b   4. a   5. e   6. d   7. b

Set B: 1. c   2. d   3. g   4. f   5. b   6. e   7. a

Set C: 1. c   2. e   3. a   4. d   5. b

Set D: 1. d   2. c   3. a   4. b   5. d   6. b

Set E: 1. d   2. b   3. e   4. c   5. a

Multiple-Choice Questions

1. c   2. b   3. a   4. b   5. b   6. d   7. c   8. c   9. d   10. a

Chapter 19

Matching Exercises

Set A: 1. e   2. d   3. b   4. c   5. a

Set B: 1. c   2. e   3. a   4. d   5. b   6. c

Set C: 1. b   2. d   3. a   4. c   5. e

Set D: 1. c   2. a   3. e   4. b   5. d

Set E: 1. c   2. a   3. d   4. b

Multiple-Choice Questions

1. b   2. a   3. d   4. b   5. a   6. c   7. d   8. b   9. b   10. d

Chapter 20

Matching Exercises

Set A:	1. e	2. a	3. b	4. c	5. d
Set B:	1. c	2. b	3. e	4. d	5. a
Set C:	1. b	2. d	3. c	4. e	5. a
Set D:	1. c	2. d	3. b	4. e	5. a
Set E:	1. d	2. a	3. b	4. e	5. c

Multiple-Choice Questions

1. b   2. a   3. c   4. c   5. a   6. c   7. c   8. b   9. a   10. d

Chapter 21

Matching Exercises

Set A:	1. b	2. e	3. f	4. c	5. a	6. d
Set B:	1. b	2. d	3. f	4. c	5. a	6. e
Set C:	1. c	2. e	3. f	4. a	5. d	6. b
Set D:	1. c	2. e	3. f	4. b	5. a	6. d
Set E:	1. e	2. a	3. c	4. d	5. f	6. b

Multiple-Choice Questions

1. c   2. d   3. b   4. d   5. b   6. c   7. c   8. c   9. d   10. b

Chapter 22

Matching Exercises

Set A:	1. e	2. c	3. a	4. b	5. d	
Set B:	1. d	2. e	3. b	4. c	5. a	
Set C:	1. d	2. f	3. b	4. a	5. e	6. c
Set D:	1. c	2. a	3. d	4. b	5. e	
Set E:	1. b	2. c	3. d	4. a	5. e	

Multiple-Choice Questions

1. c   2. d   3. b   4. a   5. c   6. d   7. a   8. c   9. d   10. b

Chapter 23

Matching Exercises

Set A: 1. e   2. d   3. c   4. b   5. a   6. c   7. a
Set B: 1. c   2. f   3. e   4. d   5. a   6. b
Set C: 1. c   2. d   3. a   4. b   5. a   6. e
Set D: 1. c   2. a   3. d   4. b
Set E: 1. b   2. a   3. e   4. d   5. c

Multiple-Choice Questions

1. a   2. b   3. a   4. c   5. d   6. a   7. b   8. c   9. d   10. c

Chapter 24

Matching Exercises

Set A: 1. d   2. c   3. e   4. a   5. b
Set B: 1. b   2. c   3. a   4. b   5. d
Set C: 1. e   2. a   3. b   4. d   5. c
Set D: 1. b   2. a   3. e   4. c   5. a   6. a   7. b   8. d
Set E: 1. b   2. d   3. a   4. c

Multiple-Choice Questions

1. b   2. b   3. a   4. d   5. a   6. b   7. c   8. c   9. d   10. a

Chapter 25

Matching Exercises

Set A: 1. e   2. f   3. a   4. d   5. c   6. b
Set B: 1. e   2. f   3. g   4. a   5. b   6. c   7. d
Set C: 1. d   2. e   3. f   4. a   5. c   6. b
Set D: 1. f   2. a   3. b   4. e   5. c   6. d
Set E: 1. e   2. d   3. a   4. c   5. b
Set F: 1. b   2. a   3. e   4. f   5. c   6. d

Multiple-Choice Questions

1. c   2. c   3. a   4. b   5. d   6. a   7. c   8. b   9. d   10. a

Chapter 26

Matching Exercises

Set A: 1. d   2. e   3. b   4. a   5. c
Set B: 1. b   2. d   3. e   4. c   5. a
Set C: 1. c   2. d   3. f   4. e   5. b   6. a
Set D: 1. d   2. c   3. a   4. e   5. b
Set E: 1. d   2. b   3. c   4. a

Multiple-Choice Questions

1. b   2. a   3. b   4. b   5. c   6. a   7. d   8. c   9. a   10. a

Chapter 27

Matching Exercises

Set A:	1. d	2. f	3. e	4. c	5. b	6. a
Set B:	1. d	2. e	3. a	4. f	5. b	6. c
Set C:	1. d	2. c	3. f	4. e	5. a	6. b
Set D:	1. b	2. c	3. d	4. e	5. a	
Set E:	1. f	2. c	3. a	4. e	5. b	6. d

Multiple-Choice Questions

1. a   2. b   3. c   4. b   5. b   6. a   7. b   8. d   9. c   10. c

Chapter 28

Matching Exercises

Set A:	1. e	2. d	3. b	4. a	5. c	
Set B:	1. e	2. f	3. a	4. b	5. c	6. d
Set C:	1. e	2. c	3. b	4. f	5. d	6. a
Set D:	1. d	2. e	3. a	4. b	5. c	
Set E:	1. c	2. a	3. f	4. b	5. e	6. d

Multiple-Choice Questions

1. d   2. c   3. a   4. b   5. c   6. d   7. c   8. b   9. b   10. a

Chapter 29

Matching Exercises

Set A:	1. d	2. a	3. e	4. c	5. b
Set B:	1. e	2. c	3. a	4. d	5. b
Set C:	1. d	2. b	3. a	4. e	5. c
Set D:	1. e	2. d	3. a	4. c	5. b
Set E:	1. c	2. b	3. e	4. d	5. a

Multiple-Choice Questions

1. b   2. c   3. d   4. a   5. c   6. a   7. d   8. a   9. b   10. c

Chapter 30

Matching Exercises

Set A: 1. e   2. c   3. b   4. a   5. d

Set B: 1. b   2. c   3. a   4. d

Set C: 1. b   2. a   3. e   4. c   5. d

Multiple-Choice Questions

1. d   2. d   3. b   4. a   5. b   6. c   7. b